SLOW RIDER

AUSTRALIA ON A POSTIE BIKE AND A 125 CC MOTORBIKE

BY

Jill Maden

Also available by Jill Maden:

Excess Baggage: One Woman, One Motorbike and a Huge
Amount of Luggage Ride Across Australia

In memory of Greg and Andy

.

Contents

EPILOGUE

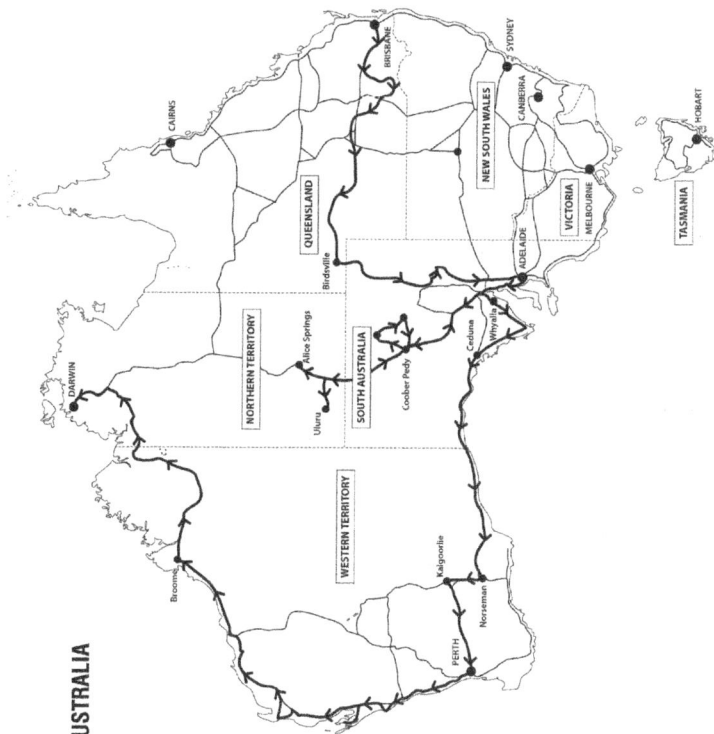

AUSTRALIA

PART 1

THE POSTIE BIKE CHALLENGE

Registration

A DESERT ROSE

"1644 Ipswich Road, please," I said to the taxi driver who had picked me up from the train station at Moorooka in the south-eastern suburbs of Brisbane.

"Where's that?" he asked.

Oh great, a taxi driver who knows less about the geography of Brisbane than I do.

"It's the old Pro Honda showroom, about 5 km from here," I said, pointing in the vague direction I'd been shown.

I'd been out the day before to do a recce and had ended up at the *new* Pro Honda showroom, where John Peterson, the owner, had told me that the bikes for the Postie Bike Challenge were being set up at the *old* showroom.

"It's in Rocklea," I added, hoping this might help.

This seemed to do the trick and after a rather circuitous route we pulled up outside a large, glass-fronted building in the middle of an industrial estate. I got out and walked into the showroom. Little red postie bikes were spread out to my left and right and a few people were tinkering about with them. I felt a jolt of excitement. It was finally about to begin. I'd waited months for this.

The Postie Bike Challenge, as the name would suggest, offers participants the chance to ride low powered postie bikes through some of Australia's most challenging terrain. It avoids the usual tourist tracks and seeks out more testing routes instead. Deserts, open plains, mountains, rainforests, river crossings, dirt tracks, corrugations and bull-dust all lead its riders through some of the most remote and beautiful places the continent has to offer.

I walked up to the counter, where a tall, slim, very good looking man, who reminded me of someone, was standing.

"Hi, I'm Jill," I said, extending my hand, barely able to contain my excitement.

"Anthony," he replied, smiling and shaking my hand.

Who did he remind me of?

As we stood there chatting, a man who looked a bit like Bear Grylls, the survival expert, came out of a walk-in cupboard, looked at me and said, "You must be Jill."

"Yes."

How did he know that?

"Are you Dan?" I enquired. Dan was the organiser.

"Yes, I am."

He ticked me off on a list, then disappeared back into the cupboard and reappeared a few minutes later carrying a blue chill bag. "You're number 24," he said, pointing to the bikes.

I took the bag and turned around to look for number 24.

"It's here," called another guy a few feet away from me.

"Thanks," I said, putting down my bag and introducing myself.

"I'm Ned," he returned.

I opened my chill bag and had a look inside. There was a road atlas, a set of running sheets with directions for each day's riding on them, a bulldog clip to attach them to the handlebars, a plastic sandwich box, two water bottles, a first aid kit, a set of ear plugs, a fluorescent green vest, a black bin bag and a Postie Bike Challenge baseball cap and polo shirt.

I put on the baseball cap and looked up. Anthony had now joined us and was starting to fiddle about with his bike.

I had a look at mine. It had a black plastic milk crate on the back with a 5 litre red jerry can in it, leaving enough space to add the chill bag. I squeezed mine in. It didn't seem to fit very well. I looked around to see how the others had placed theirs, then took the jerry can out, turned it around so it was facing sideways instead of longways, and put it back in again. This time the chill bag fitted neatly.

Next I had to make a cover for the milk crate to prevent its contents from flying out if I hit some rough ground. I opened the bag I'd brought with me, pulled out a large sheet of red and white spotted plastic-coated tablecloth material and some Velcro, and started wrapping it around the milk crate. Dan had advised us in the pre-event documentation that we'd need to create a cover for our milk crates and had supplied the approximate dimensions of the crate. I'd bought my material to slightly exceed these dimensions, but had decided to leave creating the cover until I got to the event, just in case I messed it up.

The crate was a cube with an open top. I wrapped the material around the crate, bringing the two ends together at the front, where they overlapped by an inch. I cut off a length of Velcro, stuck it to each overlap then stuck the two overlapping sides to each other, securing it round the outside of the crate. Then I took out my nail scissors (the only ones I had) and cut the two feet of material sticking up above the top of the crate down to size so that it folded over the top to make a lid. Then I stuck more Velcro in a strip about two inches below the top of the crate, around the side and front walls. A further strip under the sides of the lid meant the top would stick to the bottom.

I stood back to admire my handiwork.

"Very pretty," said Scott as he walked past. He was one of the mechanics and John Peterson's son, whom I'd met the day before.

Ned and Anthony were equally complimentary. I felt pleased with my efforts, although I was a bit afraid I'd end up pulling all the Velcro off if I opened and closed the lid too forcefully.

It had taken about an hour to complete my work of art and in the meantime the showroom was starting to fill up. People were arriving from all over the country. There was a couple from Tasmania, Silvia and Alec, who had very professional-looking mustard-coloured covers for their milk crates, which Silvia had run off on her sewing machine before leaving home. Someone else had some circuit boards stuck to the outside of his crate, and two ladies outside the building were decorating their bikes in tiaras and tinsel and had dubbed themselves the Postie Princesses. Ned's friend Greg had arrived, as had Anthony's mate Christian. A man from Canberra, Michael, who had a registration plate which included the digits 007, was also nearby.

"I should call you Bond, James Bond," I said in my best Sean Connery accent.

He laughed, but for some inexplicable reason didn't seem too keen to be named after the world's most famous secret agent, so I resolved just to call him 007 Michael in my head.

After a while I realised that out of the six women there, I was the only one who was on her own. That must have been how Dan knew who I was.

A guy I knew back home, David, who worked on the foreign exchange desk of my bank and who I'd become friendly with through our common interest in motorbikes, had given me a furry toy haggis as a mascot for the trip. I'd christened him Hamish and now attempted to fix him to the front of the bike. I didn't have anything I could use to tie him on with, so Ned made a couple of holes in Hamish's backside and gave me some cable ties to feed through the holes and fix around the forks. A few extra cable ties ensured my cover was firmly attached to its milk crate and wouldn't blow off if the wind caught it.

Every year the Postie Bike Challenge traverses a different part of Australia. This year it was going from Brisbane to Adelaide via the remote outback town of Birdsville in the Simpson Desert. For this reason, I christened my bike Rosie, as she would be my red 'desert rose'.

With Rosie's customisation complete, I took her out for a test ride.

Now the Honda CT110, or postie bike as it's known in Australia due to its use by the Australian Postal Service, isn't like any other motorbike. It's a step-through affair with a kick start and no clutch. I'd never kick started a bike in my life and had no idea how to do it. As I was sitting in the saddle attempting to press a non-existent electric starter button, John Peterson walked past.

I called out to him, "How do you start this thing?" He came over and motioned for me to get off the bike.

"Okay, first you need to turn on the choke, then pull out the kick start lever and" – he jumped down on it – "use your heel to kick straight down on the lever."

It started first time.

"Oh, right," I responded, not feeling the least bit confident about my chances of starting it so easily. I turned everything off and back on again and attempted to do the same thing. Nothing.

"Try again," he said.

I tried again, and again. After half a dozen attempts I finally got Rosie going. *Fantastic*. I was ready to head off to the practice area. *Now where's the clutch? Oh, that's right, there isn't one! So how the hell do you change gear, or pull off, for that matter?*

I tried kicking it into first gear. So far so good – the bike hadn't stalled. Maybe you just accelerate away, I thought. I revved up the engine and Rosie lurched forward. I put my feet down and jammed on the brakes. I tried again, this time being a bit gentler with the revs.

Rosie rolled away smoothly. I got up some speed and could hear that the engine was ready to change gear. I reached for the clutch. *Damn it, there's no clutch.* I rolled off the revs instead and tried kicking her up into second. It worked. That must be how you do it, I thought to myself. A few circuits of the practice area and I had it sussed.

I returned to the showroom, feeling quite pleased with myself, and rejoined Anthony and Ned. *Who on earth did Anthony remind me of?* Suddenly it struck me. Hugh Jackman. He was a dead ringer for my favourite actor, Hugh Jackman.

Oh yeah, this was going to be a great trip.

UNFINISHED BUSINESS

"How did you hear about the Postie Bike Challenge?" Dave, a guy from Alice Springs, asked me as I was making a cup of tea, waiting for Dan to start the briefing.

"Oh, I was out in Australia in 2010/11, riding a Suzuki SV650 around the country. It was an enormous bike with a high centre of gravity and I had far too much luggage piled on to it, which made it very unstable and I really struggled to keep it upright. I'd seen a few postie bikes buzzing around as I travelled and thought they would be far more my style. I'd originally come out for a year and planned to ride right round Australia, but both my parents were having health problems so I cut the trip short after seven months, having just done the eastern half, and headed home."

"But now you're back…"

"Yes, it always felt like I had unfinished business. I still had the western half of Australia to do. When I started planning this trip I thought doing it on a postie bike would be far more fun. I typed 'postie bike' into Google to find out how to buy one – and up popped the Postie Bike Challenge website[1]. That's it! I thought. I could do the Postie Bike Challenge, then buy my bike and continue around the rest of Australia on it. Well that was the plan," I continued, "but I can't do that now."

When I'd first registered for the Postie Bike Challenge, I'd phoned the organisers to see if I could buy my bike at the end of the event. The lady I spoke to advised me that this had been done by previous participants and therefore she could see no reason why I wouldn't be able to do it too.

A few months later, the second of two newsletters arrived, with a section about how you could purchase your bike. This explained that participants could buy their bikes for $800 at the end of the Challenge. It detailed how the bikes, which were registered in the state of Queensland, would have their registration plates removed at the end of the Challenge and have to be de-registered from Queensland then re-registered with the new owner's state registration authority – a process that could take ten to fourteen days with each authority. I phoned Dan to confirm this and he advised me that, because each state has its own registration

---

1 http://www.postiebikechallenge.org/

authority and you needed to have an Australian address to register a vehicle, for foreign riders it would probably take too long and therefore he didn't recommend that I attempt to buy my bike.

This left me in a bit of a pickle. How could I continue round the rest of Australia if I didn't have a bike?

When I'd originally done my 'postie bike' search, I'd also found a website by a guy called Nathan[2], who'd ridden a postie bike from Sydney to London a few years earlier. He mentioned he'd bought his bike from a company in Brisbane. As the Postie Bike Challenge was starting in Brisbane, I wanted to find out if I could buy one from this company and have them ship it to the finishing point in Adelaide. I got back on the web, found the site again and emailed Nathan for the details of the company he'd used. He kindly forwarded these to me and I had an email conversation with Joe, the owner of One Ten Motorcycles[3], and agreed I'd go and see him when I arrived in Brisbane.

I left the UK on Thursday 28 August 2014 and arrived in Brisbane about 7.30 on the Friday evening. The best thing about arriving was walking through the airport doors and smelling the sweet fragrance of the tropics. I loved that smell; it was so distinctly Australian and instantly I felt like I'd come home. It was only a mild 16 degrees Celsius, about the same temperature as Glasgow, but the air felt warm and with the smell of flowers on the breeze, I knew I was back in my favourite country.

As One Ten Motorcycles wouldn't be open again till Monday, I spent the weekend reacquainting myself with the city. I'd been to Brisbane a couple of times before but only for a day or two, and had never made it beyond the

---

2 http://www.thepostman.org.uk/

3 http://www.onetenmotorcycles.com.au/

central business district. This time, though, I'd given myself a week to get over the jet lag and do a bit of sightseeing before the Postie Bike Challenge began.

The Brisbane River cuts through the middle of the city and it's hard to go far without being near it. I took the free City Hopper ferry, which goes to just beyond Kangaroo Point. This appeared to be a very affluent area, with some beautiful old Queenslander style houses. I wandered around, taking photos, then strolled along the riverside walkway all the way back to the city, where I asked the tourist information office how to get to Caboolture.

On the Monday morning I caught the train out to Caboolture in the northern suburbs, where One Ten Motorcycles was located. Joe was very helpful but told me it would be prohibitively expensive to ship a postie bike to Adelaide. Additionally, he didn't have any postie bikes for sale at the moment, as they were all spoken for, but he might be able to get one for me if I was prepared to come back to Brisbane at the end of the Challenge and collect it. I'd just have to wait a couple of days while he made some enquiries.

On the Wednesday afternoon Joe rang to say that he'd found a bike for me but wouldn't be able to get hold of it until the following week. This meant I wouldn't be able to inspect the bike before I left for the Challenge and would be buying it blind. Having thought about it for a couple of days and realising how many miles would be involved in returning to Brisbane and then riding back to Adelaide, I decided against it.

"So what are you going to do?" asked Dave, after I'd explained all this to him.

"Well, I could either try to buy a second-hand postie bike in Adelaide or, failing that, I could get a 125," I replied.

"A 125?" he exclaimed. "You'd be better off with a 250."

"I know, but I'm not sure I can afford it. John Peterson put me in touch with a dealer in Adelaide who could do me a 125 for about £2,500. This will already cost me more than I planned and I doubt I'd be able to get a 250 for any less."

"Well, if you make it to Alice Springs come and stay with us," he said.

"Really? That would be great," I replied, astounded at how trusting he was, given that he'd only just met me.

POSTIE BIKE MAINTENANCE FOR IDIOTS

Dan called us all together. Everyone had now arrived and we were up to our full complement of forty riders. There were thirty-four guys and six women, ranging in age from what looked to be thirty to eighty, but with most appearing to be in their fifties. As I later found out, I was one of just four overseas entrants. Thankfully, Dan spared us the indignity of standing up and saying our names and where we were from, as they do at so many events these days, and left us to find out such information by our own means.

He introduced us to the four mechanics who would be supporting the ride – Andy, Scott, Richard and Mick – then split us into two groups, one with Andy, the other with Mick, to be given the low-down on caring for our machines.

Keeping the oil topped up was, according to Andy (my group leader), the single most important factor in ensuring the bike would make it to the end of the Challenge. Given that there were riders of varying experience – from ones with learner plates to ones who were on their second or third challenge – Andy took no chances and showed us exactly how to put the bike on the centre stand, locate the oil sump and read the dipstick to ascertain if more oil was required.

Keeping the tyres at the right pressure was next – 32 on the front, 36 on the back. Deflating the tyres to handle sand or dirt tracks was not recommended, as there'd be no way to re-inflate them later.

Then there was chain lubrication. This would be required at least once a day.

We were warned of the importance of checking these things every day, if our bikes were going to make it down the Birdsville Track to Adelaide.

There was just one thing he hadn't covered.

"Er, where does the fuel go in?" I mumbled, feeling like a bit of an idiot. It wasn't that I hadn't ridden a motorbike before and didn't know how to refuel it. I just hadn't ridden a postie bike before and so far all my attempts to locate the petrol tank had come to nought.

"Good question," he replied, smiling and making me feel better. He lifted up the seat to reveal the petrol cap below. "Just in here."

With the perils of neglecting our bikes drummed into us, we were free to leave, with instructions to be back again the following morning at 6.30 for a 7.30 departure.

UNDER THE WEATHER

By this time it was about 2 o'clock in the afternoon and I needed a quick comfort stop before making my way back to the hostel in the centre of the city.

As I went to use the loo another woman came out of the cubicle and started coughing badly.

"You've got the same cough as me," I said.

"Oh, it's terrible and my husband's got it too."

On the Sunday night after I'd arrived in Brisbane a woman in my room was coughing her lungs out and I thought, I bet I'm going to catch that. Sure enough, by the Monday morning I was coughing too. Nevertheless, at first it was just a minor cough so I thought I'd got away with it.

It had also become really hot since I'd arrived and the combination of walking around Brisbane in the heat and waiting for a bus back to the train station from the industrial estate where One Ten Motorcycles was located had left me very dehydrated. The jet lag had been hitting me pretty hard too, and on the train on the way back from Caboolture I had been overwhelmed with tiredness and almost passed out. By the time I got back to the hostel that evening I was coughing really badly and starting to feel feverish.

The next day I felt terrible. I decided to have an easy day at the hostel to try and shake off whatever bug I'd picked up, before the Challenge got underway.

I'd also been needing to go to the toilet a lot and when I woke up on the Wednesday morning my back was really sore. Fearing my cold might have gone into my kidneys, I got the number of a local doctor from the girl on reception at the hostel and managed to get an appointment at 9 a.m. As I sat in the waiting area, I suddenly started feeling very hot and light-headed.

The next thing I knew, I was being shaken awake by the practice nurse and having my blood pressure taken. I'd passed out.

The doctor diagnosed me with a kidney infection and a very bad cold and prescribed some heavy-duty antibiotics and some Hydralyte (a rehydration fluid) to clear it all up. I spent the rest of the week in bed, trying to shake off my illnesses so that I'd be well enough to do the Challenge. The last thing I wanted was to be going into the desert with a kidney infection.

By registration day on Saturday 6 September 2014, the antibiotics were starting to do their job and my waterworks were returning to normal, though I was still coughing as though I'd been smoking forty cigarettes a day for most of my life.

But I'd come this far. There was no way I was going to let a chest infection and the risk of developing pneumonia stop me from doing the Postie Bike Challenge.

Day 1:
Brisbane to Chinchilla

It was an early start. I was up at 4.30 a.m., with the intention of having breakfast before leaving the hostel. But the kitchen was closed and, with my food locked inside, I had to abandon it and make for the train station on an empty stomach. I got the 5.34 a.m. train to Moorooka, then a taxi back to the Pro Honda garage. This driver knew the way much better than the previous one and had me there in a fraction of the time and at half the price.

We'd all been sent a large duffle bag before we left home, into which, we'd been told, all our gear would have to fit. There would be no room for anything else, apart from a few nick-nacks which could go in our milk crates. No backpacks, except water bladders, were allowed. This posed quite a logistical challenge for me.

We would obviously be wearing our motorcycle clothing during the Challenge, but as I was coming from the UK I would need to find some way of transporting mine to the start. We had also been instructed to bring camping gear in the form of a tent, an air mattress and a sleeping bag. In addition, I would need some billy cans, a camping stove and utensils for when I continued around Australia by myself. And, of course, I'd need normal clothes and my toiletries.

My duffle bag would be transported in the support van on the Challenge, but after that I felt it would be too un-

15

wieldy to fit on the back of another postie bike or a 125, and that I'd need a better way to carry my stuff. I dug out my motorcycle panniers from my previous trip, with the idea of putting everything inside them and then putting the panniers inside the duffle bag. This meant that, at the end of the Challenge, I could pack the duffle bag away and sling the panniers over the back seat of whatever bike I ended up buying.

Unfortunately, I couldn't fit everything in. No matter how I arranged things, there was just too much stuff. I needed another bag. I bought a collapsible cabin-sized bag, which had zip-away straps that could be unzipped to convert it into a backpack. This enabled me to pack my helmet, riding trousers and gloves into one pannier, with the camping gear in the other. My clothes and wash things went in the backpack and I planned to wear my riding jacket and boots.

When I got to Brisbane, I would wear all my riding gear to the start point and transfer my clothes and wash things to the empty pannier. The backpack could then be collapsed and packed into the duffle bag for re-use at the end of the Challenge. It was a tight fit and meant a rather hot journey from Glasgow to Brisbane in my jacket and boots, but I managed to squeeze everything into the allocated space.

I dropped my tightly packed duffle bag at the support van and went into the showroom to lever my nick-nacks into the small amount of space left in my milk crate.

I wheeled Rosie outside, had a couple of quick spins around the practice area, then parked her under the canopy outside the showroom.

"I'm Walshy," said a very tall guy with white hair and a goofy smile standing next to me.

We'd been told it would be more comfortable if we put a sheepskin cover over our seats. Walshy had taken this to extremes and tied a huge sheepskin rug over his seat, which extended down to the base of his bike. He had another one over his milk crate and looked like a big white woolly mammoth. I couldn't help but laugh.

Dan set off the siren on his megaphone to get our attention and we all assembled for the morning briefing. He announced we'd already lost our first rider. James, the husband of Diana (the woman I'd met in the Ladies the previous day), had succumbed to his infection and pulled out. I hadn't met him but, given how bad I'd been feeling, he had my utmost sympathies.

Dan went on to explain how to get onto the motorway from the showroom and said that we would have a refuelling point at Goombungee. The postie bikes only held enough fuel to cover about 120 km. To supplement this, the 5 litre jerry can in our milk crates would give us a further 150 km worth of fuel. However, as the day's total mileage would be 361 km, this would not be enough to take us all the way to our destination, hence the refuelling point.

There were four support vehicles – a ute[4] with all the spare fuel in it (driven by Dan), the support van, which also acted as a workshop, carrying all the spare parts that would be required (Scott and Richard were in this), a four-wheel-drive car which would act as a roving sweeper (Andy), and another ute with a trailer attached carrying four spare postie bikes, which would be the rear sweeper at the back of the pack (Mick).

With the briefing and the obligatory group photo over, we were dispatched to collect our sandwiches for the day. Then there was a scurry for the bikes and everyone packed their sandwiches in their milk crates, donned their helmets and jumped up and down on their kick starters to get them

4 A ute, or utility truck, is the Australian term for a pick-up truck.

going. Remarkably, I was one of the first ones out of the car park.

We screamed off down the motorway, fluorescent vests flapping wildly and, for the first time, got a true feel for what these little bikes were capable of. At 110 cc each, Dan had warned us that 80 km/h was their top speed, but on a downhill section, with a tailwind, we found that even 85 or 90 was possible (though not recommended by Dan).

Although our food and lodgings were arranged for us, it was up to each individual rider to find their way to the destination each day. To assist us, we had running sheets attached to our handlebars giving us directions to follow. Fortunately these were typed in a font just large enough for me to read without my specs, but I wondered how those reliant on reading glasses would manage.

Zooming along the deserted freeway, Rosie felt very stable and it was easy to take my eyes off the road to look down at the sheets. Nonetheless, I almost missed the exit for Esk. Had I not been following a guy with a blue cover on his milk crate, which had already come undone and was flailing about behind him, I'd have shot past the turn and ended up God only knows where.

Off the motorway, it became very pastoral as we headed over the Great Dividing Range, Australia's longest mountain range. Beautiful old Queenslander houses raised on stilts with weather-boarded walls and all-round verandas were set in pretty paddocks and surrounded by tall gum trees. The Wivenhoe Dam, which had almost breached its walls during the floods of 2010/11 when I was last in Australia, was off to our right. The road gently wound its way along, not asking too much of our riding skills. I was loving it – Rosie was so easy to ride.

After about 90 km we arrived in Esk and people started to pull over. I parked my bike next to a row of other riders and, like them, pulled out my jerry can and topped up my tank. It was only 9 a.m. but already people were tucking into their sandwiches. Having missed breakfast, I did the same, keeping one for later.

Leaving Esk, I was following Michael with the 007 plates. The bends seemed to get tighter and more frequent, and packs of bikers were passing us in the opposite direction – this was obviously a popular weekend run. We were having a lovely ride, weaving through all the twists and turns, when suddenly Michael veered onto the side of the road and came to an abrupt halt.

Something was wrong. I pulled up behind him and jumped off to see what was going on. His back tyre was completely flat and was slithering around like a snake as he pushed it off the tarmac. I offered to stay with him until the support van arrived but he waved me on and reassured me he'd be all right. I later found out he'd hit a piece of metal and had a complete blow-out.

About 70 km later I came to Goombungee and our first refuelling point. Dan had the support ute parked at the edge of the road and postie bikers were pulling in around it.

I wasn't sure what to do.

"Fill up your tank from your jerry, put the empty jerry here and take a new one from here," Dan instructed. "If that's not enough to fill your tank, use one of these big jerries," he added, pointing to a 25 litre can.

Now that might sound like a simple set of instructions, but I got it all wrong. I topped up from the big jerry can, left my half-full one next to the empties and almost forgot to pick up a new one. *Time for another sandwich.*

After Goombungee, the next town we were aiming for was Quinalow. According to the running sheets, we should "Turn right @ intersection to Quinalow (Bunya Mountains on sign)", then "Follow signs to Quinalow".

I'd just passed a small sign for Quinalow with "Bunya Mountains" on it, so I had pulled over to turn around and go back. Walshy pulled up next to me, but he hadn't seen the sign and seemed to think we should go straight on. I wasn't convinced, so I did a U-turn and went back to take the turn, half-expecting him to follow me. Walshy didn't follow me, though, and soon I was on my own, wracked with doubt about my decision. But there were a lot of signs to Quinalow and, as per the running sheets, I followed them all.

Eventually, after a series of right turns, I seemed to rejoin the road that I'd left Walshy on. Another rider was coming along so we stopped and consulted my running sheets (his had blown off). We rode along together through Quinalow to the next township, Bell, where we stopped for a break.

His name was Phil and he was from Darwin. After an energy bar and a drink of Hydralyte we were off again, this time aiming for the Dingo Fence near Jandowae. A left turn at Lyndley Lane took us onto our first piece of gravel. Instantly I rolled off the power and dropped down to a cautious 40 km/h for the 2 km of skid-inducing surface to the fence.

When I was in Australia the last time, I'd developed something of a phobia about gravel roads. The weight of my motorcycle and all the luggage I was carrying meant I'd always felt extremely unstable. The thought of going anywhere near a surface that could increase my chances of falling off scared the living daylights out of me. However,

I was pleased to find that on the postie bike, with considerably less luggage, I felt a lot more steady.

The Dingo Fence is the longest man-made structure in the world. It was first erected in 1948 to keep wild dogs (dingoes) out of the fertile sheep-grazing areas of southeastern Australia. It runs from just outside Jandowae in Queensland in the north to the Great Australian Bight in South Australia, some 5,400 km away.

Apart from a plaque and a notice board giving some information about it, the fence itself wasn't overly impressive. From where we were standing we could only see the first twenty metres or so. It was only about 1.5 metres high and fabricated from wooden posts and chicken wire, hence it didn't look particularly remarkable. Later I would see it from a different perspective and change my opinion, but right now it looked like any other fence. I took a few photos, chatted to some other riders and then got on my bike and retraced my steps up the gravel road and Lyndley Lane to the main road.

Somewhere along the way I'd lost Phil, and now I was on my own again. Back on the main road, I missed the next turn, to "Warra 26", and was 20 km off course when Andy from the support team caught up with me and made me turn around and go back. Warra 26 was another dirt track, but following Andy at 80 km/h I felt a lot more confident.

Overhead was a huge dark storm cloud. We passed some other postie bikers, who had stopped to put on waterproofs, and about 20 km later we joined the main road to Chinchilla and rode right into the eye of the storm. A torrential downpour pummelled us as we dodged our way through ⌐ long line of road works. It was horrible riding, made v· by the fact that I ran out of petrol and had to pul¹ side of what was now a very busy road, full of trains, and dig out my jerry can. I hadn't topped up since the refuel at Goombungee and my earlier detour had added an additional 40 km onto my journey, causing my tank to run dry just 12 km short of our destination.

We were staying at the Chinchilla Showgrounds that night – a flat, open piece of land with a few buildings scattered about in a somewhat random fashion. As I pulled in I could see various postie bikes making their way towards a large concrete building with the support van parked behind it. I followed and, as I came level with it, saw a mixture of tents and cow sheds spread out ahead of me. These would be our digs for the night.

I came to a stop and Scott, the mechanic, came rushing up and pushed a clipboard towards me. "Sign in," he said, smiling.

I pulled out a sopping wet hand from its glove and did as I was told.

"Remember to do your checks," he continued, then rushed off to sign in the next arrival. Even though I'd gone considerably off course, I was surprised to find that I wasn't the last one to arrive that day.

I was getting pretty tired by now and struggled to haul Rosie onto her centre stand to do my checks. Suddenly, there was someone on the other side of her, helping me pull her on. It was a guy called Steve, a car dealership owner from Brisbane. He'd seen me struggling and come to my aid. *What a great guy*.

With Rosie on her stand, I got to work with my checks. The oil was okay and, with Steve pressing down on the handlebars to rock the bike forward, I was able to lube Rosie's chain by spinning the back wheel. Checking the tyres was not so easy. As I've ridden bikes for ten years this may seem like a scary confession, but I couldn't work out how to fix the pump to the tyre's air valve. At home I had an angled extension which I could screw onto the valve if it was in an inaccessible position. I'd brought this with me, but it didn't seem to fit. I shouted Dan over and asked him how to do it. He gave me a demonstration I wished I'd had years ago.

He spun the wheel so that the valve was at the back, facing forward, halfway up the wheel. He then took the pump and attached the opposite end of the connector than I usually used, so that it was pulled back onto the value rather than pressed onto it. This meant that the shaft of the pump didn't get caught in the spokes. It was a revelation.

"So that's what that bit of the pump's for," I marvelled.

As it was still pouring down, I set up my tent in a small cattle shed on top of a pile of hay and old manure. "A shit place to sleep", according to Christian.

That night, dinner was provided by the Rotary Club. Dan had arranged for local community groups to provide all our meals in exchange for a generous donation to their cause – just one of the ways the Postie Bike Challenge supported the communities through which it passed. They had cooked up a gorgeous hot stew in a giant cast iron pot called a camp oven, over an open fire. This was served with boiled potatoes, followed by fruit salad and ice-cream for dessert. It was just what we needed at the end of what had become a cold, wet ride.

During dinner I noticed some of the guys tapping numbers into calculators and writing them on their running sheets. "What are you doing?" I asked Mike, who had an 'L' plate on his milk crate and had never ridden on a public road before.

"I'm working out what number my odometer should be at for each turning point," he replied.

"Why are you doing that?" I queried.

He pointed to his running sheet. There was a column marked "odometer", another one titled "distance" and a third one with directions to the next turning point. The odometer column was blank but the distance one had numbers in it.

"The bikes don't have a trip meter so you can't tell when you'll reach the distance in the distance column," he explained. "If you add the distance to each turning point to the reading on your odometer then you know when to start looking for the next turn."

"Hmm, is that really necessary?" I asked, feeling it was a bit of overkill.

I'd eat my words the next day.

Day 2:
Chinchilla to Nindigully Pub

After a surprisingly good night's sleep, I was up at 5 a.m., with my tent down and everything packed by breakfast. I'd left my riding gear hanging over a piece of farm equipment in the shed next to my tent and thankfully it had dried out overnight. A full cooked breakfast was provided by the Rotary Club and soon we were on our way.

We were getting further from civilisation and today we only had one page of running sheets to follow instead of two. We had just 306.7 km to cover and Dan advised us there would be an early refuelling point at Condamine, only about 60 km away.

It was a good straight road to Condamine, through tall grey eucalyptus trees that pushed up through dry red earth. I was on my own at the front of the group when I saw a four-trailer road train coming up a side road on my right.

"Oh God, please turn left," I prayed, hoping it would turn away from me. I looked in my mirrors. *Oh no*. It had turned right and was coming up behind me.

I'd encountered a fair number of road trains on my previous visit to Australia and they didn't get any less frightening. They are huge trucks, with anything from two to five trailers. If you get caught in their tail wind they can blow you all over the road.

I held my breath as he got closer and started to overtake. "One, two," I counted as I watched the trailers pass and tried to hold Rosie steady. "Three, four." It was past and there was no tail wind. Fortunately, he'd not had enough time to build up sufficient speed to generate the usual tail whip.

I made good time and somehow I was first into the re-fuel at Condamine. Then I misread my running sheets and missed the next turning, "Meandarra 52". There was a col-umn on the sheets that gave the mileage to the next point but what I didn't realise was that the number given was a cumulative total, not the next distance to be covered. If I'd bothered filling in the "odometer" column, as the boys had done the previous evening, I would have worked this out, but I hadn't. Consequently, I wasn't expecting there to be a turn-off outside Condamine. The distance to the turn, as I read it, was 61.5 km. What it actually meant was that at the 61.5 km point there was a turn off and, as we were already at 58.3 km, this would be in about 3 km, not in 61.5.

Some time later, when I got to a sign saying "Mean-darra 38" and no one else was around, I figured something had gone wrong. As 38 was a shorter distance than 52, I took this road and got to Meandarra at around the same time as everyone else. It was only when Andy pulled up in the support car and asked, "Which way did you go?" that I realised my mistake.

What I couldn't understand was how Andy knew I'd taken a wrong turn. Unbeknownst to me, some of the oth-er riders had seen me miss the turn and alerted Dan. He'd gone 50 km after me before Andy was able to radio him to let him know that I'd shown up in Meandarra.

Given the chaos I'd caused, I decided I'd better ride with someone else from then on. I turned to the two guys next to me, Pete and Stu, and asked if I could ride with them. And thank goodness I did, as the last stretch to the Nindigully Pub was along 50 km of gravel track.

Stu took off at 80 km/h and as I was between him and Pete I thought I'd better keep up and whizzed along at 80 km/h too. It was a bit scary going into some of the bends and I quickly learnt that using the brakes was not the way to approach them. Rolling off the power worked better as it avoided the back wheel locking up.

When we pulled into the pub, it seemed that news of my slight detour had reached the rest of the support crew as every time I passed one of them, I got some comment like, "What way did you come, Jill?" Cheeky beggars!

Anthony was parked next to me, doing his checks as I was doing mine. I put my bike on the centre stand, checked the oil, then squatted down at the side of the bike and started spraying my chain with lube. With no one to press my handlebars down this time, I couldn't spin the wheel and had to push it round with my hand, spraying each section of chain as I went.

Seeing what I was doing, Anthony came over, took the can from me and said, "That's not how you do it." He knelt down at the back of the bike, faced the wheel and sprayed lube onto the chain from the back with one hand whilst quickly turning the wheel with the other. It was another light-bulb moment. For years I'd been doing it all wrong and had been spraying the wrong part of the chain (and most of the tyre in the process). I really needed to take some basic motorcycle maintenance classes.

We'd all got into Nindigully quite early and there was plenty of time to put up our tents, take care of some domestic chores and socialise before dinner.

I'd pitched my tent next to a man from New Zealand called Ian. We exchanged accounts of our rides and I apologised in advanced for potentially snoring during the night. Then Silvia, the Tasmanian lady, came over and handed me a bucket of soapy water, saying I could use it to do some laundry if I wanted.

I hadn't planned on doing any so early in the trip but since I now had the means, I dug out my dirty undies and gave them a quick rinse. I hadn't really thought this activity through, as once I was done I realised I didn't have anything to hang them up to dry. I took a look around and saw some space on a tree next to 007 Michael's tent. I draped my smalls over the branches and set off to the amenities to have a shower.

There was a shed with four showers in it behind the pub, one of which was empty. I stepped inside, disrobed and turned on the hot water. A trickle ran out of the showerhead. I tried the cold. This increased the volume of water but completely overpowered the hot trickle. I turned everything off and tried again. When this achieved the same result, I started to suspect that the other three showers were siphoning off the pressure and that I'd have to wait for someone else to finish before getting a decent jet. After five minutes of standing about naked in my corrugated tin shed, I heard the shower next to mine being switched off. I turned mine on again and, joy of joy, hot water cascaded down over me.

Refreshed and renewed, I hung up my wet towel on the tree with my other garments and went over to the pub for a drink.

The Nindigully Pub is purported to be Queensland's oldest continually licensed pub and it certainly had a somewhat antiquated feel about it. It was a single-storey stone building with verandahs around the edges and a tin roof. Outside was a lawn, which we had been allowed to use as our campground, and inside was a selection of animal heads, hats and other memorabilia affixed to the walls.

A girl behind the bar with a suspiciously English accent served me my bottle of Kopparberg Pear Cider and I meandered out onto the verandah. Greg, Walshy and some others were sitting chatting. Greg was talking about his business and how much he loved what he did. He was an entrepreneur and seemed to have had his fingers in many different pies over the years, with great financial success.

Pete and Stu, my male escorts from earlier, were nearby and, after a while, I gravitated over to them. They were a funny pair and I really enjoyed their company.

After a while, dinner was served – and what a feast it was. It was a full roast dinner with chicken and beef, dauphinoise potatoes, cauliflower cheese, carrots, peas and gravy, with pavlova to follow. I loaded up my plate and found a seat beside a train driver from New South Wales called Gary and an American guy called Scotty. Scotty had flown in the day before the start of the Challenge and I was surprised he wasn't suffering from jet lag.

"So what made you decide to do the Postie Bike Challenge?" I asked.

"Well, I've got a postie bike at home which I love and I've always wanted to see Australia, so I thought doing this would be the perfect way to combine the two."

"I thought you could only get postie bikes in Australia?" I queried.

"Yeah, but I managed to get one years ago and have had it ever since. I'm so glad I decided to see Australia this way."

"Yeah, it's brilliant, isn't it?" I agreed.

We chatted for a while and then I wandered off to bed. It was eight o'clock and I was done in.

Day 3:
Nindigully Pub to Charleville

The next morning, as if to make up for teasing me the day before, Scott (the mechanic) greeted me by saying, "So how's the wonderful and lovely Jill today?"

I had to give him a kiss for that, and it left me grinning all morning.

At breakfast, Anthony started talking about how he'd just refuelled his bike and it was ready to go. I didn't need to do mine as I'd filled it up the night before. Hadn't I? Suddenly I was filled with doubt. Had I filled Rosie up? I was sure I had, but now the seed of doubt had been sown and I had to go and see if I'd really done it. Of course I had. I wasn't that useless at motorcycle maintenance.

As I opened up my milk crate to pack away my day's sandwiches, I discovered I still had one from the day before in my lunch box. Each day, whatever group was catering for us would provide us with a packed lunch. The Rotary Club in Chinchilla had supplied us with two sandwiches. One was cheese and ham; the other could have been tuna or maybe corned beef mashed up with tomato ketchup – no one could figure it out. I'd eaten the cheese and ham one and half of the other one, but the second half was still in my box.

Anthony, who was now next to me, said, "I wish I'd known you had that. I was starving yesterday when we arrived." I promised to let him have any spares I didn't eat from then on.

Having learnt my lesson about riding alone, I asked the man on the other side of me, Dave, who I'd been chatting to at the Dingo Fence the day before, if I could ride with him. He seemed happy with this and we set off.

We retraced our steps back to the main road and continued up to St George, a town about 45 km away. From there we turned right onto the road towards the small township of Mitchell, some 200 km north. This would have been a glorious road to ride, with acres of green farmlands on either side, but for a debilitating headwind.

I crouched down over the handlebars, trying to make myself as aerodynamic as possible, and cranked on the power. Rosie managed to hold 70 km/h but Dave, who was ahead of me, was down to 60 km/h. Despite my decision not to ride alone, the difference in performance between Rosie and Dave's bike left me frustrated, and before long I pulled out and overtook. Next thing I knew I was tearing up the field, passing everyone ahead of me. *Woohoo!* I was having great fun but I'd completely lost Dave.

The road was straight as an arrow and after a while the farmlands gave way to huge panoramas of empty bushlands. I could see various riders ahead of me and when, after about 100 km, people started pulling over to refuel, I did so too. I was chatting away to Scotty the American and a couple of others when I noticed Dave was there too. I hadn't even seen him pull in. I was consumed with guilt. *What kind of riding buddy races off and leaves her partner for dead?* A very selfish one, I concluded. After that, I resolved to stay with him and I was very glad I did.

Dave was a gentle, soft-spoken man, with a fun sense of humour which he expressed by zigzagging his way through the white lines and riding aside me to take some photos. The wind abated a bit and after another 50 km or so we pulled over for a stop.

I discovered he was a cardiac surgeon from Sydney. "My God, this must be such a change from your normal life," I exclaimed.

"Yeah, why do you think I'm doing it?" he replied.

The day's refuelling point was at Mitchell. We pulled in, emptied the remains of our jerry cans into our tanks, topped up with the big jerry, replaced our empties and tucked into our sandwiches – cheese and ham and something with pickles.

I made the mistake of eating an apple, which left me very parched and thirsty and feeling quite odd.

"Don't you know, you should never eat an apple in the outback," said one of the others.

I didn't know if he was joking or not, but decided, just for safe measure, never to do it again.

We took a left turn at Mitchell and followed the Warrego Highway to Morven. Now we were no longer riding into the wind, I was becoming aware of how hot it was. By the time we arrived at Morven I was completely overheating and had to strip out my jacket liner and head to the public toilets to dowse myself in water to cool down.

When I got back to where I'd left Rosie, Dave and some others had decanted into the pub. I joined them for a drink and then we continued along the Warrego Highway to Charleville. I'd done this piece of road on my last trip to Australia so I felt I was coming into familiar territory, although I was surprised to find how little of it I actually recognised.

We camped at the showgrounds at Charleville that night. There was a large exhibition hall, which they'd opened for us to sleep in. This meant there was no need to pitch our tents – we simply laid our beds out on the floor. I was next to Diana and a man in his sixties from England called John.

Diana and I headed off to the showers to freshen up. There were no pegs in the shower cubicles to hang our clothes on so I left my clothes on the sink units outside and wrapped myself in my towel.

Then I screamed like a banshee, tore my towel off and hopped around naked like demented kangaroo.

What the hell was on my towel?

"What is it?" called Diana from her cubicle.

I looked down. A slimy brown slug had somehow crawled its way onto my towel.

"Argh, there's a slug on my towel," I screamed, shuddering. I picked up my towel, shook the slug off and sped into the nearest free cubicle.

Bleughhh! Where the hell had that come from?

It was only after I'd finished my shower, opened my bag full of clean underwear and discovered another slug on a pair of pants I'd washed the day before that I figured out they must have been on the tree I'd used as a washing line at Nindigully. Won't be doing that again, I thought to myself.

Feeling somewhat creeped out by the whole affair, I nearly jumped out of my skin when Scott, the mechanic, later snuck up behind me and grabbed me under the armpits. *Damn him!*

Scott was a fun guy, full of energy and a bit of a prankster. He looked to be somewhere between thirty and forty and was the type of guy I thought would make a great uncle.

"Do you want to see my cock?" he asked me after my heart had returned to a normal rhythm.

I stared at him, dumbfounded. *Surely he didn't mean what I thought he meant?*

"I shudder to think what you have in mind," I responded.

He disappeared off to the support van and returned a few minutes later with something stashed under his jacket.

He pulled out a rubber chicken.

"Phew," I sighed with relief. "You had me worried there for a moment."

I was beginning to think he might like me, and when I later saw him walking past wearing nothing but a towel, I was beginning to think I might like him too.

I don't know if it was the grubby encounter or just that I was still feeling a bit under the weather, but that night I felt strangely out of things. I sat next to Anthony, Christian and Diana at dinner and found I couldn't think of a single thing to say. They were all laughing and joking but I felt completely inhibited for some reason. Having said that, I almost cried with laughter when Pete's chair collapsed beneath him, dumping him on the floor.

Day 4:
Charleville to Windorah

WEDNESDAY 10 SEPTEMBER 2014

As there were only six turns to make on our running sheets for the day, I started off alone, thinking even I couldn't go wrong with that.

Leaving Charleville, the next 215 km to Quilpie were on a long, straight, sealed road which ran parallel to a railway track for most of its distance. The ground was getting redder now, as we got further inland, and stubby shrubs bordered the road. Scattered along its shoulder were the remains of hundreds of kangaroos, and a series of triple road trains passing us in either direction indicated the most likely culprits for their demise.

I hadn't gone far before I caught up with another rider. Rosie was on good form, having had a service the night before, and I quickly overtook him. Only he wouldn't let me pull free. He seemed to be riding right behind me. What's he doing? I thought. Eventually I dropped my speed and let him pass me.

But once again he stayed with me and didn't seem to want to pull away. What's he up to? I kept thinking. Then, when two others passed us, one riding very tightly behind the other, I figured it out. *Slipstreaming.* This is the act of one bike hitching a free ride off the tailwind of the other. If the second bike positions itself just right, the tailwind of the first one acts as a slingshot and drags the second one along behind.

This, together with overtaking on the inside, was a practice outlawed by the event organisers. If the lead bike was to stop suddenly then the tailing bike would go straight into the back of it. This didn't seem to put anyone off, though, as after that I noticed loads of people doing it.

I followed my companion as far as the roadhouse at Cooladdi. Here, Diana noticed that there was oil all over my front mudguard. Fortunately, Andy the mechanic was there and tightened Rosie's "tappet", which seemed to fix the problem.

Some distance further on, Andy passed me in the support car and indicated for me to pull over. *What now?* It would seem my brake light was jammed on. He fiddled about with it and came to the conclusion that I must have been riding along with my foot on the back brake pedal. I was pretty sure that I hadn't.

Pulling back out from the side of the road, Pete and Stu came up behind me. We all rode along together for a bit, but clearly I was going too slowly for them, as suddenly Pete overtook me on the inside just as Stu passed me on the right.

"That was a risky manoeuvre," I said to Pete when I got to the refuel in Quilpie, "passing me on the inside."

"Hmm, I know. Sorry about that," he said with a sheepish grin. "I won't do it again."

As I fuelled up, Scott came over to see what was wrong with my brake light. He wiggled a wire about for a while and proclaimed it to be sorted.

In Quilpie I had a bottle of Powerade in a café with Pete and Stu, who then invited me to ride with them the rest of the way to Windorah. We set off in formation: Pete first, Stu next and me bringing up the rear. Pete was possibly the most relaxed rider I'd ever seen. He was leaning back with his legs straight out in front of him and his feet resting on his indicators.

From Quilpie it was a straight 250 km to Windorah along the Diamantina Development Road. This was a narrower piece of road and when a triple road train came up behind us and started overtaking, it was a bit of a tense moment, as I counted the trailers squeezing past us. Even Stu, who'd been so fast on the dirt on Day 2, wiped his hand over the top of his helmet and made out he was flicking sweat from his brow, as if to say "Phew". It didn't seem to bother Pete at all though, who kept his feet up through the entire manoeuvre.

Unfortunately the Powerade went straight through me and within 50 km I had to leave them and head into the bush for an emergency comfort stop.

After that I was on my own again. But I didn't mind; it was beautiful riding. I saw my first live kangaroo (as opposed to all the road kill), some emus, lots of cows and sheep, some wild horses and two emergency airstrips painted on the road. Every once in a while I'd pass a group of postie bikers who'd stopped at the side of the road for a rest and I'd beep my horn and wave merrily as I rode by.

The light was stunning, too. There's something about the light in Australia that is so vivid. It brings out an amazing purity in the air and every leaf on every branch of every tree is silhouetted with pristine clarity. The colours pulsate – azure blue skies, red sandy earth and smooth silver tree trunks.

The wildlife is harder to spot. Emus were the same colour as shrubs, kangaroos blended into the long, straw-like grasses and cows looked like boulders from a distance.

As I was cruising along, breathing in the colourful vista around me, I became aware of a large shape on the horizon. It was a road train. As it got closer, I thought it would pull off the road so I didn't have to, but it didn't. Suddenly, I realised that if I didn't pull off, I would be flattened. I swung Rosie onto the gravel shoulder as the beast thundered by. That snapped me out of my reverie and taught me a lesson I'd need to remember – road trains stop for no one.

Riding into Windorah, the light was at its most vivid. Small houses were adorned with pink and white bougainvillea, silhouetted against the flaxen grasses behind. There were two main roads lined with a few shops, a petrol station and a hotel, plus a number of smaller streets providing housing and a sports ground for the population of eighty.

We were staying at the sports ground and I turned in there, did my checks and set up camp under the covered outdoor basketball courts between 007 Michael and Pete and Stu. I wandered over to the café area, found a free table and sat down to write up my journal.

From a neighbouring table, another guy called Dave, with an Akubra hat, called over, "So how you finding riding with all these men, Jill?"

"What, are you kidding? I'm loving it. Helpful? Handsome? Funny? What's not to like?"

I was in heaven. Back home, I seemed to spend most of my time in female company. I worked with women, my friends were all women, and I hadn't had a boyfriend for seven years. This seemed to have the effect of bringing out my masculine side and I spent most of my time avoiding the types of things women usually did and taking on more manly pursuits. Now, however, being with all these men really brought out the feminine in me. For the first time in years, I was lapping up all the help and attention the menfolk were giving me. This is the natural way of things, I found myself thinking. It brought out a sense of fun in me and I found I was making all sorts of flirty comments without getting the least bit embarrassed about it.

As if to confirm my new-found femininity, a few minutes later Steve, a dentist from New South Wales, sat down beside me, followed shortly after that by a retired teacher called Mike, then by L-plate Mike. In a matter of minutes I was surrounded by men. *Ah, this is the life.*

Dinner was provided by the Windorah Rodeo Club. A choice of spaghetti bolognese or an indeterminate rice dish, which could have been curry but I'm not entirely sure, was on the menu.

After we'd finished eating, Dan announced that Scotty the American had withdrawn from the Challenge. I'd seen him in the hall at Charleville that morning with normal clothes on and had almost said, "Are you going home?" to tease him, but had thought better of it. Now I felt terrible. I hadn't even noticed he'd not been around all day and, judging by the stunned murmur that followed, neither had anyone else. Apparently he hadn't given a reason; he'd just told Dan, "I'm out."

The nosey parker in me went almost insane trying to figure out what could have made him drop out. *Was it the distances? Was it not what he was expecting? Did he feel that he didn't fit in? Had someone said something to upset him? Had he had a call from someone back home?* All that any of us could do was speculate. I was sad that he'd left, as I'd enjoyed his company.

Later, mechanic Scott came up and informed me that my footpeg had fallen off my bike and been found in the street outside the sports ground. I couldn't believe it. Surely I would have noticed something like that? But right enough, when I went to have a look, it was gone. Once again, I had become the butt of the support crew's mirth.

Day 5:
Windorah to Birdsville

We'd reached the edge of civilisation. Windorah was the last town we'd see for about 1,000 km that could be reached by a sealed road. After four days of relatively easy riding, we were about to hit the dirt.

After leaving Windorah, the first 110 km were on bitumen, as we entered the stunning scenery of the Channel Country. An immense blue sky arched above us and only a few escarpments in the far distance stood in the way of uninterrupted views of vast, flat plains covered in spinifex and small, stubby shrubs.

The Channel Country is an area that spans about 150,000 sq km, from Queensland to South Australia and New South Wales. It is made up of numerous channels flowing from the ancient river systems that crisscross the region. It is arid country, which only has occasional rainfall, but when it floods the landscape is transformed from dry scrub into huge flood plains which leave the ground rich with nutrients. For this reason it is able to support a massive cattle industry. In the Queensland section alone, it is estimated that there are between half and one million head of cattle.

There had been rain recently and the plateau was blooming with verdant flora. We could see cattle on either side of us, grazing amongst the grasses. Some would stop and poke up their heads as we passed, while others roamed casually, looking for the next succulent patch to chew.

Ahead, I could see a group of three cows walking towards the road. There was a line of postie bikers in front of me and I felt sure the cows would see us. But just as I came level with them, something seemed to catch their attention and they broke into a trot and ran out in front of me. I slammed on the brakes and narrowly missed going straight into the side of one of them. Clearly target fixation exists for cows too – there was nothing going to stop these fellas from getting their next meal.

At the end of the bitumen, just before we hit the dirt, we all rallied together. Dan warned us of the dangers of riding on dirt roads. There would be gravel, sand and deep corrugations to contend with, not to mention a gruelling distance of almost 300 km before we reached our destination of Birdsville. We were counselled about the risks of going too fast and told how every year several riders came to grief for not heeding his words.

Consequently, there was a mixture of great excitement and abject terror amongst our motley crew. I, of course, was in the latter category and from then on, my riding fell apart. I'd asked Dan the night before for some pointers on riding the dirt and he'd said the main thing is to keep the centre of gravity as low as possible by putting pressure into the footpegs. If the bike started to wobble I should let it, and it would usually right itself.

We turned off the main road onto the Birdsville Development Road, crossed a cattle grid, and then we were on it – a ribbon of pale grey gravel, disappearing into the distance.

Now you may wonder why on earth I had decided to do an event that included five days of riding on dirt tracks, when I was petrified of gravel. Well, it's amazing what a nice fat juicy carrot dangling at the end of a stick will do for you.

When I was in Australia on my previous trip I'd read a book called *Birdsville* about a Sydney journalist and his wife who went to live in the town for a year. Because it was in such a remote, inaccessible location, life was very different there and I wanted to see all the places and people he'd mentioned for myself. When I saw that the Postie Bike Challenge would be going to Birdsville, it seemed like the perfect opportunity. The town was only accessible by dirt roads therefore the only way to get there under my own steam would have been to hire a four-wheel-drive or to fly (there were no bus or train services to that part of the country).

The fact that there would be several hundred kilometres of gravel road to cover in order to get there was glossed over by the prospect of sharing the experience with other riders and having a support team to help us if we ran into trouble. This had clearly blinded me to the reality of what riding a postie bike down a dirt track would actually be like.

I started off down the track at 60 km/h. But it was terrifying. The Birdsville Races, the annual horse racing meeting that attracts people from all over the country, had taken place the week before and the mass exodus of hundreds of spectators in their four-wheel-drives and caravans had carved up the road, leaving huge trenches across its entire width.

I battered my way over the blitzed surface, vibrations shooting up my arms as if I was holding onto a pneumatic drill. Man, I thought, this is murder.

Within a couple of miles, a rider was down. He was lying face-down at the side of the road, with a group of other riders gathered around him. It seemed there were sufficient people to help him and I rode on, a knot in my stomach.

A few miles later, another rider was down, also lying face-down. This time a four-wheel-drive vehicle had pulled up and seemed to be taking care of him. Again, I rode on.

More vibrations, then I hit some soft sand and Rosie went into a wild wobble, lurching violently from side to side. Jesus, I thought, clinging on for dear life.

"Weight into the pegs," I commanded myself. More wobbling. "*Weight into the pegs*," I almost screamed, and thrust my legs downwards.

Miraculously, Rosie righted herself. *Hell, that was close.* I dropped back to 50 km/h.

Before long, the pack spread out and it seemed I was falling to the back of the group.

Silvia caught up with me. "Do you want to ride with me?" she asked as we came to a stop.

"I was thinking of riding alone today," I replied. "I think I need as much space around me as possible. I don't want to crash into anyone. Aren't you riding with Alec?"

"No, he wants to ride with the boys. I would just slow him down."

For a while we rode together, but even she started to gradually pull away from me.

Batter, batter, batter. Wobble, wobble, wobble. I was all over the place.

By the refuel point 100 km later I was down to 40 km/h.

Going up the hill to Deon's Lookout, where the refuel was taking place, was worse than the main road itself and completely blew whatever confidence I had left. Rocks the size of footballs were strewn over the track, which had the worst gouges yet, sinking to almost a foot deep in places.

My front wheel got caught in one and I got thrown to the side.

"Shit," I muttered, thinking I was going to go over, but again Rosie managed to stay upright. By the time I got to the top, I was shaking like a leaf.

I refuelled, had a sandwich (more pickles), took some photos and tried not to think about how terrifying it was going to be going back down again.

I couldn't put it off forever, though, and soon I was back on Rosie, making my descent.

The remaining 200 km into Birdsville was the most punishing riding I've ever done. The road became a carved-up mess of deep grooves lined with endless corrugations, sand pits and rocks. I had to weave from one side of the road to the other to find the smoothest surface. This often meant crossing a series of grooves, which would be strewn with loose purple rocks along their apex. Steering Rosie over them became an exhausting ordeal. It seemed the best way to avoid them was to ride down the shoulder, which was formed from compacted sand. But this, inevitably, would turn into soft drifts every few kilometres, meaning more wobbles and an immediate return to the harder gravel surface to regain control. Here, however, the corrugations practically shook my teeth out of their sockets.

The Aussies drive on the left, but the right-hand side of the road seemed a bit less treacherous than the left or the middle, so I manoeuvred Rosie over. Every time I went round a bend or approached a summit I prayed that nothing would be coming in the opposite direction.

I was down to 30 km/h. The corrugations were bone-shaking and my arms were aching with gripping so tightly. It seemed I was the only person on the road. I pulled over for a drink. Shortly after, Andy drew up in the support car and rolled down his window to enquire if I was okay.

"Just remind me why I wanted to do this?" I said.

He laughed and carried on.

About 40 km from Birdsville, I saw Linda and Kylie, the Postie Princesses, ahead of me. Linda was standing next to her bike and Kylie's bike was on the ground at the side of the road. Had she come off? I couldn't tell what had happened. I stopped next to Linda and asked her. She seemed a little confused and didn't really answer me. Just then, Kylie came up and said Linda had had a bad fall and caught her leg under the handlebars of her bike. Seeing this, Kylie had thrown her bike aside and rushed to her aid. Fortunately Linda was just badly shaken and hadn't broken anything, but she was still a bit dazed.

As we were talking, John, the Englishman, passed us. Being a nurse Kylie assured me that she could look after Linda, so I carried on. After a while I caught up with John and we rode the last stretch into Birdsville together.

With 30 km left, the road turned back to bitumen. "Oh God, thank you," I uttered under my breath. "Please let this last to Birdsville."

But it was not to be. Within a few kilometres it changed back to gravel. *Oh no.* My heart sank. And so the last few kilometres to the town were a tantalising mixture of gravel and bitumen surfaces. Just when I thought I was finally on bitumen for good, it would change back to gravel. It seemed like a tortuous way to greet visitors to the place.

It was 5 o'clock by the time I finally got there. I'd been on the road for ten hours and was completely wasted. On the final stretch, John had pulled away from me and, as I had removed my running sheets from my handlebars to prevent them flying off, I didn't know how to get to the caravan park where we were staying.

I saw 007 Michael walking along the road and stopped to ask him. I could hardly speak, I was so parched. But I was too exhausted to take in what he said and missed the turn. I ended up amongst some houses.

Realising I'd gone wrong, I turned back and screamed, "Where's the fucking campsite?" at Steve the car dealer, who was walking by.

Clearly terrified by this assault, he pointed a quivering hand down a side street and said, "Over there."

As I rolled into the campground, Scott told me I'd have to go back out and fuel up at the petrol station, as Dan had had to take two people to hospital and wouldn't be doing the refuel in the camp.

I thought I was going to collapse. But with no other option, I hauled Rosie around and went to the service station across the street. John was already there. I pulled up behind him, took off my helmet, put my head in my hands and burst into tears. I was completely shattered and the emotional and physical pounding of the day had left me feeling very fragile.

007 Michael came out of the shop, handed me a bottle of water and patted me on the back.

"Here, have this," he said.

It was a kind gesture, but I could barely even say "thank you". I stood there sobbing for the next five minutes, until I managed to compose myself enough to lift the pump off its cradle and start refuelling. John seemed a little concerned at my outpouring and attempted to comfort me, but I couldn't quite pull myself together.

I had been really looking forward to seeing Birdsville, but I'd arrived so late in the day, I barely had time to do my checks and set up camp before running across to the bakery where dinner was being served, let alone explore the town.

I could hardly eat my food, my hands were so weak. Hand Mike (a physiotherapist who specialised in hand and arm injuries) advised me I'd got "arm pump", a build-up of lactic acid in my forearms. I'd also badly strained the ring-finger of each hand, and the rest of my fingers were so cramped from gripping too tightly that I couldn't straighten them out again. They were injuries that would plague the rest of my trip.

I really struggled to keep my emotions in check during dinner, and when I discovered that the two riders I'd seen at the side of the road had been air-lifted out by the Royal Flying Doctor Service to a hospital in Mount Isa, 700 km away, it shook me up even more.

Ian, the New Zealander I'd been talking to at Nindigully, had a head injury and was badly concussed. Hugh, a man I hadn't met, had broken his collar bone and bruised his kidneys.

I was so worn out by the time I finished dinner that I went straight to bed, having seen nothing of the town I'd come to see. I had no idea how I was going to survive the next few days, if the roads continued to be this bad.

Day 6:
Birdsville to Mungerannie

During breakfast, John, my English compatriot, told me he was pulling out of the Challenge. He'd had a bad fall the day before and this, together with seeing me in such a state, had really shaken him.

"It's okay for you women," he said. "You can let it show on the outside, but us men have to keep it in. Just because I didn't let it out like you did doesn't mean I wasn't feeling it too."

This really upset me and left me feeling very shaky about the whole Challenge. *Perhaps I should pull out too? I mean, wasn't seeing Birdsville one of the main reasons I'd wanted to come? If I stayed on here with John, then I could see all the things I wanted to see.*

By the time I got back to camp, I was a mess. Anthony was camped next to me and as I was packing up he started chatting. I have no idea what he said, as the next thing I knew I was bubbling again.

We were starting the Birdsville Track today, an epic outback road which runs from Birdsville in Queensland to Marree in South Australia, 529 km away. Today we would be doing the first 321 km of it, followed by another three days on more dirt roads. If they were anything like the one we'd just covered, I wasn't sure if I'd make it. We were six days into the Challenge and already we'd lost five riders. *I could be next.*

"What's wrong?" said Anthony.

"I'm just having a bit of moment, that's all," I said, trying to make light of the situation, whereas in actuality I was feeling completely overwhelmed. *How the hell was I going to manage this?*

During the briefing that morning I was still sobbing, and when Dan announced John's official withdrawal it was all I could do to stop myself wailing out loud. I felt that John and I had bonded, somehow, and I was very sad to see him go. I gave him a huge hug and wished him well.

"What are you going to do?" I asked.

"I'll stay around here for a few days, then I'll meet up with friends in some other parts of the country," he replied. "I'd always planned to spend a few weeks in Australia."

I was glad his trip wouldn't be wasted and almost envied him for having the chance to see Birdsville, but something inside told me I wasn't ready to quit just yet.

As I let John go, someone turned to me and said, "You're the only foreigner left now."

Learning this steeled my resolve and I felt, somehow, that I had to stay in the race.

Before leaving Birdsville, Dan wanted to get a photo of us all lined up outside the Birdsville Hotel, an outback icon. As we lined up our bikes for the photo, Anthony came up to me and said, "I'm just going to take it easy today, if you want to ride with me."

I could have kissed him. He was an experienced dirt biker and was always one of the first ones into camp each day. Part of me worried that I'd be depriving him from having fun with his mate Christian, but when God sends you an angel in the form of a Hugh Jackman look-alike, you don't say no.

"I'll pick out some lines and you can follow me," he promised.

But as we left town and joined the Birdsville Track south, we got separated in the mass of other riders and I ended up on my own again. I was all over the place. I had no idea how to handle the ruts and was even stopping and manually paddling my way over ridges and troughs with my feet to try and find smoother ground. After about half an hour I became aware of someone ahead of me, at the side of the road. It was Anthony. True to his word, he'd waited for me.

He watched me ride for a bit, then pulled me over and told me what to do. I was struggling with the trenches.

"Whenever you come to a set of grooves, pick your line, keep your speed up and power through it," he said. "If you develop a wobble, the momentum will carry you through."

He set off and I started to follow. "Oh, and try not to strangle the grips," he shouted.

We hit the grooves at 60 km/h and, amazingly, he was right. It was actually much easier to ride the ruts at speed than it was to take them slowly (I'd been slowing down every time the surface got uneven). It even smoothed out the corrugations a bit. But it took nerves of steel.

Every time I had a wobble I remembered his words: "Keep the power on and the momentum will carry you through." I twisted the accelerator and my back wheel steadied, regained its grip and pushed me forward. *God, I love momentum!*

We had a stop after a while and I said, "You really need to keep your eyes fixed on the road ahead. If you look down, then it gets much harder to pull the bike through."

"Yes. As soon as you start looking down, you know it's time to have a break."

With this in mind, every time I stopped, I waited till I got onto a smoother patch so that I could slow down without skidding. When I started again, I got up to speed as quickly as possible so that I hit the trenches fast.

By the time we got to the refuel 185 km down the track I was feeling much better. I climbed off my bike, went over to Anthony and put my arms around him. "Thank you," I whispered.

"No worries" he said. "You'll be up at 70 or 80 by tomorrow".

"Ha, not likely," I replied.

There was a road gang in the parking area where we'd stopped to refuel, who were out grading the road. This is when they use huge tractor-like machines with large steel blades to scrape off the tops of the corrugations to smooth the road out. From this point on, the road got a bit easier to deal with.

Anthony stayed with me for the rest of the day – sometimes letting me ride ahead, sometimes letting me fall behind. It transformed my riding and we were amongst the first to arrive at the campsite at the Mungerannie Hotel.

I was elated. I felt like Nicole Kidman in the film *Australia*, where Hugh Jackman plays the handsome Drover who helps her drive her cattle through the Never Never to Darwin. I had gone from being a game but slightly hopeless rider, into a confident, fearless dirt biker, all because my very own Hugh Jackman look-alike had taken me under his wing and shown me how to ride the dirt.

I felt utterly indebted to Anthony. He had put his own needs aside to help me, and turned what could have been a nightmare journey into something I now felt capable of handling. To say that I was developing a bit of a crush on him would be something of an understatement. Anthony was now, unequivocally, my hero.

That afternoon in the pub, I was a transformed woman. Gone were the tears of the night before, gone was the sense of dread and in came a new confidence. I was chatting to anyone who would listen and boy, did I have a story to tell. I couldn't praise Anthony highly enough.

Alas, despite my best efforts not to "strangle the grips", my hands were still like claws. But it didn't matter. I was halfway down the Birdsville Track and I was still alive. Better than that, I was actually beginning to feel I knew what I was doing.

The Mungerannie Hotel lies about halfway down the Birdsville Track. Apart from a few cattle stations off the track, it's almost the only structure between Birdsville and Marree and provides a number of services to travellers. As well as offering a few rooms, it has a campground, a pub, a restaurant and a couple of petrol pumps. On approach, it looks like a single-storey wooden shack, but as you get closer you see a number of buildings scattered behind it. But Mungerannie's secret treasure is that it is built on top of the Great Artesian Basin, Australia's huge underground water supply. Despite being in the middle of a desert, it has its very own hot spring.

After regaling everyone in the pub with my tale of salvation, I put up my tent and wandered over to see what the hot spring was like. It was a small rectangular pool, about 3 metres wide by 10 metres long and a metre deep. It had been faced with wooden boards and had a small ladder leading into it. I was a bit overweight and too self-conscious to wear my swim-suit, so I just clambered in with my shorts and T-shirt on. Even though the external temperature was now in the low thirties, it was a delight to float about in that glorious hot water. It was the closest thing I'd had to a bath since arriving in Australia.

However, like water heated in the earth's subterranean pressure cookers all over the world, these springs contained sulphur and smelt strongly of it. After luxuriating in its healing fluids for a while, I climbed out and went to the showers to rinse off. All the showers were occupied and, as I waited, a couple of ladies from a tour bus came in to use the toilets.

"Aww, it stinks in here," one of them said, covering her nose.

"I'm afraid that might be me," I proffered. "I've just been in the hot springs."

She looked at me in disgust and they turned on their heels and walked straight back out again.

As my clothes were also stinking, I washed them in the shower before drying off and wrapping myself in my towel. I walked outside and started hanging my clothes over the railings of the shower block to dry out. I heard a wolf-whistle and looked up. Scott and Andy were at the support van, watching me and grinning like a couple of schoolboys.

"Nice dress," said Scott.

"It's a towel," I replied, grinning back and sashaying past them, letting a bit of leg show. It was lovely to get a bit of male attention.

That night the staff at the Mungerannie Hotel put on an amazing barbeque for us. They laid out trestle tables with white tablecloths in a yard behind the hotel. Overhead, the black sky was impregnated with a million glittering stars. With nothing to obscure our view, it was like being beneath an endless celestial chandelier.

I was sitting beside Pete, Stu and Dr Dave the cardiac surgeon, and the banter was flowing. Dave had a huge grin on his face and looked as if he couldn't have been happier.

It was a great end to an amazing day and I went to bed that night feeling truly blessed to be with such wonderful people.

Day 7:
Mungerannie to Marree

The grounds of the Mungerannie Hotel were scattered with a few old trucks that looked as though they would never make it back to civilisation. There was a set of notice boards giving information about the Great Artesian Basin and cattle farming in the area. I got a bit distracted taking it all in, and when I looked up, half the team were off and I hadn't even started Rosie yet.

Being considerably down the field and feeling more confident after my lesson with Anthony, I blasted it down the rest of the Birdsville Track at 70 km/h. Soon I was catching and passing other posties. One by one, I made my way up the field. God, it was so much easier now I knew what I was doing.

But this was no place for complacency. There were still numerous traps to catch out the unwary. Huge rocks were embedded in the corrugations, long sweeping bends had piles of gravel heaped on their edges which could flip you if you weren't careful, and soft sand pits lay hidden from view.

There were also a surprising number of surfaces to cope with. After three days on the dirt I was beginning to recognise the different ones and how to deal with them.

Firstly, there was your standard, light grey gravel surface. This was generally quite solid and reasonably smooth, unless there had been a lot of traffic, in which case it could become very corrugated.

Next, there was what I called purple gravel. Here the surface had been pounded into deep trenches or grooves, where multiple vehicles had used the same lines. The surface was broken up and the pulverised stones would be thrown onto the top of each trench, creating numerous purple-lined grooves to choose from. This was the surface that had been so prevalent on our first couple of days and which had had me in such a state. Trying to cross from one groove to another was very scary, as I'd have to cross all the loose stones on the top. After following Anthony, though, I discovered it was definitely easier hitting these at speed, as if you went too slowly your wheels would sink in and there was a higher chance of flipping over.

Then there was clay. This usually seemed to be red or light brown and in dry conditions was a joy to ride, as it provided a smooth, tightly compacted surface. When it's wet, apparently it's a different story, but luckily I didn't have to deal with that.

There was also a brilliant white surface that looked like concrete. Again, this was quite compacted and relatively easy to ride, but in the bright sunlight of the desert it could be blinding.

Finally, there was sand, the most dangerous of all the surfaces, in my view. Whereas all the other surfaces are reasonably compacted, sand gives no resistance whatsoever. If you hit it, your bike is absolutely guaranteed to be thrown into a violent wobble that will invariably fling you out of the saddle like a bucking bronco.

I could see Dan's ute up ahead, parked sideways on the crest of a hill, blocking the left-hand side of the road. I slowed down and pulled over to the right. On the other side of the summit was a two-metre drop into a huge sand pit, where the road had collapsed. If he hadn't been there to ward us off, I'd have gone straight into it and would, no doubt, have become the fourth person to end up in hospital.

The day before, Greg, Ned's friend, had had a really bad smash on his bike coming out of Birdsville. No one had seen what happened; he'd been discovered on the side of the road with his bike on the ground. An ambulance crew from Birdsville stabilised him and he was airlifted out by the Royal Flying Doctor Service to a hospital in Adelaide. He was our third casualty.

We only had 208 km to cover today, so there was no need to rush and take unnecessary risks. After recognising the hidden dangers ahead, I decided to have a few stops to absorb the scenery and take some photos.

I was behind the guy with the blue milk crate cover who I'd been following on the first day on the motorway, leaving Brisbane. His name was also John so, in my head, I called him Aussie John.

There was an unexpectedly high number of people with the same names. There were eight Mikes, three Daves, two Johns, two Steves, two Phils, two Scotts and three guys called one of Alec, Al or Alan. Hence the reason I was having to prefix them all with some sort of qualifier.

Aussie John and I seemed to be on the same time clock and were pulling in at all the same places. He was a nice guy and it was good to shoot the breeze with him. Our first stop was outside a homestead at the Etadunna station. There was a small creek ahead, which, for once, actually had some water in it (most of the creeks we'd crossed had been dry). John had stopped to film us all going through it. I did my best to create an impressive splash as I hit the water, but didn't manage to raise much more than my own eyebrows.

At one point we could see an escarpment near the roadside. John bumped his bike onto the tiny track that led through the scrub to the base of the hill, and I followed. The fact that I even considered doing such a thing showed how much more confident I was feeling. We parked the bikes at the base of the hill (although I noticed some people had actually ridden all the way up) and walked to the top. Below was an endless panorama of flat plains, interspersed with salt lakes. It was breathtaking and took several minutes to absorb.

By 1.30 p.m. I'd made it to the end of the Birdsville Track at Marree. There was a sign on the opposite side of the road marking the beginning of it (from the southern end) and Gary, Hand Mike and some others were already there taking photos of themselves. I jumped off Rosie, whooped with joy and ran over to celebrate with them.

"I'm going to start calling you Zena, Warrior Princess," said Gary. "Well done."

It was a triumphant moment. We had just completed one of the toughest outback roads in Australia. Not only that, we'd done it on 110 cc postie bikes, not big 4 x 4 Land Cruisers.

We were staying in the campground at the Marree Hotel. It was one of the oldest buildings in the town, having been there since the town was founded in 1883. It was a square, two-storey, sandstone building, which seemed to have had a variety of extensions added to it over the years. I found the campground, did Rosie's checks and pitched my tent. Then I had a shower and headed for the pub.

Anthony, Christian and Ned were already there and gave out a big cheer as I entered.

"I hear you overtook half the field coming out of Mungerannie?" said Anthony.

I smiled and nodded my head.

"See, I told you you'd be up at 70 today," he said with a glint of pride in his eye and I knew he'd got something out of the experience too.

A couple of bottles of pear cider later and I was starting to feel very tipsy. As it was still early in the afternoon I decided to have a look around Marree before I got completely plastered.

Central Australia, in which Marree lies, was opened up in 1862 when the explorer John McDouall Stuart mapped out a route for the Overland Telegraph Line between Port Augustus and Darwin. Towns sprang up along the line and soon a railway followed, linking these towns.

Originally called the Central Australian Railway, this was a narrow-gauge railway that ran from Port Augusta in South Australia to Alice Springs in the Northern Territory. Construction began in 1878 and followed roughly the same route as the Overland Telegraph Line. This took it east of a small mountain range called the Pichi Richi Pass, through the towns of Quorn, Hawker and Parachilna, among others. Construction got as far as Marree in 1883, followed by Alice Springs in 1929. It was nicknamed the Afghan Express or, more commonly, the Ghan, after the Afghan camel drivers who transported many of the raw materials needed for its construction.

There were seventy-nine stations along its length, with a particularly twisty section between Marree and Alice Springs. This became notorious for delays, usually caused by flash floods, which would wash away bridges and rails. Passengers often had to disembark and help reconstruct the track.

I wandered around the now abandoned railway station, looking at some of the old diesel locomotives that were still sitting on what remained of its tracks. Marree was once a major railhead for the cattle industry, but no trains had run there since the line closed in 1986 and the town was now, judging by some of the photographs on display, something of a shadow of its former self.

Marree has a population of about sixty people, apparently mostly involved in mining, agriculture and accommodation services. It sits at the junction of the Oodnadatta Track and the Birdsville Track, so a lot of tourists pass through. This explained the need for accommodation, but given what a dry, barren area it was, it was difficult to believe there was any agriculture apart from cattle farming. There were a few shops, a police station, and the rather misplaced Lake Eyre Yacht Club. Lake Eyre was another 100 km to the north-west and it was so dry it was usually a large salt flat rather than a saturated basin.

Coming back to the hotel, I saw Ned sitting outside. "How's Greg?" I asked.

"Not good. He's in an induced coma."

"What?" I gasped. "What on earth happened to him?"

"He's got six broken ribs, two punctured lungs, a burst spleen and a head injury."

"Oh my God. I had no idea his injuries were so bad."

Ned looked very forlorn and I realised he must be worried sick. I gave him a hug. "Hmm, you smell lovely," I said, catching the whiff of some gorgeous cologne.

This made him smile and I hoped he wasn't agonising over his friend too much.

I made my way back to the campsite and moved Rosie from the grassy area where I'd left her over to the other bikes, next to the support van. I was in the middle of putting her onto her stand when Bob, the oldest member of our group, rode in. He pulled onto the grassy area I had just vacated and toppled to one side. Scott, who was standing nearby, sprung over and caught his bike just in time.

"Whoopsie," said Scott, holding it steady. "You all right?"

Bob smiled back wryly. "Hmm, yes, thanks. Just a bit tired."

I couldn't help but be impressed that, at eighty years old, he was doing the Challenge at all. I'd be happy just to make it out of the house at that age. But Bob had just done the Birdsville Track, for heaven's sake – he was allowed to have a wobble if he needed to.

The mechanics were gathered around the support van, changing a tyre on a bike. I realised I didn't have any photos of them, so I took out my camera and fired off some shots.

They were a phenomenal team who before, during and after each ride, fixed and, if necessary, serviced our bikes. They were all volunteers who helped out for the love of it and they were a joy to be around. Andy had been involved right from the start of the Postie Bike Challenge in 2001.

"How's it going?" he asked me. "You seem a bit happier today." The last time we'd spoken was when I'd asked him to remind me why I'd wanted to do the Challenge on the Birdsville Development Road.

"Yes, Anthony gave me a lesson on how to ride the dirt yesterday and it completely transformed my riding," I answered.

"Ah, I saw you give him a hug at the refuel. I wondered what that was about."

"What do you do when you're not doing this?" I asked him.

"Oh, I'm retired now, but I love bikes. In fact, I've got a shed full of them at home. Classics that I've restored over the years. My wife and I both love them."

He told me about his wife and how they'd both been divorced before, and had met later in life. His eyes shone with love as he told me about his lady and how blessed he felt to have found her.

"You know, I'm really glad you're here," he continued. "You bring a certain charm to the group and it's just really good having you around."

"Aw, thanks," I replied, touched by his kindness. He was such a warm person.

That night in the pub everyone was in high spirits from having survived the Birdsville Track. Linda (who, I was amazed to discover, was only on her 'L' plates) and I decided we'd had enough of dirt roads and attempted to find a way to avoid doing any more. There was a map on the wall which showed all the roads and tracks in the region, but try as we might we couldn't find a route that would take us all the way to Arkaroola, our next stop, on sealed roads. We eventually resigned ourselves to the fact that we were in it for the long haul.

The pear cider was going down a treat and before long everyone was my best friend and I was dishing out hugs left, right and centre.

Ned got another one and I couldn't help but utter, "God, you smell good."

Anthony was nearby and started laughing.

"Basic instincts," I muttered, trying to justify myself.

By the time dinner finally came round later that evening we were more than ready for it. An array of roast meats and a chicken curry were on offer. I decided the roasts were for me, but the staff had other ideas and piled our plates high with a bit of everything.

I'm not a fan of hot, spicy food and would never usually have eaten curry, let alone mixed it with a roast dinner, but when someone else is doing the serving, there's not a lot you can do about it. I tried to leave the curry at the side but it had seeped into everything else and some of it got into my system. During the night, I noticed I was exceedingly flatulent.

I was obviously not the only one affected by its potency as, in the morning, I overhead L-plate Mike complaining that the noise being produced by the campers around him was "like being in the shootout at the OK Corral".

Day 8:
Marree to Arkaroola

Despite the joys of completing the Birdsville Track, I was feeling emotional again the following morning. The hotel TV was full of reports about the forthcoming referendum on Scottish independence from the UK and somehow it made me sad. What if the country voted in favour of independence? What on earth would life be like after that, separated from the rest of the UK by politics but not by geography?

Even though the roads in Marree were sealed, all three roads leading in and out of the town (the Birdsville Track, the Oodnadatta Track and the rather unimaginatively titled B83) were gravel.

We took the B83 south from Marree and rejoined the dirt. It seemed a lot smoother, but maybe I was just getting better at riding it. After about 55 km we came across Farina, a ghost town situated half a mile off the road.

Originally called Government Gums, Farina had been settled by farmers in 1878. Like many early European settlers who happened to come across a new region during a rare period of high rainfall, they assumed it was always like that and thought it would be suitable for growing wheat and barley. To reflect these aspirations they changed the name to Farina (the Latin for flour). Unfortunately, after several years of good rains, normal weather patterns resumed and harvests failed, quickly bankrupting the farmers and destroying the thin and fragile layer of topsoil.

Initially plans had been laid out for 432 quarter-acre housing blocks in Farina, but these never came into being as the normal rainfall was insufficient to cultivate crops and there was barely enough water to support the population. However, while the wheat and barley crops failed, Farina flourished as the railhead for the Ghan, until the railway was extended to Marree. For a short time it benefitted from cattle farmers driving their stock there for transportation south to Adelaide. Several silver and copper mines were also dug in the surrounding area, expanding the population to 600 at its peak.

Despite the harshness of the environment, the town grew big enough to have two hotels, an underground bakery, a bank, two breweries, a general store, an Anglican church, five blacksmiths, a school and a brothel.

However, by the 1930s Farina was declining and by the early 1960s the post office was closed, followed by the railway in the 1980s.

Nowadays nothing but the ruins of the old bakery and the railway's water tank remain. The town is deserted, with the closest residents living at Farina Station, a few miles to the west.

We continued on, through the rocky plains to Lyndhurst, a tiny town with a roadhouse, a couple of houses and not much else. Lyndhurst's main claim to fame is that the Strzeleckie Track, another great outback gravel road, starts/finishes here. But the best thing about Lyndhurst was that we left the dirt behind and rejoined a sealed road all the way to Copley. Admittedly, it was only 35 km away, but, oh, the sweet joy of being able to ride without having your arms vibrated out of their sockets.

I wouldn't have minded a stop to have a look around Lyndhurst, but everyone else seemed to be riding on and, as I was still feeling a bit fragile, I followed, not wanting to be left on my own.

Approaching Copley we could see the outer edges of the Telford open-cut coal mine. A wall of tall black slag heaps marked its perimeter, but from the highway we could only catch a glimpse of its full size. Hidden from view was a huge open-cut pit descending several hundred metres into the ground.

Copley itself proved to be a rather uninteresting town. The main road through the village was lined with somewhat dilapidated square houses, most of which seemed to be white or grey in colour. Against a sandy background, they gave a somewhat bland appearance to the place.

I was still following some of the others and still craving security, when they pulled into the bakery for a cup of tea, so I did the same. Getting closer, I realised it was Pete, Stu, 007 Michael and Alice Springs Dave. We'd only done 116 km but it was nice to have a rest and take in the mountains that were now around us.

When I left, Michael decided to ride with me. I was quite relieved, as I was worried about the next stretch of dirt we'd have to tackle. So far we'd mostly been on flat, straight tracks, but now we were going to climb into the hills of the Northern Flinders Ranges to Arkaroola. Dan, during his morning briefing, had advised us there would be lots of steep ascents and tight bends, so we should be extra careful. Before leaving Marree I'd asked my riding instructor Anthony how to handle the bends.

"Okay, as you approach a bend, pick your line, roll off your speed and then keep the speed steady through the bend," he advised.

Michael and I crossed the railway line as we took Copley Road out of town and immediately found ourselves back on the dirt for the next 150 km up to Arkaroola. I was ahead and as I came to the first bend, I talked myself through Anthony's instructions. *Find your line, adjust your speed and keep it steady through the bend.* It worked well and I was able to maintain a fairly steady 60 km/h through the winding track ahead.

It was a beautiful trip up through the mountains. Jagged peaks surrounded us, with the occasional small homestead nestled in a clearing set back from the road. I marvelled at how many long dirt roads exist in Australia and wondered how on earth they'd come into being. Not only must there have been a huge amount of manual labour involved, but how did they discover all of these places to begin with, given how little water and food there was around to sustain the explorers of the time?

The road continued through the mountains. The track was reasonably smooth and soon I was in a flowing rhythm through the twists and turns – *line, adjust, steady... line, adjust, steady.*

We stopped at Nepabunna, home to the Adnyamathanha aboriginal people. It was a pretty, well-kept village with a Mission, run by the local people, which assisted with housing, schooling, health and other facilities and provided a dormitory for Aboriginal children.

Dentist Steve and Silvia came up behind us. Together we shared a drink and gazed in wonder at the stunning peaks around us.

A few miles later, the road descended into Italowie Gorge, a dry creek bed flanked with tall gum trees and littered with large boulders. A few posties had stopped there but we continued. By the time we reached the campground at Benbonyathe Hill, nature was calling. I pulled off, and a few minutes later Michael, who'd been ahead, appeared round the corner to see if I was okay.

"Just need the loo," I explained.

He nodded understandingly and carried on while I wandered into the bush.

I was getting back on Rosie when Aussie John passed me. Ahead was another long incline and by the time I set off I could see John in the distance. After a while the road flattened out and I came to a grassy plateau. There was a field of wild horses to my left and John was pulled up at the side, taking some footage with his GoPro camera. I carried on and soon I arrived at the Arkaroola Resort & Wilderness Sanctuary, relieved that the road hadn't been as bad as I'd expected.

The resort was situated in a natural amphitheatre at the foot of a set of tall, striated, russet granite mountains. It comprised a central building housing a bar, restaurant, shop, information centre and a couple of petrol pumps. Along a trail to the left were a campsite and caravan park. Beyond the main centre was a square accommodation block with motel-like units around the outside and a central gallery and seating area on the inside. Opposite that, on the other side of the road, was a series of stand-alone cabins. Between the main building and the accommodation block was a swimming pool and barbeque area.

Once again, we'd arrived quite early in the afternoon and a row of postie bikes was lined up outside the accommodation block with no riders to be seen. I figured I knew where they would be.

In the bar, the usual suspects had gathered – Anthony and Christian, Ned, Aussie John, L-plate Mike and my companion for most of the ride, 007 Michael. I was starting to really love this life. I sat on a bar stool, my back resting against Aussie John's, sipping an orange juice. I felt so comfortable with these guys. They were becoming like a family of big brothers to me and gradually I was falling for every one of them.

After a while, news reached us that the mechanics had set up shop at a shed behind the main building. We rode our bikes round to do our checks and then left them so the mechanics could give them all a quick check over.

Dan had arranged for us to stay in proper beds in the accommodation block for the night. Before we left Marree, he had asked us all who we'd like to share with, so that he could allocate rooms accordingly.

"I'll share with Jill," Diana had yelled out.

Damn, I thought, thinking of the many men I'd have happily shared a room with that night. But I didn't mind really. Diana was great fun, full of laughter and possibly the most cheerful person I'd ever met.

It had been another hot day and with Rosie's needs taken care of and our accommodation not yet available, I made my way to the swimming pool. Silvia and Alec, Dentist Steve and IT Mike (the one with all the circuit boards on his milk crate) were already there. Various toes were dipped in to test the water but no one seemed game enough to take the plunge. After a fair bit of havering myself, I steeled my courage and dived in fully clothed.

God, it was freezing. Almost immediately, I rocketed straight back out. *Man, that was cold!*

Silvia was next in, and after a while I decided to have another go. This time it didn't feel quite so bad and the two of us managed to bob about for quite a while until we heard that our rooms were ready.

I grabbed my gear and raced to my room. There was no sign of Diana yet so I bagged my bed and jumped in the shower.

By the time I'd finished, Diana had arrived. She'd been sightseeing again with her pals Alan and Akubra Dave. They'd become known as the Sandwich Club as they were always stopping off for cups of coffee, a nibble on their sandwiches and to see whatever sights were to be seen.

After she'd had a shower we went off to explore. There was an observatory on the hill behind the centre. We took a walk up there but it was closed. Not surprisingly, it wouldn't be open until that evening, when a star-gazing tour would take place.

After dinner, a bunch of the boys disappeared behind a curtain at the end of the restaurant. *What was going on?* I walked over and stuck my head round. There was Anthony, Christian, Walshy and Aussie John, all crowded round a glass box that looked like a fish-tank, with looks of wonder on their faces.

"Men's business," they joked, pulling the curtain closed.

"Yeah, right," I said, poking my head back round.

Inside the box was a collection of beautiful iridescent rocks, lit by a single light. Aussie John was filming them with his GoPro.

"Are you really filming a bunch of stationary rocks with a video camera?" I asked.

This raised a laugh and, for a moment, I felt like one of the boys.

Back at the accommodation block, I bumped into Ned. Even without hugging him I could smell how lovely he smelt. "What *is* that aftershave you're wearing?"

"Oh, it's just a body wash."

Best bloody body wash I'd ever smelt.

Day 9:
Arkaroola to Orroroo

MONDAY 15 SEPTEMBER 2014

Our morning briefing started with a stern warning from Dan about the treacherous condition of the roads ahead.

"I've actually put 'Beware dips, sand, gravel' on your running sheets and I haven't done that for any other days, so be warned – this is not a good road surface to ride."

With the fear of God instilled in us, we backtracked the first 30 km to a junction we'd passed the day before, then took the road to Blinman. This led us onto a high, exposed ridge with a cross-wind like a jet engine. For the next 30 km our little row of postie bikes leaned over at a forty-five degree angle, trying not to be blown off the road.

At one point the Squash Club, two younger guys in motocross gear who did a lot of dirt biking and had squash racquets wedged into their milk crates for reasons which I never got to the bottom of, were standing by the side of the road waving at us. At first I thought they were just being friendly. As I got closer, I realised they were signalling for us to slow down, as there was a huge sand pit right across the road. I just managed to roll off enough power not to hit it at full throttle. I bounced through the air, lurching one way and then the other as I landed on the other side.

This marked the start of the "dips, sand and gravel" Dan had been warning us about.

A few kilometres further on, Anthony was standing by the side of the road at a junction, signalling for us to go right. That's funny, what's he doing there? I thought. Anthony was usually so far ahead of everybody else that you could go the whole day without seeing him. It was only later that I found out that Christian had broken two of his spokes when he landed in the sand pit. Anthony must have been waiting for him while his bike was being repaired.

Further on again, Dentist Steve was sitting at the edge of the road. I stopped. "Are you okay?" I called out to him.

"Yes, I just stopped to refuel and discovered I'd lost my jerry can and everything in my milk-crate. It must have fallen out when we went into that sand pit. I'm just hoping someone's picked it up."

I waited with him, and a few others pulled over to see what had happened. As we all gathered by the roadside, a couple in a four-wheel-drive pulled up and asked us what we were doing.

"We're doing the Postie Bike Challenge," said one of the guys and explained a bit about it.

"Are you doing it for charity?" said the lady.

"Well, sort of. The bikes will be donated to the Rotary Club at the end, who will auction them to raise funds."

At this point the lady took out her purse and pressed a $20 note into his hand. He put it in his pocket, promising to pass it on to Dan.

As the contents of Steve's crate had now been delivered by another rider, we all got going again.

The next 100 km were a nightmare. The road slowly descended into a valley through a series of steep drops, tight bends and carved-up surfaces, but surprisingly I found I wasn't thinking about it anymore. No longer was I talking myself through every twist and turn; I was just doing them. Even a couple of wobbles didn't freak me out, as I knew the momentum would carry me through.

Having said that, there was a new hazard to contend with here – floodways.

If you haven't figured it out already, Australia is an extremely dry country, especially away from the coastal areas. However, when it does rain, it usually deluges, causing extensive flooding. Flood waters flow into creeks and rivers, which invariably cross the many roads and tracks that crisscross the outback. The points at which these creeks cross the road are known as floodways.

On sealed roads, they usually take the form of a concrete dip, with an indicator at the side of the road showing the depth of any waters flowing across them. On dirt roads, though, there is seldom any warning, and it's only through reading the land that you get a sense of where they will be. Here they aren't lined with nice smooth concrete; they are usually lined with soft sand or are strewn with rocks and small boulders. Very, very occasionally there will be some water in them, too. If you don't see them coming, crossing them inevitably results in a very rough ride.

This road was full of them. Every dip and hollow would have one, and even some of the flatter sections would spring them on you, too.

As I came over the crest of a small hill, the road dropped steeply down to the valley floor and I plunged into another sand-lined floodway. I bounced out of it, straight into another one. "Oh, Jesus!" I couldn't stop myself from shrieking as the bike swerved left and right. This time I really thought I was a goner. But it's a testament to how hardy these little postie bikes are that not only did Rosie's tyres stay intact but, once again, she stayed upright.

On the other side, the road rose steeply. I cranked on the power and grinded my way through a narrow ribbon of bends. The Engineering Club (we were all starting to get nicknames by now), a group of three engineers – Kate, Al and another Mick – caught up with me and started overtaking me on both sides. Shit, I thought as they squeezed past and I tried to stop Rosie drifting into their path.

Up on a high plain I was alone again. I needed to top up Rosie's tank and empty my own. I pulled out my jerry can, filled up and then made for a bush on the other side of the road. Now why is it always the way that you can go for miles in the outback without seeing another soul and then, whenever you need to bare your all, someone comes along? In this case, about half a dozen other posties went by. Thankfully, the straightness of the road at that point meant they were going along quite quickly and weren't subjected to an unduly long exposure.

When we finally arrived at Blinman, a small town whose main claim to fame was that it was the highest surveyed town in South Australia, we rejoined the tarmac. I was so happy to see it, I prostrated myself on the road and kissed its beautiful, smooth, solid surface.

A few of us stopped by the roadside for a while, celebrating our return to civilisation, but it had clouded over and the temperature had dropped considerably. Posties were arriving dressed in just motocross shirts and armour, and were shaking with the cold. There was no time to waste. We still had 100 km to go to the refuel at Hawker, where they'd be able to get jackets and jumpers from the support van, so no one hung about for long.

You'd think rejoining the tarmac would be a joyous occasion, but the wind was now blowing a gale and the ride south was a tortuous battle into a strong headwind, keeping Rosie down at 60 km/h.

We were riding through the spectacular Flinders Ranges, the highest mountain range in South Australia. They are thought to have formed as the result of tectonic activity along the Adelaide Rift Complex – folding, buckling and forcing strata upwards. They comprise mostly limestone, shale and sandstone, with hard quartzites (compressed sandstone) forming most of the high ground and ridgetops. From afar they present a long, pointed range with clear, sloping lines of strata in their sandy surface.

It was gorgeous countryside but oh, so cold and when I saw Engineer Mick pull up ahead of me, I stopped beside him. As he was usually with the other engineers I hadn't really spoken to him much – only a few passing comments like the fact that we had the same tent and helmet. But now I got to have a bit of a chat. He was nice guy and very funny, but it was too cold to stand about for long. I put on my windproof jacket (which had been strapped to the outside of my milk crate since Brisbane) while he pulled out a jumper, and soon we were on our way.

I lost him when I pulled over to take some photos of the peaks below.

The road descended through pretty meadows filled with delicate lilac, yellow and white wild flowers and viridian pine trees, eventually flattening out at the junction to Wilpena Pound.

What on earth is that? I thought. The name intrigued me and, as it was only a few kilometres off route, I decided to take a detour and have a look. Seeing my bike, a man in a car at the junction rolled down his window and shouted, "Your friends are down there."

I didn't know who he meant – it could have been any of the posties – but when I arrived I saw three postie bikes in the car park. Often I could tell whose bike was whose by their milk crate covers, but I didn't recognise any of these. I parked next to them and went over to the visitors' centre. Outside, sipping coffee and eating their sandwiches, were the Sandwich Club – Diana, Dave and Alan.

I joined them for a cup of tea and ate my sandwiches too (more bloody pickles – I hated pickles), then went in search of an explanation. Wilpena Pound, it turns out, is the name given to a set of mountains within the Flinders Ranges which form a large circular basin. Because of its shape, it was initially thought to be some kind of ancient volcano, but it has now been identified as two mountain ranges – one on the western edge and one on the eastern – joined by a long bluff at the south. The level floor of the Pound is approximately 8 km long by 4 km wide. The word 'Wilpena' is thought to come from the Aboriginal meaning "place of bent fingers" and 'pound' is an old English word that means "an enclosure for animals". This, in fact, was how the pound was used by early farmers, as a place to keep their horses.

With my curiosity satisfied, I headed back to the main road and continued south to Hawker. I was starting to leave the Ranges behind me and when I arrived at my destination, the land was levelling out again.

Dan's ute was at the side of the road and I pulled over to refuel. There was a helmet on the kerb with hair trailing out of it. It looked as though someone had been decapitated.

I did a double-take and heard a peal of laughter as Dr Dave came over, sniggering. He'd found a wig by the road and thought he'd see how many people he could catch out by stuffing it inside his helmet and leaving it on the ground.

It was another 100-odd kilometres to Orroroo, our target for the day, and the wind wasn't getting any easier, so I pressed on. We were entering farming country now and huge pastures full of wheat spread out to either side. I stopped in the odd village to have a quick look around, but mostly I tried to keep going.

Walshy was up ahead of me and I crouched down to improve my aerodynamics and pushed past him. *Yes!* Then the Squash Club boys sped past me and stole my thunder. I crouched down again and caught up with some others.

"Come on," I harangued Rosie. She responded and we passed them too. I was bobbing up and down like a sewing machine. It was great fun.

Eventually the flour silos of Orroroo came into sight. This was another place I'd been to on my previous trip. But I had no inclination to go down memory lane; I just wanted to find the campsite. We were staying at the Sports Grounds and I looked at my running sheets – left, right, left. *There they are!* I'd made it. I pulled up by Anthony, who was visibly shaking.

"Did you ride all the way here just wearing that?" I asked. He was wearing a thin motocross top.

"Yes," he admitted sheepishly. "I think I was on the verge of hypothermia."

"Didn't you get your jacket out of the support van?"

"No, it hadn't arrived by the time we were leaving, so we just carried on."

I found it deeply comforting to know that even Anthony could be a bit of an idiot sometimes.

I did my checks and made my way into the clubhouse. But all was not well. The water supply to the building had been cut off and the toilets were out of use. Nevertheless, some tea and beer had been provided by the Orroroo Football Club and we all huddled around the tables, sipping our beverages and trying to warm up.

The wind was still raging and I noticed that a few people had already started to pitch their tents in the exposed grounds around the clubhouse. *Surely they'll get blown to pieces?* I had a look around. Aussie John had pushed three benches together in front of a metal building and laid his bed out on top of this. This seemed like a good idea, as the building's wall formed a wind break. As there were another three benches there, I claimed them and did the same thing. With my bed sorted for the evening, I went to see what could be done about having a shower.

By this time some additional showers, which had running water, had been identified in a shed across the playing fields. However, as these would have to accommodate both the male and female members of our party, Dan said he'd arrange for us women to be called when the men, who had already started using them, had finished.

Diana, Silvia, Linda, Kylie and I gathered in the dugout by the side of the playing fields, towels at the ready. It was the first time all the girls had been together as a group since the start of the Challenge. We larked about, shouting out things like "foul" or "offside" to an imaginary football team as we waited. Then, when mechanic Mick gave us the signal, we herded into the bleakest shower block I've ever seen.

Judging by the collection of massage tables, benches and assorted sports equipment scattered around the building, these showers hadn't been used in quite some time. There were two rooms, with three showers along the back wall of each. We split into two groups – Linda and Kylie in one and Diana, Silvia and I in the other.

Now men are used to stripping off in front of their team mates and using shared showers in locker rooms around the world, but we ladies usually have individual cubicles to maintain our modesty. No such luck here. After a few minutes of debating our options, we realised we were in for a long wait if we each went in separately, and accepted we were just going to have to swallow our pride and go in together. Looking anywhere but at each other, we disrobed and headed in. Despite their grubby exterior, the showers actually turned out to be quite good and we all returned feeling a little warmer.

On my way out, I caught sight of Linda's bare leg. There was a huge purple bruise running from her hip to her knee, marking where she'd fallen on the Birdsville Development Road.

"God, look at your leg!" I couldn't help exclaiming. "Is it sore?"

"Oh, it's okay now. It probably looks worse than it feels."

I was amazed she hadn't been limping, with a contusion like that.

Returning to the clubhouse, we found that the local people had prepared some hot soup, which they were dishing out as an aperitif to our dinner. It was just what we needed. An hour or so later they served up a fantastic meal for us, so we all had nice warm bellies to fend off the cold winds whistling through the campground.

They'd also arranged for a local folk singer to come and serenade us but I decided to duck out at this point and head to bed. I had bought two sleeping bags with me, one made from down, the other from a thin synthetic material. So far I'd only needed the down one, but tonight I dug out the synthetic one and put the down one inside it. I then snuggled in for what turned out to be a remarkably cosy night's sleep.

Day 10:
Orroroo to Adelaide

Australians are known for their barbequing prowess, and the following morning the Football Club outdid themselves by preparing an entire cooked breakfast on the large barbeque plate outside the clubhouse. I filled up my dish and sat down beside Scott, the mechanic. I hadn't seen much of him for the last few days and had missed his attentions.

"So what will you do when this is over?" I asked. "Will you go back to working at Pro Honda?"

"No, I don't work there anymore. I'm going to go sailing around the Whitsundays."

The Whitsundays were an island group off the coast of northern Queensland. We chatted a bit about this and then he said, "If you don't mind me asking, how old are you, Jill?"

"Fifty-one" I replied.

I have never seen anyone look so stunned in all my life. His face literally froze in shock. "I thought you were about the same age as me," he mumbled.

"And how old is that?" I enquired.

"Thirty-eight."

"I thought you were more like thirty-five or forty," said Elton Mike (another Mike, with a bike called Elton), who was sitting next to me.

I turned to thank him for the compliment, but when I turned back around, Scott had vanished. Any thoughts he might have been having about staying in touch were obviously quashed in that moment.

Given how cold it had been the previous day and that the morning's temperature wasn't much better, I decided to zip my removable lining back into my jacket while we waited for Dan to start the briefing. Anthony and Christian were standing next to me. I laid the outer jacket on the ground and started feeding the arms of the inner jacket down its sleeves. They weren't going in very easily.

"It's easier if you wear the liner, then put your outer jacket on over the top of it," said Christian sarcastically.

"No it's not," I said, "coz I need to zip it all together and I can't do that if I'm wearing it!"

I wasn't angry – merely a little exasperated, but Ned, who'd just arrived, seemed to think I was getting a bit uptight and came over. He put his arms around me and said, "You need a hug."

Even though I hadn't felt particularly agitated, it was so nice and it immediately calmed me. *And God, he smelt so good.*

Dan told us we were on a deadline to reach Adelaide by 2 p.m. because the Rotary Club would be waiting to meet us to take the bikes away. We would have a refuel at Clare, about 130 km away. This meant that if we didn't fill our tanks right up to the top we might run out of fuel before we got there and have to do an additional refuel from our jerry cans, which would waste time. Therefore, we should all shake our bikes to ensure our fuel sank as low as possible in our tanks and then top up the remaining space before we set off.

Anthony started shaking his bike wildly from side to side.

"That's not how you start it, mate," joked Christian.

"Ha," I laughed. Christian was a funny guy.

It was an intense day's riding. We were accompanied by another strong headwind, although not quite as bad as the one the day before.

We were definitely starting to rejoin civilisation now and the towns were becoming more frequent. After 55 km we passed through Jamestown, then 40 km after that, Spalding. Another 40 km along the Horrocks Highway and we were at Clare. I could see the refuel point ahead at the side of the road.

This was like a Formula 1 pit stop, with Andy waving us in, us filling our tanks, then jumping straight back on the bikes again and rejoining the carriageway.

We were in the Clare Valley now, an area rich with farmlands. Lush emerald and yellow canola fields lay on either side of us. The towns were getting bigger too, often preceded by a new housing estate or two.

Coming into Gawler, things started to get complicated. We were back up to two pages of running sheets and I was about halfway down the first and kept losing my place. It's not easy trying to read them while you're riding and at the same time looking for the landmark they refer to.

Dan had warned us things would start getting tricky at this point and that he would tie pink and orange ribbons to trees or signposts to help us find our way. I couldn't see any, though, and when Hand Mike passed me, I decided the best thing to do would be to follow him into town. We crossed a bridge and then he pulled over. I pulled up beside him. The instructions said "Left turn at Seventh St signed One Tree Hill (just over bridge)".

"Was that the bridge?" I asked.

"I'm not sure. What do you think?"

Just then, another group of posties passed us. We abandoned the sheets and took off behind them. Shortly we came to another bridge and there was the sign to One Tree Hill, with a set of ribbons attached to it.

This took us out of town again and up into the hills. Gary the train driver was ahead of me but was struggling to keep his speed up. Rosie was pretty nifty in comparison and we raced past him. Fifteen kilometres later we came to an intersection with a gravelly stopping place on the other side. A dozen or so posties were already there, so we pulled over and joined them for a rest.

I overheard someone saying, "That was a steep hill," to which Gary responded, "Yeah, I knew things were getting bad when even Jill overtook me."

"Oi, what do you mean by that?" I exclaimed in mock indignation.

Wisely, he didn't reply.

I was dying for the loo, but as the only female in the pack I wasn't about to go bush.

We got back on the bikes and I suddenly found myself in the lead. The road began to rise again, and for a few glorious miles I was the undisputed leader, racing ever upwards along the road.

But it was a short-lived victory. When we came to another junction, I couldn't find where we were on the running sheets or work out which way to turn. Hand Mike raced past me and I fell back.

This terrain seemed vaguely familiar and I wondered if we were entering the Adelaide Hills, where I'd been to visit my friends Pete and Susie on my last trip. We were going downhill now, along a very narrow, twisty road. This quickly separated the men from the boys. And when I say "boys" I really mean me. I was rubbish at cornering. I did my best to keep up with the guys, riding much faster than I was comfortable with, but one by one they all passed me.

Soon I was on my own again. Then I saw Pete and Stu, my male escorts from Day 2, in my mirrors. Pete whizzed past on the first straight stretch but Stu seemed happy to take a slower pace and stayed behind me as we descended the last few kilometres into Adelaide. It seemed fitting that I should be finishing the Postie Bike Challenge with them.

We pulled up at a set of traffic lights, then Pete suddenly veered off to his left into a shopping centre car park. This was the rally point where we were all supposed to re-group before riding into the city together.

Pulling in behind Pete, the first thing on my mind was to find a toilet. After extensive investigations I found one at the back of the shopping centre. It was one of those stand-alone boxes with a sliding door that's opened by inserting the appropriate fee and pressing a button. Years ago I'd been taking a train to Aberdeen that had a similar sliding door arrangement and as I sat with my skirt hoisted round my middle, doing my business, I suddenly realised I hadn't pressed the "lock" button – just as someone pressed the "open" button.

Mortified, I turned scarlet as I sat there, helpless to do anything, while an equally embarrassed man stood, stunned, in the doorway. "Oh, excuse me" he blurted, and we both scrambled to press the "close" button.

Although I could see the funny side of this, and the man had discreetly removed himself from the scene by the time I re-emerged, it had left me with a deeply ingrained mistrust of toilets with sliding doors. But needs must and it looked as if it would be some time before everyone arrived and we did the final run into Adelaide, so I used it.

With that taken care of, I returned to our ever-increasing band of riders. It was strange, standing there waiting. The Postie Bike Challenge was almost finished.

Slowly, in twos and threes, the last riders gathered, with the exception of Walshy, who rode right past without noticing us. This was somewhat ironic as he was the only one who lived in South Australia and had any knowledge of Adelaide.

Finally, we were ready to go. Dan and Scott swapped cars with Andy and headed up our cavalcade in the four-wheel-drive car. We fell into two lines behind them. As soon as the lights changed, we were off. Thirty-four of us and four support vehicles made our way in formation through the streets of Adelaide. Anthony and Christian were first, followed by the motocross boys (that is, the Squash Club plus motocross Phil), then me and Elton Mike, then everyone else.

Every time we stopped at a set of traffic lights, the motocross boys started doing wheel spins. Being right behind Phil, this meant I got a face full of burnt rubber every time they did it.

"Oi, gonnae no dae that!" I yelled in my best Glaswegian after they did it for the tenth time, fanning clear the cloud of smoke in front of my face.

A few km later we were making our final turn onto Goodwood Road and entering the park at South Terrace.

And that was it. The Postie Bike Challenge was over. We'd covered 3,384 km in ten days, through some of the most beautiful and remote country on earth.

It should have been a jubilant moment, but it actually felt like something of an anticlimax. There was no final gathering of the troops to congratulate us, just a rather hurried clamber to get the bikes handed over to the Rotary

Club as quickly as possible. We were staying in the five star Rydges Hotel, which was immediately opposite the piece of grass we were assembled on, and people wandered off as soon as they had been relieved of their bikes.

I took a few photos, hugged a few people and emptied Rosie's milk crate for the final time. I removed Hamish, my haggis mascot, from Rosie's forks, gathered my running sheets, key ring and clothing and made my way to the hotel. *Was it really over?*

My room overlooked the park and I could see the last of the postie bikes being loaded onto trailers and utes outside. I sat down, put my head in my hands and cried. It had been the best ten days of my life and I was so sad it had come to an end.

I had never done anything quite like it before. Never had I been with such a great group of people. Often, where groups of people are involved, there will be at least one who gets on your nerves, but I couldn't say that about any of the postie bikers. They were all wonderful people and, for the first time in my life, I felt I'd truly fitted in.

The organisers were fantastic, too. This was the thirteenth Challenge they'd arranged, so they'd obviously got it down to a fine art, but I was still staggered by how well organised it had been, right down to how the sandwich box fitted inside the chill bag, which fitted inside the milk crate. They had thought through every detail and it meant we always felt secure, knowing we'd be in good hands should we come to grief.

But it wasn't quite over yet. That night, Dan had arranged a celebration dinner for us all.

I was one of the first to arrive in the bar. Anthony and his wife were already there, but as I ordered a drink Ian, the guy who'd had the head injury on the Birdsville Development Road, came in and started chatting. I was glad to see that he looked all right, but as he rattled through an account of what had happened he was speaking very quickly, something I hadn't noticed during our previous conversations and I couldn't help wondering if he hadn't fully recovered.

Quite a lot of the riders had been joined by wives and partners so there was a fair-sized group for dinner. Dan gave a speech, warning us of how we'd all find riding at anything over 80 km/h a terrifying experience now, and how we'd keep seeing people we thought were postie bike riders. Then he gave us all certificates marking our achievement and, I swear, my round of applause was just a little bit louder than everyone else's. Or maybe it just seemed that way to me.

The next morning as I came out of my room, Scott was passing by.

"What time is it?" I asked him as we waited for the lift.

He grabbed me and gave me a huge hug.

"Oh, it's cuddle time." I laughed as he squeezed the life out of me. He'd obviously got over the shock of how old I was.

Downstairs a few people were checking out and some were having breakfast. I said farewell to those who were leaving and joined the others for some food. I swapped addresses with Alec and Silvia, and 007 Michael gave me his card. Phil from Darwin reiterated his invitation to come and stay if I made it that far and I took his details. Sadly, Anthony wasn't about and I wasn't able to thank him again for all the help and support he'd given me. I hoped he'd know what a difference his instruction had made to me.

After breakfast I wandered back upstairs to get organised. A couple of hours later I was back in the foyer. This time the two Steves were there and we said our goodbyes. Then it was just me and Walshy left.

"So what happened to you yesterday?" I asked. "You missed the rally point."

"Yeah, but I was first to arrive at the finish so that means I won."

I laughed. "It wasn't a race, you know."

"I don't care, I still won!" He beamed happily.

"How are you getting home?" I said.

"I've got my car in the car park," he replied. Then he added, "Where are you going from here?"

"To the youth hostel. In fact, I should really order a taxi, unless..." I added cheekily, "you could give me a lift?"

"Aw no, I don't really like driving in the city," he replied.

"Never mind. It was worth a try."

He seemed to change his mind. "Is it nearby?"

"Yes, it's just along the road."

"I guess I could do that."

"That would be great." I smiled.

We piled my gear onto the back seat of his ute and I noticed a familiar object in the utility tray at the back.

"Is that your postie bike?" I asked.

"Yeah, I decided to keep it."

He drove me round to the hostel and I told him about my plans to ride round the rest of Australia on a 125 cc bike.

"I think you're mad!" he exclaimed.

This seemed a bit weird, given we'd both just done the maddest thing of all and ridden postie bikes down the Birdsville Track. Nevertheless, he took out a pencil and paper and wrote down his details. "If you get into any trouble, phone me," he said intensely. "If I can't help you, then I'll probably know someone who can, so just call me."

"Thanks," I said.

We got out the car, gave each other a hug and I was off. Off for the next part of my adventure. The Postie Bike Challenge was over and I had survived.

PART 2

IS THAT A 125?

Ruby Wednesday

It was Wednesday 17 September 2014. No sooner had I checked into the youth hostel than I went straight back out to find Moto Adelaide, the Honda showroom. After realising it was going to be too complicated to buy my postie bike or to go back to Brisbane and collect one from One Ten Motorcycles, I'd decided to buy a new bike.

When I was in Brisbane and had accidentally ended up at the new Pro Honda showroom, John Peterson had shown me a Honda CB125e.

"If you're going across the Nullarbor you're going to want something that can do at least 100 km/h," he said.

"And this one can do that?" I asked in slight disbelief. *Surely not with all my luggage on it?*

"Oh yeah, no bother. Let me call Martin Guppy, the Honda dealer in Adelaide, to see if he can get you one."

He called Martin, who advised me that he could provide the same bike for $2,350 on the road and told me to get in touch when I arrived. This was three times what it would have cost to buy my postie bike but it was still a lot cheaper than any other new bike. Additionally, buying it through a dealer meant that they could register it for me through their computer system and I wouldn't need to mess around with sending forms away and waiting for the appropriate documents to be returned, as I'd need to do if I bought a second-hand bike.

I still needed to have an Australian address for Martin to get the bike registered to, so I'd asked my friends Pete and Suzie if I could use their address. They'd agreed and Martin had told me that one of them would have to come to the showroom with proof of their identity in order for the sale to be completed.

The only time one of them would be available was that afternoon. I had no time to waste. I found the tourist information office, who told me which bus to catch to Moto Adelaide. Shortly after that I was at the showroom. I had a look around and saw they had a couple 250 cc bikes as well as the CB125e, but these were sports bikes with dropped handlebars and were about twice the price of the 125 and so weren't suitable.

The CB125e, apart from being somewhat low-powered, was ideal. It had upright handlebars, a petrol gauge so you could see when the tank was getting low, a centre stand, which would help with checking the oil and lubing the chain, a gear indicator so you'd know which gear you were in (which is always handy, even if you're an experienced rider and should be able to tell), and a rack onto which a top box could be fitted. Plus they had three colours to choose from – red, white or blue.

Trying to decide which colour to get was the hardest thing. The blue one was lovely and reminded me of the Triumph Bonneville I'd had at home but had had to sell to finance this trip and was still feeling very sad about. Buying one this colour might evoke too many memories of my beautiful Bonnie and upset me every time I looked at it. The white one was obviously going to be far too impractical, as it would no doubt end up covered in dirt. That just left the red one. Rosie, my postie bike, had been red and I'd rather liked that. It seemed a good idea to have a red theme for this trip and I went for that one. I knew immediately what I would call her – Ruby.

Martin and I talked through the details, and while I waited for Pete to arrive they fixed up the bike for me to test ride it. It was a nippy little thing but I did wonder how she'd fare under the weight of all my luggage.

When Pete arrived he provided the necessary paperwork and, because the bike would need a top box fitted, we arranged that I'd come back and collect her two days later, on the Friday.

With that taken care of, Pete dropped me back off in town and I returned to the hostel to tackle my laundry.

All my riding gear was thick with dust. It had got in among everything. I didn't have a single piece of clothing that wasn't affected by the stuff. I took my bags down to the laundry room and emptied all my possessions onto the floor. Everything that could be washed was washed and everything that couldn't was thumped and shaken until it was clean. Then I put it all back into its bags, carried everything up to my room and collapsed.

What a day. I'd said farewell to all my wonderful new friends, I'd bought a new bike and I'd spent most of the evening washing everything I owned.

The next day was a bit gentler and I occupied my time writing my blog. I'd had quite a few emails from friends back home, checking I was still alive, because I hadn't updated it since I'd set off on the Postie Bike Challenge.

On the Friday I went to collect Ruby and took her straight up to the Adelaide Hills, where Pete and Suzie had invited me to stay the night. Ruby was a lovely little bike to ride – nice and light and smooth on the clutch. She just didn't have a lot of power. *But that wouldn't matter too much, would it?*

I had a great visit with Pete and Suzie. They were friends of my brother Chris and lived in the gorgeous Adelaide Hills area of the city. I'd first met them on my previous trip to Australia and had instantly liked them. Back then, they'd been in their fifties but now I was astonished to learn that Suzie was about to turn sixty. She looked more like forty.

They were a fun couple and had another two friends staying. We had an easy afternoon, lazing around talking, nibbling tasty salads and wandering around their huge gardens. In the evening Suzie made a delicious dinner of barbequed salmon and dauphinoise potatoes. The taste was exquisite and it took every ounce of will-power I had to stop myself from having a third portion. Pete then hooked up his TV with his camera and showed us photos of various outback trips they'd done.

Suzie turned to me and said, "You'll need to be careful crossing the Nullarbor. You'll start getting four-trailer road trains there."

"I know," I replied. "I'm just hoping Ruby doesn't get blown off the road by one of them."

Pete showed a video about Tom Kruz, the legendary outback postman who used to drive the Birdsville Track between Marree and Birdsville. Every fortnight he would drive his beat-up old truck up and down the track. This was back in the 1950s and 60s, when it was mostly sand, and it was something of a miracle that he managed it all, given there were no four-wheel-drive vehicles in those days.

The next day I made my way back to the city. The last time I'd been to the Adelaide Hills I was on my giant Suzuki SV650 and was a nervous wreck because it was so big and heavy. On the way down the steep, twisting hill from Pete and Suzie's home to the city, I'd been overtaken by a guy on a push bike because I was going so slowly. Therefore, I couldn't believe it when it happened again, at exactly the same point on this ride. I looked at my speedometer and I was going at 50 km/h, which was quite a bit faster than last time, but still I was appalled to be passed by a pedal-powered two-wheeler. I hoped this wasn't a sign of things to come.

Back in the city I spent the afternoon buying various bits and pieces for my onward journey. Quite a few of my postie bike companions had been wearing a hydration pack – that is, a backpack with a water bladder inside. I knew I was going to be covering huge distances and that the temperature could get very high, so one of these was the first thing on my list. Knocking my tent pegs into the parched earth had also been a problem on the Challenge, and a decent hammer was the second thing I wanted.

More Hydralyte was on the list, too. Although my kidney infection was now better, I didn't want to run the risk of getting dehydrated again, and the Hydralyte sachets had proved a good way to keep my electrolyte levels topped up. By the end of the afternoon I'd got everything I needed and went back to the hostel to plan the route to my first stop, Port Augusta.

New Directions

SLOW RIDER

On Sunday morning I loaded up Ruby and left Adelaide. Although I had considerably less luggage than on my previous trip to Australia, you wouldn't have known it from looking at the bike. I had my two panniers slung over the back seat, one dangling at each side (one with my clothes, the other with my camping gear). My backpack, with my tent, jacket liner and some other bits and pieces, was sitting on the back seat and resting against the third item, the top box. This contained a 5 litre jerry can full of fuel (a necessity when travelling on a small bike in a huge country), my chill bag and its contents from the Postie Bike Challenge, my laptop, a spare set of gloves and a few other miscellaneous items. I didn't have any more cable ties to attach Hamish to the handlebars and had to put him in the top box, where he acted as a cushion for my hammer to rest on.

On my person I had all my riding gear, with the addition of my hydration pack. It didn't really feel as though I'd mastered the art of travelling light on a motorcycle.

Nevertheless, in spite of needing a bit more power to pull away, Ruby handled her load admirably. Or at least it seemed that way to begin with, as we made our way through the relatively slow streets of the city. But as soon as we got onto the motorway it was a different story. I had to crank the accelerator onto full lock just to get her up to 90 km/h. It looked as if the 100 km/h John Peterson had promised back in Brisbane would only ever exist in his mind. But after a top speed of 80 km/h on the postie bike, 90 didn't feel too bad at all.

It wasn't only the bike that was going slow, though; I was as well. I hadn't really been ready to leave Adelaide. After all the rushing around, I could have done with another day to recover, but I didn't want to be trying to find my way out of the city first thing on a Monday morning and had reckoned a Sunday departure would be a better option. And it was, but I found I was reluctant to do any long distances and kept stopping for fuel, for something to eat or to look at the sights.

I was missing my postie biker friends, too. I'd become used to being part of a crowd and never being far from one of them. I loved them all; they were such fun, warm people, and it had been strange waking up alone the last few days and not having a tired, smiling face staring back at me. And, just as Dan had predicted, I'd kept thinking I was seeing them as I walked about Adelaide doing my shopping. In some ways it was good that I hadn't had too much time to dwell on the Challenge ending but, in another, I needed some time to adjust and I think my restlessness was a reflection of that.

The ride south through the Flinders Ranges at the end of the Postie Bike Challenge had been gorgeous and I was really tempted to take a similar route north, going through them again, to get to Port Augusta. But I wanted to re-visit the pink lake I'd seen on my previous trip, and decided to take the same route out of Adelaide as I had done then, up the A1 to Port Wakefield.

On my previous trip I'd passed a crimson lake called Lake Bumbunga, just north of the town of Lochiel. However, because the only place to pull in and look at it was a gravel parking area, and I'd been too frightened about dropping my bike, I'd ridden past without being able to stop and absorb the view. After a week on the dirt though, I now felt capable of riding onto a gravel car park to have a proper look.

Lake Bumbunga is a salt lake and the pinkness is caused by white salt overlying red earth. With the addition of water on top of this and sunlight from above, it creates a strong pinkish hue. Perhaps one of these elements wasn't as strong this time but, alas, it didn't look as pink as before. I was disappointed and, because it was a road I'd travelled before, I wished I'd gone through the Flinders Ranges instead, which would have provided some new fodder for my scenery-hungry eyes.

One thing I found funny was that somebody had laid out on the salt flats a set of seven halved tyres, which increased in size and had a trolley at the end, making them look like the Loch Ness Monster.

I stopped at Crystal Brook, a sleepy farming village with a wide high street lined with hanging baskets full of colourful flowers. A huge set of flour silos dominated the skyline and a railway station served by the Sydney–Perth and Adelaide–Darwin passenger trains was at the bottom of the high street. There was also a butcher who, rather disturbingly, claimed to carry out "Contract Killing", according to a sign on his wall.

I had a sandwich and then continued on to Port Germain to see "The Longest Wooden Jetty in the Southern Hemisphere". I'd seen this on my last trip, too, but as I was passing I thought I'd take another look.

In its heyday, Port Germain was the largest grain shipping port in Australia, but as it was a shallow water port the jetty needed to extend for 1,676 m (5,500 ft) to get to greater depths. Sadly, there wasn't much evidence of its illustrious past now, with only a couple of hotels and a few houses making up the town. But the jetty was still in good condition and I walked the first couple of hundred yards along it.

From there I travelled on to Port Augusta, where I planned on staying for the night. The sun was setting by the time I got there. I found a campsite, pitched my tent and raced back into town to get some food before the light completely faded.

The next morning, a man in a massive caravan next to me came over for a chat. He was a resident of Port Augusta and he and his wife had been travelling around Australia in their giant mobile home. They were now waiting for the tenants who'd rented their house to move out, so they could move back in. As this was not for a few months yet, they were living in the caravan at the campsite.

He stared at Ruby and said, "Is that a 125?"

"Yes," I replied.

"Are you going around Australia on it?"

"Yes," I said again.

"Struth, that's a gutsy thing to do."

"Hmm, foolhardy may be a better word for it," I mused.

WHAT NEXT?

It was a pleasant day with a light breeze and as I still felt in need of some rest and relaxation I decided to stay for another night.

I found a picnic table in the campsite and sat down. It was the first time I'd had to reflect since I left Brisbane.

Getting to Australia at all had been an adventure in itself. After returning from my previous trip in 2011, I'd drifted for a few years. I hadn't really been sure what to do next. Before going, I'd been a massage therapist for nine years, but it had always been a struggle to make ends meet and when I got back my heart just wasn't in it anymore. I started doing some temporary work for the National Health Service (NHS) and then, in the summer of 2012, I got a job running a youth hostel in Inveraray.

Inveraray is a pretty village located at the top of the Kintyre peninsula on the west coast of Scotland. It is a long trunk of land, looking out to the islands of the Inner Hebrides to the west and across to the high peaks of the Isle of Arran in the east. An intricate tapestry of single-track roads thread their way through a mixture of moorlands, forests, lochs and seascapes, weaving past ancient villages and all manner of monuments and attractions. I knew the area really well from exploring it on my motorcycle, and happily imparted this knowledge to all our guests.

I'd enjoyed this aspect of running the hostel so much, I decided a career as a tourist information officer was obviously for me. I approached the local tourist board for work, but inexplicably I didn't even get an interview, let alone a job.

This really threw me. After all, I was an experienced traveller myself and knew what it was like to be tired and weary and how a kind word can lift one's spirits. Ever since I'd got my motorcycle licence I'd been riding around the west coast of Scotland and knew it like the back of my hand. And now I had a season's experience of running a youth hostel, and countless appreciative comments that people had left about me in our guest book. If this wasn't what they wanted, heaven knew what they were after.

As a result, I'd fallen back on temporary work again. The lure of paid employment, however transitory, was much more appealing than the constant worry of not earn-ing enough to live on as a massage therapist. I was good at administrative work but it didn't inspire me and I really didn't see it as a long-term option. I needed something more interesting, more fulfilling and a lot more active, but I didn't have a clue what that might be. I was almost fifty and I needed a proper career – something with a pension, paid holidays and sick leave.

After getting back from Australia I'd been adopted by a gorgeous little black and white cat. He'd turned up outside my front door, which was pretty good going, given that I live on the top floor of a block of flats with dogs on each of the floors below. He was in a terrible state – half starved, riddled with fleas and with raw sores on his skin where he'd scratched the fur away.

The local vet established that he had a microchip in his neck and that his owners lived just a few streets away from me. I took him back, but the owners had moved away. The new tenant left a message on their answering machine to say I'd found him, but they never got in touch so I kept him. I decided to call him Cozy (after Cozy Powell, the Rainbow drummer).

Nursing him back to health was one of the most satisfying things I'd ever done. As I loved animals, it put the idea of working with them into my head.

It was with this in mind that I started looking for jobs that involved animal care. Somehow, I chanced upon a website that mentioned veterinary nursing. On investigating further, I discovered this was something I could do relatively easily. Unlike a lot of jobs these days, you didn't need a university degree to do it. All you needed were some school leaving qualifications, and you could apply for a vocational training course which would teach you everything you'd need to know.

It seemed ideal. I could work with animals, I had the appropriate qualifications to do the course, I'd get paid a decent salary when I finished and it would, in effect, be an extension of all the medical knowledge I'd acquired as a massage therapist.

I started looking into which colleges in Scotland provided veterinary nurse training. Unfortunately, as it was already May 2013, it was too late for me to get into the September intake, as all the places had been taken. Now, when I get an idea in my head, I find it very hard to shake it. I mean, just look at Australia. It was two years since I'd got back from that adventure and I was still trying to figure out a way to get back there and do the western half.

That was it! Maybe I could train to be a veterinary nurse *in Australia*. I started looking into it.

There were three courses open to international students, one in Sydney, one in Adelaide and one in Perth. The only trouble was that as an international student you had to pay much higher fees and you also had to prove you had enough money to cover your living expenses for the duration of the course.

This would amount to a huge sum of money. The only way I could possibly afford it would be to sell my flat – but if I did that I'd lose all my equity and have nowhere to come back to. Not to mention, I'd be off the property ladder and in the current economic climate it wouldn't be easy to get back on.

It was a huge risk, but the start date was in February 2014, which meant I wouldn't have to wait until the next academic year started in the UK in September 2014. And it would get me back out to Australia and allow me to do another motorcycle tour.

In the summer of 2013, I turned fifty. My mum, whose seventy-fifth birthday was two days later, came up to mine to celebrate. I told her about my idea to study in Australia and some of my doubts.

She was very supportive and encouraged me to do it. She even offered to look after Cozy for me while I was away. But the whole plan still gave me the heebie jeebies. I mean, I'm pretty adventurous, but if it didn't work out I'd be left with nothing and, even for me, that was an enormous risk.

Probably because of the risks, for once, instead of charging in blindly, I decided to do an introductory veterinary care assistant course to make sure I'd enjoy it first. By the end of July 2013 I'd finished the course and decided veterinary nursing was definitely what I wanted to do.

I applied for the course in Perth, Australia and got a place. It was a fantastic opportunity – I'd be a fool to turn it down. But the risks were still worrying me.

I talked it over with my friends Teresa and Pablo. Teresa is great at playing devil's advocate and put me through the wringer, asking about all the pros and cons of going. At the end of it, I remembered how, early on in my massage career, I'd thought about selling up to go and study in Australia. I'd got as far as putting my flat on the market, then lost my nerve and chickened out. But I'd always wondered what would have happened if I'd done it. And you know what they say: "It's the things you *don't* do that you regret." I didn't want to have regrets again, so I swallowed my fears and accepted the place.

Within a couple of weeks I had my flat on the market. However, the decision wasn't sitting entirely comfortably with me, not least because I only had until the end of September (less than two months) to sell it, if I was going to get back out to Australia by mid-November. (Although the course didn't start until February 2014, I wanted to get there early and settle in before it began.)

What I didn't anticipate was what would happen next.

By the end of September 2013, I'd only had one viewer for my flat and no offers. It usually takes about six to eight weeks for a property sale to go through in Scotland which, had I had an offer, would have tied in with my planned departure date of the middle of November.

This left me with a choice. Either I could go to Australia and leave my flat on the market, in the hope that it would sell while I was away. But that would leave me with two sets of bills and financially would have been a very risky strategy. Or, I could borrow the money to do the trip. But as I already had quite a bit of debt, I didn't want to add to it. I would also have to rent out my flat. As I'd now done it up and it was much nicer than it had been the last time I went to Australia, I didn't want to run the risk of having bad tenants and getting it trashed. Plus I had a problem I couldn't overcome.

My mum had been told she wouldn't be able to have Cozy at her retirement village. I tried to find someone else who could take him, but to no avail. It was a deal-breaker. I couldn't possibly go and leave him behind without someone to look after him. After all, that was the reason I'd adopted him in the first place, because he'd been abandoned. It would hardly make a fitting start to my career as a veterinary nurse if I left my own cat behind.

I cancelled my place on the February 2014 course in Perth. I was gutted.

A couple of weeks later, the job I was filling temporarily was advertised as a permanent position. By this time I'd decided to see if I could get into the September 2014 intake for a course in Scotland. I tried for the main course in Edinburgh, but unfortunately I was refused.

Maybe I would be better off taking the job here at home? It was local, it was with a great crowd of people that I really liked, I'd be fairly autonomous and the work was reasonably interesting. Plus it was being advertised at a grade higher than my current one and would be the best salary I'd had in years. But did I really want to sign up to do admin work for the rest of my life? I couldn't decide.

Eventually, I decided to go for it and submitted an application. It took three weeks for the interview to come through, by which time I'd talked myself out of it again, and withdrew.

Two weeks later, the interviews were completed and someone else had been appointed to my job. I felt like an fool. This was the first good job I'd had in years and, in effect, I'd just blown a bird in the hand for one in the bush. I was raging at myself.

Now what?

Would I have to keep temping for another year? Would I ever make it back out to Australia or was the universe telling me it was time to settle down? I had one more option to try.

I applied for the other veterinary nursing course in Scotland, located in Thurso on the north coast (an eight-hour drive from Glasgow). I was offered a place – but this wasn't going to be easy, either. Not only would I have to attend classes in Thurso for two weeks every two months, but I also had to get a placement with a veterinary practice. I might be able to get a placement in Glasgow, but I couldn't leave Cozy every time I had to go up to Thurso.

It seemed there was no easy way for me to become a veterinary nurse after all. I'd now spent a year trying to make it happen, and when something is that difficult to bring about, you have to ask if it's really meant to be. I decided it wasn't, and pulled out of this course too.

It's funny how, when you finally let something go, another path presents itself. Shortly after that, I got the email from Dan setting out the details of the next Postie Bike Challenge. The dates and route matched what I wanted to do. I'd get to go to Birdsville, I'd be able to keep the bike and continue on it afterwards and, as the Challenge ended in Adelaide, I could continue around the western half of the country from there. Plus my friend Carol had offered to look after Cozy. It was all falling into place.

All I had to do now was raise the money to finance it. I took out a massive bank loan, my mum leant me some money and my brother gave me some, too. But I still had a shortfall of £3,500. There was only one thing for it – I'd have to sell my beloved Triumph Bonneville T100.

I put an advert on the internet and, three weeks before I was due to leave, I finally got an offer from someone who I felt would give her a good home and love her as much as I did. I couldn't bear to sell her to some boy racer who would trash her within a week.

The new owner's name started with "Ewan MacGregor" and ended in a colour, so the sting of selling my prize possession was slightly soothed by the fact that it was going to the namesake of one my heroes. But it still hurt. We'd been together for eight years and she had taken me all over Europe. I loved that bike and I had to wipe away the tears as Ewan rode her away. But I'd managed to get the cash I needed, even if it had been a close call.

After I'd paid the cost of the Postie Bike Challenge plus my airfare and insurance, bought some equipment and put aside enough money to cover my bills back home for the three months I'd be away, I was left with a budget of £5,000 (that equated to $8,620.89) to take with me. It didn't seem much – over three months it would work out as about $100 a day – but I figured I could survive on that.

So, all in all, it had been a pretty turbulent few years and I wasn't any further forward with finding a perfect career for myself. But that was part of the reason I'd come away, to give myself a break and see if a change of scene would help to clarify things and help me find a new direction.

Sitting at my picnic table, I switched on my laptop and opened my budget spreadsheet. After I'd paid for Ruby and deducted the money I'd spent so far, I had $5,000 left for the rest of the trip. Not being able to buy the postie bike and having to buy a new bike had completely blown my budget. With ten weeks to go, it meant I had $500 per week.

Fortunately, I only approximated the next calculation. Instead of dividing $500 by seven days (which would have given me $70 a day, a terrifyingly low amount), I worked out that if I budgeted for $90 a day, with a couple of non-riding days a week (these would cost less), then I should be okay. There's nothing like blissful ignorance to help you on your way.

POWER, TRAINS AND TOURISM

Having worked out my budget and reflected on how I'd managed to get here, I decided to stop worrying and make the most of the time I had.

I took Ruby for a ride around town. It was hot, 29°C already, and it was only the middle of September, which is officially still springtime in Australia. The last time I'd been here at this time of year it had been freezing, and I wondered if today's heat was just an aberration or if we were in for an early summer.

Port Augusta's main industry is electricity generation and its two huge power stations are where the coal mined at the Telford Cut Mine is delivered, via what is left of the Old Ghan railway.

In 1957, to facilitate the movement of coal between Telford Mine and Port Augusta, the Old Ghan line south from Marree was rebuilt in standard-gauge and rerouted down the west side of the Pichi Richi Pass, closing off the stations to the east and effectively cutting off many of the remote communities the original route served.

In 1980 the whole Ghan was replaced with a new standard-gauge track which ran much further west, from just east of Port Augusta, via Tarcoola, to Alice Springs. But to support operations at Telford Mine the upgraded track between the mine and Port Augusta was retained and renamed the Telford to Port Augusta Railway. The section between Telford and Marree was closed in 1986 and Marree lost its railway line completely.

Railways form a major part of Port Augusta's landscape. The Transcontinental Railroad from Sydney ends here and joins the Trans-Australian Railway, which originally ran from Port Augusta across the Nullarbor Plain to Kalgoorlie in Western Australia. From there, the Westland Railway, a narrow-gauge line, continued to Perth. When the Westland was converted to standard-gauge in June 1969, the Trans-Australian was extended to Perth, providing one single transcontinental line all the way from Sydney. The passenger service that runs on that route is called the Indian Pacific, as it runs from the Indian Ocean in the west to the Pacific Ocean in the east.

In addition to the Telford to Port Augusta Railway and the Trans-Australian, the New Ghan, which commences in Adelaide, passes through Port Augusta on its way to Alice Springs and Darwin. This and the Trans-Australian line follow approximately the same route as the Stuart Highway until Tarcoola. Here the lines split, the Ghan going north and the Trans-Australian going west. As well as passenger services, both lines form important freight routes between western, central and northern Australia and the eastern states. I discovered this when I got caught at a railway crossing for about twenty minutes as an enormous, mile-long train hauled its numerous wagons over the tracks. With some of the containers stacked two-high, it was quite an awesome sight.

Although Port Augusta is South Australia's seventh largest town, it only has a population of about 13,000. However, with its coastal location and access to western, central and northern Australia, tourism is another of its main industries. It lies on the Spencer Gulf and the town is divided by two large sea inlets. The first one is as you enter the town from the east and has sea on one side and dried flats on the other. The second is more like a river and bisects the town in two. Along the shore of the second inlet, a pleasant esplanade has been developed, with grassy lawns and picnic areas leading down to sandy shores.

There is also a very comprehensive tourist information office call the Wadlata Outback Centre. It was here that I discovered it was possible to visit the Royal Flying Doctors Service at the airport. I hopped back on Ruby and we went off to have a look. Unfortunately, it was closed for some reason that wasn't explained, and I had to return to the campground disappointed.

By this time I had pretty much exhausted Port Augusta's attractions and was ready to move on. It was time to head north, to the Red Centre.

Northbound

LONE RIDER

When I'd originally been planning this trip I had intended making my way to Alice Springs on the Oodnadatta Track. This is another famous dirt road that starts in Marree and follows much of the same route as the Old Ghan railway. At the town of Oodnadatta you can either continue on the track to Marla, where it joins the Stuart Highway, or you can take the Finke Desert Road all the way to Alice Springs.

I had planned on taking the track to Oodnadatta, where there is a pink roadhouse which, for some inexplicable reason, I really wanted to see, then on to Marla. But having survived the thousand-odd km of dirt tracks on the Postie Bike Challenge, I didn't want to risk doing it alone. It's one thing doing a dirt track when you're in a supported group, but quite another when you're on your own and your bike is weighed down with luggage. What would I do if I had an accident like Greg? I'd never survive alone.

Instead, I decided to take the Stuart Highway all the way to Alice. I wasn't sure how far I'd go today. I could stop at Glendambo (about 285 km north of Port Augusta), where there was a caravan park, or I could go all out and try for Coober Pedy, 537 km away. I'd wait and see how I felt.

Coming out of Port Augusta, the road passed through a beautiful flat plain with the Flinders Ranges behind me and small mesas and escarpments in the distance ahead. It was chilly – the temperature had dropped again – and the open plain provided no protection against the strong headwind.

Soon Ruby was down to 80 km/h. Given the wind, I was surprised to see a light aircraft circling the road, and wondered what it was doing.

About halfway to Pimba, four dark men in black leathers on Harley-Davidsons passed me. They didn't wave and, acknowledging their undoubted dominion over the road, neither did I. A few kilometres further on, they had pulled over and were walking back toward a small salt lake at the side of the road. This time, as I chugged past, they all waved and smiled at me.

The road seemed to be rising and Ruby was down to 70 km/h. A series of heavy road trains passed me in the opposite direction and I got walloped by a wall of wind as they passed. It was like being hit in the chest with a cricket bat. I soon discovered the best thing to do was duck down on my tank, to reduce the surface area provided by my torso for the wind to hit. Even worse was being overtaken by a road train – then you'd get caught in the tailwind and be towed in a zigzagging dance behind it.

The Trans-Australian/Ghan Railway line was parallel to the road and, to my delight, an enormous train appeared from behind a hill and slowly pulled past me. There must have been at least a hundred wagons on it. To my left and beyond was a mixture of rough scrub, hills and, some miles further on, a massive white salt lake. I pulled into a parking area and watched, mesmerised, as the wind whipped up the dust into a tall vortex, which danced across a white salt stage.

At Pimba I stopped at Spud's Roadhouse to fill up and the four Black Angels were there (they had passed me again). Immediately one of them came up and advised me that after Glendambo there was a 250 km stretch to Coober Pedy with no fuel, and to make sure I had enough. I wasn't sure I was going that far, but I had a full 5 litre jerry can on board so I knew I'd be all right if I did.

Inside the roadhouse we got chatting. The boys were on their annual two-week ride together and were on their way to Alice Springs.

"Did you see that plane flying over?" one of them asked.

"Yes. What was that all about?"

"Cops."

"Cops?" I queried.

"Yeah, doing speed checks."

"Really? Oh well, I've got nothing to worry about, then."

They looked at me, puzzled. "Is that a 500 you're on?" one of them asked.

"Ha, no, it's a 125," I replied.

"What? Are you going to Alice Springs on a 125?"

"Not just Alice Springs. Across the Nullarbor and then up to Darwin."

"You're mad!" he exclaimed. "I like you already."

I left them having their coffee and went to use the Ladies. By the time I got back out to Ruby, they were gathered around her, staring in disbelief.

"Well, at least it's a Honda," one of them said. "You'll have no problems with that – you just won't be able to go very fast."

"Really? I hadn't noticed," I replied sarcastically.

"Good luck!" they shouted as I rode off.

The wind was getting stronger and Ruby was struggling to stay at 70 km/h. I heaved the accelerator round again and crouched down over the tank. *Whack* went another road train, batting me to the side of the road. *Whack* went another one. This was becoming hard work.

After about 50 km of getting smacked about like a tennis ball, I saw a huge white salt lake, Lake Hart, to my right. I pulled in and did my best to capture its enormity on my camera, but it was useless. As soon as you put a frame around any immense landscape you immediately cut off its edges and reduce its size.

My Harley friends arrived just as I was pulling out, and twenty minutes later they all sailed past me again, completely oblivious to the battering I was taking.

At Glendambo I caught up with them and we had lunch together. They were a fun bunch and were headed for Coober Pedy that night. It was 1 p.m. and I had a decision to make – would I continue to Coober Pedy or stay at Glendambo? I knew I couldn't ride with them. I was far too slow, but catching up with them every once in a while had given me a sense of security about being alone on such an exposed piece of road. And, if I'm entirely honest, I quite fancied one of them and liked the idea of seeing them again.

I reckoned it would take me another four hours to get to Coober Pedy, but it would mean I could then complete the remaining mileage to Alice in two days, not three. All in all, there were more reasons for going than staying, and I decided to press on.

Not far out of Glendambo, the Harley Boys passed me again, but that was the last time our paths crossed. Despite my secret hopes, I never saw them again.

It was a long four hours to Coober Pedy. Save for the railway line and a few stray animals indicating that there might be a sheep station somewhere nearby but not within sight, there was nothing between Glendambo and Coober Pedy. The wind and the gradual incline of the road had me down to 60 km/h in some places, and fatigue meant I was stopping more often. My accelerator hand was aching from holding the power on. But the landscape was captivating. There may not have been much to see in the way of landmarks but I loved the long stretches of empty plains. And BIG, BIG skies. I would never tire of Australia's vast, open spaces.

About 40 km from Coober Pedy, I saw a guy walking along the roadside. I slowed down to see if he was all right.

"Are you okay?" I shouted.

"Yes, I'm fine," he replied, and marched on with no intention of stopping.

I carried on but I couldn't figure out what on earth he was doing there, miles from anywhere, walking along. A few kilometres further on I saw what appeared to be some mining works and presumed he must have been making his way there – but where had he come from?

As I got closer to Coober Pedy, I started to see lots of small heaps of rubble, with the occasional vehicle parked amongst them. They looked like rows of miniature pyramids. It was a flat plain and the pyramids, silhouetted against a darkening sky, gave it the appearance of a lunar landscape. *What were those heaps? Were they something to do with the mining operations?* I knew there was some sort of mining at Coober Pedy but I didn't know what type. It could have been anything from coal to gold as far as I was concerned.

It was 5.15 p.m. when I finally rolled into town. I found a caravan park and the lady behind the desk asked if I'd like to take a bus tour of the town the following day. Given I didn't know anything about Coober Pedy, except that it had some underground houses and a mining industry, this seemed like a good idea and I booked a place.

The booking entitled me to 10% off anything in the camp pizzeria. By the time I'd got my tent up and used the hammer

I'd bought in Adelaide to whack the pegs into the concrete-like ground, I was more than happy to take advantage of the discount and devoured a 12-inch ham and pineapple special.

That night the wind got even worse. I could hear my flysheet flapping and a tent peg or two getting whipped out of the ground. Then, halfway through the night, my flysheet almost blew off completely. I jumped out of bed and removed it before it was carried away forever. I spent the rest of the night curled into my two sleeping bags, protected only by the inner net of the tent, which I'd had to weigh down with my bags at either end.

By the morning I felt as if I'd spent the night inside a giant vacuum cleaner.

GEM OF THE NEVER NEVER

Not surprisingly I was up early, so I walked into town to get some food. It was still windy but pleasantly cool.

Coober Pedy sits at the foot of a small range of hills called the Stuart Ranges, in the middle of a large desert. The town itself is quite hilly, but as soon as you start going west it levels out into a flat desert plain.

It looked like a bit of a shanty town, with many of the small hills having strange wooden, plastic or metal structures attached to them and shabby yards filled with what, at a glance, appeared to be wrecked cars and scrap metal. Walking down the main street, shop after shop revealed the type of mining Coober Pedy was famous for – opals. *Of course, I knew that.* I'd just completely forgotten. In fact, Coober Pedy is known as the "Opal Capital of the World". It is the largest opal mining area on the planet, with over seventy opal fields.

During the tour that afternoon I learnt more about the town. Coober Pedy (or Stuart Ranges, as it was originally called) was founded in 1915, when opals were found there by a fourteen-year-old boy called Willie Hutchison. He was a member of his father's prospecting party, who were looking for gold. While the rest of the party were off searching, Willie was left in charge of the camp. After he'd finished his duties he went exploring himself and stumbled upon what became the richest opal field in the world.

This prompted something of an opal rush, which is still going on today.

After the First World War, an influx of miners caused a major increase in opal production. The town reached its peak in the 1970s, when the introduction of mechanised mining methods made it possible to extract enormous quantities of opals. It attracted migrants from all over the world, but mostly from southern Europe. Hence there are a large number of clubs and churches representing the many nationalities and faiths.

Many of the early migrants were former soldiers who had served and lived in the trenches during World War I. Legend has it they introduced the idea of living in abandoned mines, known as "dugouts", as a means of escaping the unbearable summer temperatures. It was this style of living that gave Coober Pedy its current name, from the Aboriginal word "kupa-piti" meaning "white man's burrows".

We set off through the town down Seventeen Mile Road to the Coober Pedy Opal Fields Golf Club. This is an 18-hole course, which is somewhat unique in that it has absolutely no grass. Golfers take a small piece of artificial turf to use for teeing off, but otherwise it consists of a series of circular black "greens" made out of sand, spread across the plain. They look like craters on the surface of the moon. To avoid the daytime temperatures, most games are played at night with luminous balls.

In 2002, after the clubhouse was burnt down and a new one was built, the president of the club sent St Andrew's Golf Club in Scotland a photo of the course and asked if they would like reciprocal membership. Much to his surprise, St Andrew's agreed, on the proviso that Coober Pedy Golf Club granted St Andrew's an opal mine as well as reciprocal rights. These were duly granted, making the Club the only course in the world to have reciprocal rights with St Andrew's. These rights were, however, granted for the Balgove Course, the 9-hole course at St Andrew's. This seemed like a bit of a raw deal to me, but I wasn't a member and didn't even play golf, so my views were irrelevant.

We continued across country to the Fourteen Mile Opal field, where John, our guide, explained how anyone can become a miner. All you have to do is go along to the Opal Mining Registrar's Office, pay about $150 and state which lot you'd like. You can either have a small lot at 50 m x 50 m or a large one at 50 m x 100 m. They give you a set of plates to peg out your plot with. You, and preferably a couple of friends, then go off to your site and start mining. Simple as that.

I was surprised to learn that the vast majority of miners in Coober Pedy were one- to four-man bands, and very few companies operated there. In fact, early in the town's development the Council took the decision to restrict the size of the lots available to discourage corporate mining. Consequently, the chance of any Tom, Dick or Harry making their fortune was very real and even today people are still selling up their city lives and trying their luck on the opal fields. Having said that, it costs around $1,000 a week

just for the diesel to power the equipment needec
price, you need a fair bit of cash behind you to surv
you strike it rich. Consequently, a lot of miners no
day jobs and just mine their plots at the weekend.

John told us various stories of boom and bust, ir
ing his own. His brother came out to Coober Pedy
Melbourne in the 1970s and soon persuaded John to sel
pizza business there and join him. For years they plug
away at their plot but didn't discover anything of any r
value. Eventually John abandoned hope and opened up th
town's only pizzeria, the rather creatively named "John'
Pizzeria", an altogether more profitable line of work by all
accounts.

He ran this for many years. When he sold it, this enabled him to buy the caravan park I was staying in. Here, he
set up the camp pizzeria and started doing tours as another
profitable side-line.

Driving through the opal fields was fascinating. Hundreds of white slag heaps like the ones I'd seen riding into
town were dotted around the site. Every once in a while
there'd be a group of vehicles churning waste out of the
ground. Signs warned of the perils of entering the fields
without supervision and falling down a mine shaft. Although the slag heaps were easy to spot, the mine shafts
were usually hidden behind a mound and it was clear how
easy it would be to miss one and disappear without a trace.

There are two ways to mine for opals. Either you can
dig a shaft or you can develop an open-cut mine. All the
original mines were shafts, which the miners dug out with
pick axes and shovels. Opal only occurs down to a depth
of 30 metres and is usually found in veins between seams
in the rock, so a shaft would be sunk straight down to this
level until a promising seam was discovered. The miner

ould then branch out sideways, following the seam, using icks and dynamite to drive out a tunnel along the level. A 1andpick or screwdriver would be used to delicately extract any opal found. Most mining was a two-man operation, one man in the hole and the other on the surface, winding up the winch and hauling out the dirt.

Nowadays, most shafts are sunk by Caldweld drills, which are used to drill vertical holes about one metre in diameter. Tunnelling machines with revolving cutting heads are then used to drive the tunnels, while waste material, known as mullock, from the shafts and tunnels is removed using strange-looking truck-mounted vacuum cleaners called "blowers" (unique to Coober Pedy). It was these blowers which were responsible for creating all the pyramid-like slag heaps I had seen on my way into the town. Although less labour intensive, the price of such machinery increases the cost of opal extraction significantly, as it all has to be powered.

Open-cut mines are where bulldozers are used to remove the top surface or "overburden", to expose the opal level. Spotters follow behind, watching for traces of opal, and any seams found are then worked over by handpick. Of course, it can be devastating when the opal is spotted only after it has been crushed by all this heavy equipment.

We stopped at a huge open-cut gouge. Although very neatly cut out, it left a large scar on the landscape and I much preferred the appearance of the mullock slag heaps, poking up like inverted cones of salt against the clear blue sky.

When mining first started in Coober Pedy it was unregulated and there was no requirement for mines which had been fully excavated to be backfilled. Although regulations on backfilling have since been introduced, they could not

be retrospectively applied to abandoned mines, hence the existence of so many slag heaps.

No one is quite sure how opals are created, but the most popular theory is that they are formed from a solution of silicon dioxide and water. When it rains, water runs down through the earth and picks up silica from any surrounding sandstone. This silica-rich solution is carried into cracks in the rocks and, as the water evaporates, it leaves a silica deposit behind. This cycle repeats over millions of years, building up layers of silica, and eventually opal is formed.

Given that Coober Pedy is in the middle of a desert and rarely sees rain, you might wonder how it ended up with the largest opal field in the world. Well, fossil evidence suggests that Australia was originally part of an ancient super-continent called Gondwana. At this time, it is believed, central Australia was covered by a huge inland sea, as evidenced by the presence of the Great Artesian Basin, and silica-laden sediment was deposited around its shoreline. Then, 30 million years ago, lots of silica was released into a solution which filled the cracks and voids in the area.

There are two main types of opal – common opal and precious opal. Precious opal, as its name suggests, is the more valuable of the two. What differentiates common opal from precious opal is the way it is structured.

Opals are composed of minute spheres of silica. In common opal, where there is no play of colour, the spheres are of varying sizes and are not uniformly arranged. In precious opal, the spheres are uniform and arranged in an orderly three-dimensional grid which diffracts light into the colours of the rainbow.

The actual range of colour in a particular opal is determined by the diameter and spacing of its silica balls. Smaller spheres bring out the blues; larger spheres produce the reds. The regularity of the balls makes its colours and patterns richer. The more uniformly the spheres are placed, the more intense, brilliant and defined the colour.

From the opal fields we continued to The Breakaways, a conservation park a few kilometres north of Coober Pedy. It consists of several low hills and flat-topped mesas, which rise out of the stony gibber desert. These mesas appear from a distance as if "broken away" from the higher ground of a nearby escarpment.

John pointed out a tiny white dot in the distance on the plain below us and explained that this was the pumping station for Coober Pedy's water supply, which was located on Oodnadatta Road, north of the town. With a population of around 3,500 and an average annual rainfall of only 129.5 mm, I wondered how on earth they managed to get enough water to support them all.

From the lookout we drove down through the mesas to the desert floor and stopped off at the Dog Fence. This was the same fence I'd seen on the first day of the Postie Bike Challenge, when it had been called the Dingo Fence. From here it looked a lot more impressive, running for miles in either direction. Judging by the map on the signpost, we were now about three-quarters of the way along it. Originally, the fence was a series of smaller fences built by individual farmers to keep dingoes from destroying their stock. But soon the farmers started to merge them together into bigger district fences, until 1946 when they were all linked together to form one single Dog Fence.

The fence stood about two metres high and seemed to be in very good condition. I'd wondered when I first saw it in Queensland whether it was still a functional barrier, and learned that it was still very much in use, with several maintenance teams patrolling different sections of it every week to ensure no holes or damage had occurred.

Back in town, the mystery of the shabby homes was revealed. What I had been looking at were not junk yards but "dugout" homes in which people lived. As they are burrowed into the hillsides, many of them have canopies shielding their entrances from the blazing daylight sun. Covered plastic pipes stick out of the tops of the hillsides to provide ventilation shafts. The scrap or junk I'd seen was not rubbish; it was mining equipment kept in their driveways or yards. Despite their somewhat scruffy external appearances, John assured us that some of the underground homes were worth over $350,000.

We went to a museum based in an old mine. A large, open cavern housed cases of dazzling opals and an eager sales assistant enthusiastically told me about the different ways in which opals can be cut and polished, depending on the nature and thickness of the colour band. A singlet is a pure opal with no backing. A doublet is a single layer of opal bonded to a black backing. A triplet is a single layer of opal bonded to a black backing with a protective crystal dome (usually quartz) glued on top. A singlet is the most valuable, as it contains the thickest band of the gem.

They were all beautiful and if I'd had a spare few hundred dollars I'd have gladly bought one. Alas, much to my sales assistant's disappointment, I had to settle for a book on opal mining instead.

Beyond the cabinets of jewels a series of tunnels took us into the old mine. The tunnels were just large enough to stand up in, and our guide showed us a seam in which some common opal was located.

There were also some living quarters. These had all the usual amenities one would expect from a house – a bathroom, kitchen, bedroom, lounge and hallway, together with electricity and running water. None of the tunnels or rooms had any form of joists supporting them and our guide explained that the walls were self-supporting. I didn't entirely trust this statement and couldn't help worrying that the whole place would collapse on top of us.

Small holes were drilled through the roof to the outside to provide ventilation. I didn't think it felt significantly cooler than it did outside, but it wasn't a particularly hot day. I thought I would find the whole living underground thing quite claustrophobic, but knowing how hot Australia can get, I could understand why people did it.

I had thought the whole town of Coober Pedy would be underground, but there were also quite a lot of surface homes and businesses, including a drive-in cinema which, John told us, used to have a sign asking patrons to leave their explosives outside.

Below ground there was an array of businesses. Hotels, bookshops, cafés, galleries and even a bar existed in dugouts of varying sizes. We visited the Serbian Church, which had been tunnelled out of a hillside and had intricate sculptures carved out of its walls as well as a large congregational area and balcony.

Coober Pedy was a fascinating place. It was like the set of a science fiction movie (in fact, it had been the set for several science fiction movies). I'd never seen anything like it. The landscape, with all its vivid colours and glistening mounds of mullock, its deceptive housing secreted into the hillsides and, of course, its glittering prize – the Gem of the Never Never, the opal – had entranced me. It had been an unexpectedly interesting stopover and I loved the place.

TRICKS OF THE LIGHT

Next morning was very cold again and I layered up all my jackets to keep warm. It took me a while to leave Coober Pedy. I wanted to go back and see some of the things we'd passed on the tour but hadn't had time to stop at. We hadn't actually got to see any dugout homes close up, or the drive-in cinema or the Big Winch.

I also wanted to stop and take some photos of the opal fields. I wouldn't be allowed back in by myself, but those mullock mounds had intrigued me and I wasn't ready to ride off without at least taking some photos from the roadside.

When I finally got going, it was mid-morning. The first 151 km to Cadney Park Roadhouse was a reasonably quick hop. Because the winds had now abated, I managed to keep Ruby at a fairly constant 90 km/h. I had a cup of tea to warm myself up, used the facilities and carried on.

I was passing through miles of desert. This isn't the type of desert you get in Arabia or the Sahara, where tall, windswept white sand dunes roll off to the horizon. In Australia, the desert has quite a lot of vegetation.

Stubby little bushes poked up through dry earth, topped with rocks and gravel. Occasionally a silverback lizard would creep from the undergrowth and sun itself on the road, but there wasn't much wildlife to be seen. Sometimes I'd spot the rotting remains of a kangaroo that had tried to take on a road train and lost, and once I saw a snake that had been ground into the tarmac, but that was about all.

Except, that is, for a beautiful golden horse standing with its head over a fence by the edge of the road. It looked so lonely as I rode by, I wanted to stop and stroke it. But my hands were seized to the handlebars and I couldn't react quickly enough.

An hour and 80 km later I was at Marla, where the Oodnadatta Track ends. I could see the track and its rubble surface as I rode into town, and was glad I'd decided against taking it. It had taken me two days to get this far on a sealed road and it probably would have taken twice that long to do on dirt.

I stopped at the roadhouse and filled up.

A guy with a caravan came over. "Is that a 125?" he asked, pointing at Ruby with an expression of utter disbelief on his face.

"Yes, it is," I answered proudly.

"Where are you going?"

"Alice Springs then Darwin, via the Nullarbor," I replied.

His eyes just about popped out of his head.

"I've come from Brisbane," I added, to see if I could make his head explode.

But I was to be punished for my mischief. On the way back from paying he stopped me again and, as I opened my mouth to greet him, a fly flew in and got caught in my throat. I choked, gagged, then coughed up and spat out my aerial assailant. When I looked back up, the man was hurrying away with a look of revulsion on his face.

The next 186 km to Kulgera was a long, empty stretch. It was very dry and I wasn't sure if I hadn't been drinking enough or what, but the light seemed to have been playing tricks with me all day. Firstly, packing up my tent, I kept seeing a shadow out of the corner of my eye, but when I looked there was no one there. Now, on this piece of road, I had a weird sense of someone watching me whenever I stopped.

The light was also creating mirages on the road, making it look as if there was water ahead. Of course, I never reached it; it stayed the same distance from me. And, as if all that wasn't enough, I kept feeling I was going to fall asleep in the saddle (probably the result of not sleeping very well last night).

I eventually pulled into a parking area to have a rest, but couldn't find a clean enough picnic table to lie down on (there was no way I was going to conk out on the ground, not with snakes about). I downed some Hydralyte and that seemed to put an end to my delusions. (My hydration pack just had plain water in it and I stored a bottle of Hydralyte and a spare bottle of water in the pockets of my backpack. This was on the seat behind me so it wasn't easily accessible when riding and I had to wait until I stopped.)

Then, about 40 km from Kulgera, once again a man was walking along the roadside, this time in the opposite direction to me, pushing a sort of trolley. After miles of being the only vehicle on the road, I saw a 4 x 4 appear behind me. It overtook me just as I got level with the guy, so apart from tooting my horn in greeting, I wasn't able to stop and find out what on earth he was doing there. What was it with men walking along deserted highways 40 km from a town?

Twenty km further on, I crossed the state border from South Australia into the Northern Territory. There was a large car park with a set of information boards and a big monument welcoming visitors to the state. I did the obligatory set of photos and was getting ready to leave when a bunch of young lads pulled in next to me.

"Hey, how you doing?" they asked.

"Good, thanks."

"Is that a 125?" They gaped.

"Yep." This was fun, but starting to get a bit predictable. "Where are you guys from?" I asked, trying to divert the conversation.

"The States," one of them replied.

"Are you out here on a working holiday?" I asked.

"Yes, we've just been fruit picking near Adelaide. Now we're off to see the Rock." (The Rock being Ayres Rock.)

I offered to take some photos of them and they all clambered over the monument as I snapped away. I got back on Ruby and rejoined the highway.

A signpost advised that "Unless otherwise indicated the speed limit in the Northern Territory is 110 km/h". Immediately after this sign, there was another one telling us we could now go at 130 km/h. Apparently, for the 200 km stretch between Alice Springs and Barrow Creek, the speed limit had been removed altogether, but I wouldn't get to see that on this journey. Not that it would have made any difference to my progress. Ruby wouldn't even be able to get up to 110, let alone anything above that.

A few miles later, the Americans raced past me, screaming and waving wildly as they did. It was a funny moment and had me smiling for miles after.

I got to Kulgera Roadhouse by mid-afternoon. I could have continued to Erldunda, 74 km further north, where the road turned off to Ayres Rock, but I'd had enough for the day and decided to take advantage of the soft grassy campground, where I could gently press my tent pegs into the earth instead of having to sledge-hammer them in like in Coober Pedy. There was a strong smell of marijuana in the camp and by the time I'd finished setting up my stuff I was feeling remarkably mellow.

Kulgera, like Marla before it, consisted mostly of the roadhouse. Both towns had, in addition, a few houses and a railway station for the Ghan – otherwise there wasn't a lot to see.

It had been a lonely day. I hadn't spoken to many people and the barren scenery offered little to occupy my thoughts.

With all this time on my hands, my mind had been roving. I kept thinking about the guys from the Postie Bike Challenge. Although they all seemed to be married, just being around so many men again had reawakened a deep longing in me. I loved that male energy and so much wanted to be with a man again.

When I'd got back from my last Australian trip I'd realised that adventure was the thing I loved to do and that I should abandon my search for the perfect job and just use whatever work I could get to finance my next expedition. However, the temporary work I'd been doing was generally quite poorly paid and left me with barely enough to cover my expenses, let alone save for another trip.

Despite my best efforts, I'd got caught up in the survival treadmill again and in my attempt to keep enough money to live on coming in, I'd been denying my real needs. It was seven years since I'd last had a boyfriend. On the road, without all my usual activities to distract me, I'd started to feel my need for love again. I would drift into fantasies about what it would be like to have a boyfriend once more, and I hoped I would meet someone on this trip.

That night a guy on a Harley-Davidson arrived at the roadhouse. I was in the bar having dinner when I saw him pull up at the petrol pumps outside. My heart jumped as I thought of the possible romance we could have. But it wasn't to be. He checked into one of the cabins in the campsite and that was the last I saw of him.

I heard him leave, though. At 5 a.m., before the sun had even started rising, he fired up his Harley and woke the entire campsite with the sound of his Screaming Eagle exhaust pipes. Clearly he wouldn't have been a suitable match for me – I don't like noisy bikes.

The Red Centre

A TOWN LIKE ALICE

Unlike the day before, which had been freezing, it was a good ride up to Alice Springs from Kulgera – fewer road trains, sunny but not too hot and, best of all, no wind. By Australian standards this was going to be quite a short ride, at 279 km. I was going to visit Dave, who I'd met on the Postie Bike Challenge, and his wife Cecily (or Cec as she was known).

My first stop was the Erldunda Roadhouse.

Roadhouses aren't like the service stations we have in the UK. Often they are the only inhabited outpost for 200–300 km, so they offer a wide range of services to travellers. As well as fuel, they usually have a restaurant, toilets and a shop selling everything from cereal to insect repellent and from maps to jerry cans. There is usually a caravan park or campground and often there are small motel-style rooms that can be hired. In some really out-of-the-way places, they act as the local post office as well.

As this one sat on the junction to Ayres Rock, and obviously catered for all the tour buses that passed through, it had a huge forecourt, a caravan park, a motel, a large restaurant and a small wildlife enclosure with emus roaming about in it.

I filled up Ruby's tank, knocked back some Hydralyte and went on my way.

Alice Springs sits at about 600 m (2000 ft) and the road was slowly rising again. Bland bush gave way to rugged hilly outcrops and the earth became redder. The road had started to twist gently through the hills, and another 80 or 90 km brought me out at the oasis that was the Stuarts Well Roadhouse and Camel Farm. It was set in a valley full of lush eucalypts and pink bougainvillea. I was sucked into its charm and stopped for breakfast.

I was developing a pattern for riding. I'd get up early, ride for a few hours, then stop mid-morning and have breakfast at a roadhouse. This would satiate me until I got to wherever I was going, where I'd have a good dinner (either cooked on my camping stove or purchased from a roadhouse, depending on what facilities were available).

My breakfast usually consisted of bacon and eggs – some better than others. The Stuarts Well's bacon and eggs were quite the best I'd ever eaten. Two fried eggs with a mound of perfectly grilled bacon were presented on four slices of golden toast, with a tuft of parsley to top it off. An urn of hot water was set on a table, from which one could make oneself tea or coffee as desired. Savouring every mouthful, it was one of those simple joys one starts to appreciate as one's mind relaxes from the rush and bustle of city life and settles into the slower pace of the outback.

I arrived in Alice about 12.30 p.m. and went straight over to Dave and Cec's place. Dave had sent me a text message giving a flawless set of instructions, which I followed to the word. It was only when I got to his street that I got a bit confused about what a "unit" was.

I ended up in a very pleasant lady's back garden. She explained that a "unit" was a flat or apartment and that I should go back to the start of the street, where I'd find the "units" to which Dave had referred.

It was great to see them again (Cec had been at the celebration dinner in Adelaide) and, after supplying me with lunch, Dave took me off to Desert Edge Motorcycles so that I could put Ruby in for her 1,000 km service (she'd already done 1,700 km). It was Friday 26 September 2014 and they couldn't take her that day. The servicing department was closed at the weekend, forcing me to book her in for the following Monday instead.

We went back to Dave's, where we spent the afternoon catching up and swapping stories of adventures we'd had. They were both retired and had moved to Alice Springs from Canberra, after visiting one of their daughters who was living there. They'd liked it so much they'd stayed, even though the daughter had since gone back to Canberra. Cec had been a GP and Dave an IT consultant.

Dave was an experienced dirt biker and he and Cec had both done the Postie Bike Challenge before. He'd also been a marshal on the Finke Desert Race a few times. *The Finke*, as it's commonly known, is a two-day event held in June each year. I had thought it was just a dirt bike race, but Dave informed me that cars, buggies and quad bikes all take part. Participants hurtle down the old South Road from Alice Springs to Finke and back again, as fast as they can. It is one of the biggest annual sporting events in the Northern Territory and has the reputation of being one of the most difficult off-road courses in the world. According to the Finke's website[5] it is "the most fun you can have with a helmet on!"

It looked terrifying to me, but I've never been very keen on being in situations where I feel out of control. But Dave obviously liked them, as he was signed up to do a motorcycle trip down the Canning Stock Route in 2015.

The Canning Stock Route is another famous outback dirt road. Named after Alfred Canning, who surveyed the route for the track, this runs from Wiluna in mid-west

---

5 http://finkedesertrace.com.au/

Western Australia to Billiluna on the Tanami Track, then on to Halls Creek in the Kimberley in the north of the state. It runs for 1,850 km (roughly the distance from London to Helsinki) and is the longest historic stock route in the world. It was constructed between March 1908 and April 1910, and forty-eight wells were sunk along the route to provide water for cattle and their drovers. It was never very popular and the last droving run was completed in 1959. Since then it has become more of a four-wheel-drive adventure track. But considering how long it was, I took my hat off to Dave for wanting to give it a go (secretly, it was something I'd love to do, but not on a motorbike).

He showed me lots of photos of his adventures and I showed him my photos of the Postie Bike Challenge.

"Have you heard how Greg's doing?" I asked.

"Er, he died," replied Dave.

"What! Are you sure?"

"Yeah, I'm pretty sure it was him. There was something on one of the websites about it. It was a man about his age, so I presumed it was Greg."

I couldn't believe it. He must have been mistaken. Greg was such a passionate man, with so much to live for. I couldn't comprehend that he wouldn't have survived. With no "proof", I cast aside this information, thinking Dave must have got the wrong man.

That evening they took me up to Anzac Hill, a local viewpoint, to watch the sunset. The hill gave great views of the town and the general lie of the land.

The following morning, Dave took me on a tour of the local surroundings. We stopped at the Transport Museum to see how much it would cost to get in, should I want to go back myself, then the Uterne Solar Power Station – a mass of solar panels which Dave informed me is due to be quadrupled in size over the next few years.

Alice Springs is surrounded by the MacDonnell Ranges, long escarpments which run for hundreds of kilometres to the east and west of the city. We headed out of town to Honeymoon Gap, a place where ancient rivers carved a gap through the limestone ridges of the Ranges when the continent was still forming. Today the river was dry, though it still flows in times of heavy rain.

From there we went to Simpson Gap, another place where a space in the Ranges has been formed by erosion. There was a group of rock wallabies at the foot of the cliffs, but sadly they were too quick and too far away for me to get a good look. I did, however, manage to get a close view of a baby dragon lizard, when a Park Ranger called us over and pointed it out.

After that we went back to Dave's to collect Cec and went out to the Ellery Creek Big Hole, a gorgeous permanent swimming hole 88 km west of town. The temperature had risen quite a bit since I'd arrived and a swim in its surprisingly chilly waters was utterly delightful. We had some lunch, swam some more and then returned to Alice. Where else would you do a 176 km round trip just to have lunch and a swim? That would be like driving from Glasgow to Perth for a sandwich.

Back in town we went to see the old Telegraph Station. In the mid 1800s, Australia consisted of six separate British colonies – Victoria, New South Wales, South Australia, Queensland, Western Australia and Northern Territory (which was under South Australian rule). There was no centralised government and it took at least two months for news and mail from Europe to reach the continent by sea. The colonial governments agreed that it would be beneficial for Australia to join the new world telegraph network (the technological equivalent of the internet in its day), whose cable ran from Europe to Java. But they could not agree on how to share the costs or where it should come ashore.

In 1858 Sir Richard MacDonnell, Governor of South Australia, proposed landing a cable from Java on Australia's north coast and building an overland telegraph line all the way to Adelaide. Initially, the Superintendent of Telegraphs in South Australia, Charles Todd, was sceptical about this plan, doubting that an overland telegraph line could be built across the unexplored centre of the continent. However, his opinion was changed when (a) John McDouall Stuart successfully crossed the continent in 1862 and provided a route for the line to Adelaide and (b) the South Australian Government succeeded in establishing a settlement at Port Darwin on the north coast. This would provide a landing point for the overseas cable and a base for constructing the line south.

After fighting off opposition from the other colonies, South Australia began constructing the line on 29 April 1870. It was completed by 1872.

The telegraph line was strung across 3,000 kilometres of country. There were no towns along the route so everything had to be transported overland. Although the line was insulated, small amounts of electricity leaked out, thus weakening the signal, so repeater stations containing large banks of batteries were needed every 250–300 km to boost the signal.

Each station was staffed by telegraph operators based at the station and linesmen, who would travel along the line mending faults and clearing debris. Because of their isolation, the repeater stations were built like small farms to ensure that the staff had enough food to live on.

The construction of the Overland Telegraph Line is recognised as one of the greatest engineering achievements of the 19th century and Alice Springs is its only remaining original telegraph station.

Not content with what had already been a pretty busy day by my standards, Dave and Cec took me out to some claypans just out of town for a barbeque.

Dave, like most Aussie men when it comes to barbeques, took control of proceedings and cooked up a splendid feast while I wandered about the claypans looking up at the clear, starlit canopy above me. It was a delicious meal and I could barely keep my eyes open by the time we got home.

On Sunday, Dave and Cec had other commitments so I took myself off to explore the city. I had been there before, in 1989, but it was too long ago for me to remember anything very clearly. It was hot, 34°C, and after a morning of wandering around the shops and the craft market, buying things to make dinner with, I decided to take shelter from the sweltering heat in the Royal Flying Doctor Service (RFDS) museum.

The RFDS is another amazing Australian institution, which has developed to look after the people living in remote parts of Australia. It started life as the Australian Inland Mission (AIM) in 1912, when a Presbyterian minister, the Rev John Flynn, who had lived in the outback for most of his life, was commissioned by his church to visit the Northern Territory and report on its missionary needs. His report resulted in his being appointed as Field Superintendent of AIM.

The vast distances of the Territory and the lack of adequate medical facilities concerned Flynn, and from 1917 onwards he founded a series of nursing services in remote locations.

In 1917, Lieutenant Clifford Peel, a young medical student with an interest in aviation, wrote to Flynn. Peel suggested using aviation to bring medical help to the outback. Flynn immediately saw the potential of this idea and for the next ten years campaigned for an aerial medical service. Unfortunately, Peel was shot down in France at the age of twenty-four and never knew that his letter became the outline for the RFDS.

Flynn's vision became a reality when his long-time supporter, H. V. McKay, left a large bequest for "an aerial experiment". At this time, Flynn also met Hudson Fysh, a founder of QANTAS, and discussed the possibility of leasing planes from the airline to form an aerial medical service.

In 1927, QANTAS and the newly founded AIM Aerial Medical Service signed an agreement to operate an aerial ambulance from Cloncurry in Queensland. Its first flight took off on 17 May 1928. Flynn had managed to get his Flying Doctor Service off the ground.

After several name changes, the AIM Aerial Medical Service became the Royal Flying Doctor Service in 1954. From its humble beginnings back in 1928, the RFDS now has sixty-one aircraft and twenty-one bases across the country, meaning that no one is ever more than two hours from a major hospital. I found this very comforting to know as, I'm sure, did most of the outback residents.

The RFDS was also responsible for a number of spin-off services. In the 1920s, the service lacked the communication technology to deliver its services efficiently. In 1929 Flynn worked with Alfred Traeger to develop the Traeger pedal radio, a pedal-operated generator which powered a radio receiver. Each remote homestead was allocated one of these, to allow them to call the Flying Doctor Service if an emergency occurred. At the time, there was a major problem with farmers becoming depressed because of their isolation from other people, therefore, the radio service enabled station owners and residents to contact friends and families scattered over thousands of kilometres, outside normal transmission hours.

In 1951 the School of the Air was established in Alice Springs. It used the Flying Doctor Service radio network to provide outback children with the opportunity to receive lessons with teachers located in other parts of the country. It also enabled pupils to interact with other children and work on projects together.

I was amazed at the resolve of people like John Flynn and the pioneers who had opened up the outback. Their vision and determination had made Australia the unique country it is today and I was humbled by their achievements.

That night I made dinner for Dave and Cec, to say thank you for their wonderful hospitality. Dave and I shared an interest in industrial heritage and he had been filling me in on all Alice Springs' attractions since I'd arrived.

"You should be a tour guide," I said to him as he showed me a book about the Snowy Mountains Scheme, the huge hydroelectric and irrigation scheme in south-east Australia.

"Hmm, maybe."

"In fact, that's what I should do," I exclaimed. "I should start running industrial heritage tours back home. I mean, Glasgow's got a fascinating history but no one is out there telling it. I could do that."

THE HEAT IS ON

On Monday, after taking Ruby for her service at Desert Edge Motorcycles and being served by the rather delicious-smelling Dallas, I headed back down the Stuart Highway for Ayres Rock. It was 10 a.m. before I was on the road and already the temperature was over 30°C. I had 443 km to cover and it just kept getting hotter. It was going to be a long, hot slog.

As I retraced my steps southward down the Stuart Highway, I recalled what Dave had told me about its construction.

"It only took ten months to build," he had said.

"What, the whole thing took just ten months?" I replied, incredulous. The entire Stuart Highway was 2,834 km. To build it from scratch in ten months seemed like an impossible task to me. They'd have had to have done 283 km a month to do that.

"Well, once the army got involved, they got a gravel road down in ten months."

While wandering around the town centre the day before, I'd dropped into the tourist office and found out the full story. The Stuart Highway, named after John McDouall Stuart of Overland Telegraph Line fame, began as a dirt track for servicing the line in the 1870s. It enabled supply vehicles to travel with loads of building materials along its length. It was approximately 40 metres wide and became known as "the track".

The need to bring in provisions to telegraphers based at the repeater stations and to undertake maintenance work along the line meant that traffic along the track was ongoing after the O/T Line had been completed. It was the only track through central Australia and became a path for travellers, drovers, and adventurers crossing the continent. When gold was found, miners used it to get to the mines and pastoralists brought cattle and sheep up the track, establishing stations along the way. Contractors tapped into underground water and the track became a line of wells and bores, bringing more people to the region. The importance of water holes is reflected in many of the place names, like Daly Waters, Tennant's Creek, Alice Springs and Adelaide River.

Some repeater stations along the O/T Line grew into small towns and with their growth came government administration, law and customs, and further development of the road.

From 1936, a low-standard dry-weather road was developed from Darwin to Adelaide River, and then from Adelaide River to the railhead at Larrimah. This followed much the same route as the present day highway. However, it was an unsealed track, which meant it became a quagmire in the wet and a dust bowl in the dry.

During World War II the gravel track between Alice Springs and Larrimah was upgraded to bitumen. By early 1943, traffic between Darwin and Adelaide River had increased so much that the gravel surface had disintegrated. Hence this was also upgraded to bitumen. By 1944, the remaining sections down to the South Australian border were sealed. I was surprised to learn that the section from the border south to Port Augusta was not sealed until the 1980s, which seemed quite recent to me. Work only began on sealing this part in 1978 and took five years to complete.

By 1987, the whole wartime highway had been further upgraded to national highway standard, providing the surface I was now riding on.

The temperature was rising and I was guzzling water like there was no tomorrow. If I was struggling in this heat on a motorcycle, heaven knows what it must have been like for John McDouall Stuart, *walking* this route all the way from Adelaide to Darwin back in the 1800s.

John McDouall Stuart was a man of great fortitude. He was a Scotsman, born in Fife, who immigrated to Australia at the age of twenty-three after he graduated from the Scottish Naval and Military Academy as a civil engineer. He arrived in South Australia in January 1839 and soon found employment with the colony's Surveyor General, the famous explorer Captain Charles Sturt. Working in the semi-arid scrub of the newly settled districts, he marked out blocks of land for settlers and miners. Stuart left the Survey Department in 1842, when he became a private surveyor and grazier.

In 1844, Captain Sturt embarked on an expedition into the arid interior and engaged Stuart as a draughtsman. When Sturt's second-in-command, James Poole, died of scurvy, Stuart took his place. Sturt and Stuart survived to return to Adelaide, but suffered greatly from scurvy. Stuart was unable to work or travel for a year after that, but he eventually returned to his trade as a private surveyor, spending more and more time in remote areas.

Stuart undertook six expeditions. The first three mainly explored the north-west of South Australia, but when the South Australian government offered a reward of £2,000 "to any person able to cross the continent through the centre and discover a suitable route for the telegraph from Adelaide to the north coast", Stuart decided to attempt this. It took him three attempts, but he finally reached the northern coast near modern day Darwin on 24 July 1862.

Stuart was one of Australia's most accomplished inland explorers. His expeditions resulted in the Overland Telegraph Line being built, the Old Ghan railway being established and the Stuart Highway from Port Augusta to Darwin being constructed.

Despite all his achievements, the severe hardships he suffered on his expeditions affected his health badly. He returned to Scotland on 25 April 1864 and lived with his sister. They moved to London, where he died on 5 June 1866 at the age of fifty. His funeral was attended by only seven people.

It made me sad that, after all his achievements, Stuart had died such an anonymous death. If he had lived to see the results of his endeavours, I'm sure he would have been happy that it had all been worthwhile.

By noon I was back at the Erldunda Roadhouse, dripping with sweat. I pulled up at a petrol pump, dismounted and threw my riding gear to the ground.

"Must be hot on the bike today?" a man said, on the way back to his caravan.

I panted for a moment. "Yes," I gasped, and grabbed my water bottle.

He looked at Ruby. *Here it comes.* "Is that a 125?"

I nodded and reached for the pump. I was too hot to have this conversation again.

I paid up and made for the Ladies. Inside there were a number of elderly women, but I didn't care. I needed to cool down, so I turned on the tap, cupped my hands under the flow and threw the water over my head. I took off my T-shirt and ran it under the tap too, much to the horror of my elderly audience. I threw more water over my head and face, put my top back on and went back out to Ruby.

For the next half hour or so, the wet T-shirt acted as an air-conditioner, cooling my way. But it didn't last long and by the time I got to the next roadhouse at Mount Ebenezer I had to repeat the whole procedure. It was the hottest part of the day and I still had almost 200 km to go.

The first time I'd visited Australia, in 1989, I'd taken a tour to Ayres Rock, the Olgas and King's Canyon. I remembered that on the way to the Rock we'd seen a tall, flat-topped mountain rising out of the desert and had all thought this was Uluru. In fact, it had been Mount Conner. About 15 km from Curtain Springs I saw it again. It was every bit as striking as I remembered and I pulled into the viewpoint to have a proper look. It had a wide base, which tapered in before sheer rock faces rose straight up and then flattened into a smooth table-top.

Some people in a tour bus pulled in and, after taking their photos, all scampered up a sand path on the other side of the road. I wondered where they were going but was far too hot to follow.

I had a 2 litre hydration pack on my back, a 750 ml bottle of Hydralyte and another 750 ml bottle of water. By the time I got to Curtain Springs I'd sucked every one of these dry. Even a chilled bottle of Powerade in the road-house didn't cool me down. In fact, I was starting to feel decidedly weak. Part of me thought I should stay there the night and give up trying to get to Uluru for sunset (especially seeing as there was a free campground at Curtain Springs). But the other part of me didn't want to pitch my tent and then have to do it again at Ayres Rock the following night.

The woman behind the counter seemed to recognise my plight and pulled out a bar stool for me to sit on. "Pretty hot, isn't it?" she said.

I nodded.

She was a nice lady, in her late thirties or early forties, I guessed.

"Have you been working here long?" I asked.

"No, just a couple of weeks. I was up in Queensland before this."

"Doing the same thing?"

"No, I was working on a cattle station."

"Wow, that must have been interesting?"

"Hard work, but yeah, it was good."

We could see Mount Conner from the roadhouse and she told me that the path the bus party had taken looked out over a giant salt lake. I resolved to take a look on my way back.

I ate a chocolate bar in the hope that this would revive me, and made the decision to keep going.

But I'd drunk so much fluid I had to keep stopping to relieve myself. There was very little cover, only a few small shrubs, but I'd had to use nature's bathroom quite a lot now and was getting less self-conscious about exposing my wares by an empty roadside.

When I eventually arrived at the Ayres Rock Resort in Yulara at 5.45 p.m., I was a heaving, sweaty mess. The girl at reception said, "Ah, it's only 34.8 today – that's nothing."

"We don't even have temperatures that high in Scotland," I replied, but she thought I was kidding.

It had taken me almost eight hours to get there and by the time I'd put my tent up I was completely exhausted. Even a cold shower didn't really revive me, meaning that a trip to the base of the Rock for sunset photos was out of the question.

All I could manage to do was cook up a tin of stew for dinner and go to bed. But I slept like a baby. It was the first good sleep I'd had in days. I'd been on an airbed at Dave's, which had been slightly under-inflated and was like sleeping on a jelly.

ULURU

There are some things in life that truly take your breath away and Ayres Rock is one of them. To avoid the worst of the midday sun, I'd left it until mid-afternoon before venturing out to see this unique monolith.

You start to catch glimpses of it about 30 km before you reach the Ayres Rock Resort, but it's not until you enter the National Park that you get its full impact. It is huge. I don't think there is anything else quite like it in the world. It makes you want to fall to your knees and prostrate yourself in awe. It is quite the most spiritual thing I have ever seen and seems to have a power about it that radiates out into the landscape around.

It is considered a deeply spiritual place by the Aboriginal people and I can completely understand why. Photographs cannot even start to capture how utterly holy it is.

Although I had been there before, it was twenty-five years ago, and seeing it again was like seeing it anew. Its vermillion sandstone surface rose out of the desert floor like a petrified mammoth. Dimpled with crevices, stained channels marked where millennia of heavy rains had left their black and white residues. At its base, partly filled water holes were hidden behind clusters of trees and shrubs. Sheer surfaces showed where sections had cleaved away from the main rock and fallen to the ground. A lattice of hollows formed a brain-like structure at its rear, and bulges and chasms broadened and narrowed its width in no set pattern.

It was stunning and I felt both overjoyed and utterly humbled in its presence. I rode around its base, jumping on and off Ruby to explore it from every angle. Although you can still climb the Rock, it is strongly discouraged and it is

156

often closed due to high winds or extreme temperatures. I had no desire to do this. It would have felt like sacrilege to do so.

The local Pitjantjatjara people call it Uluru. It has no meaning – it's just a name – but it seemed so much more reverent than the name it had been given by European settlers and I vowed to call it Uluru from then on.

There is a Cultural Centre in the National Park that says something along the lines of "White fellas come and take their pictures and want to climb Uluru, but if they just sat in its presence for a while they would experience so much more". After I read those words I stopped taking pictures and did just that.

As I left, it was approaching sunset. For a short while I joined the rows of tourists lined up in the viewpoint to take pictures of how Uluru's colour changes in the fading light. But taking more photos seemed irreverent now and I made my way back to the campsite.

I am not a religious person but I do believe there is some force of goodness out there that we can all tap into if we chose to do so. Today I felt I had done just that. Uluru had cradled me in its goodness and I felt truly blessed.

Southbound

BREAKING THE RULES

The number one rule of the outback, apart from "never drive past fuel" and "never walk past a toilet" (as I was beginning to learn) is "don't drive at dusk or dawn", as this is when all the wildlife comes out. I was about to break this rule – big time.

I was heading back to Coober Pedy. I'd had a brief glance at my map and worked out that it should be about 675 km. At 80 km/h, this would take about eight and half hours, not including stops, and would mean a seriously early start.

I'd filled up Ruby the night before and was up at 5 a.m. and on the road for 6.30 – dawn. I was heading east into the rising sun, which meant I could hardly see a thing – a sure fire way to hit a kangaroo. Plus there was another headwind.

I was down to 70 km/h and had 245 km of this before I joined the Stuart Highway south again. It wasn't all bad, though. I saw my first ever dingo, and what appeared to be a piglet running across the road in front of me. I also saw three huge eagles rise up from the roadside as I passed. And I stopped at the Mount Conner lookout again and saw the salt lake. It was dazzling. The wind blew gently across my face as I turned my head to observe a huge white basin, spreading for miles in every direction, sparkling in the sun. I was the only one around and I felt like the luckiest person alive, to be able to see such a wonder in its pristine state.

I made it to the Erldunda Roadhouse and the junction with the Stuart Highway at 10.30 a.m. It had taken four hours and I wasn't even halfway. A quick fill up with fuel and I was on my way south.

The wind wasn't so bad here, but it seemed the road was continually rising. This was confusing, as it had seemed to be rising on the way up and it couldn't be rising in two opposing directions at once. It should have been descending now. Was this another trick of the light? Ruby was struggling to maintain 80 km/h and it was hard to tell what the cause was.

By 12.15 p.m. I'd made it to Kulgera. I did another refuel and asked the man behind the counter how far it was to Coober Pedy.

He said, "Four hundred and twenty k."

What? Surely that wasn't right? But the sign on the way out of the town confirmed it. *Oh God, I'd miscalculated.* I'd only done 319 km. If I added 420 to that, it made a total of 739, not 675 as I'd thought. Now that's only 64 km more, but going at 80 km/h, it was going to add another hour to my already tight schedule. If I was going to make it to Coober Pedy by nightfall, I'd better get a move on.

As I pulled out of the roadhouse, Ruby seemed to be dragging. Now that the wind wasn't so strong, I wondered why she was going so slowly. *Was it her tyres? Had I got a slow puncture?* I turned back to the service area and checked her tyre pressures. Nothing was wrong; I must have been imagining it.

By 4.40 p.m. I was at Cadney Park Roadhouse and still had 153 km to go. "What are the chances of getting to Coober Pedy before sunset at 80 km/h?" I said to the man as I paid for another tank of fuel.

"Yeah, you should be right. It's only 4.40 p.m. just now and it will only take two hours at the most."

Yeah, two hours, if you can go over 100 km/h.

115 km out of Coober Pedy I saw the guy I'd seen walking along the road on the way up, the one pushing the trolley. As I was on the same side of the road as him this time, I pulled up to find out what he was doing. "Are you walking across Australia?" I yelled at him.

"Er, yes, I am," he replied.

Where else could you stop on a major highway and have a chat with a complete stranger? It turned out he'd walked from Sydney to Uluru in three months, spent three months there working with an Aboriginal community, and was now walking home again, via Adelaide – a journey that would take him about four and a half months. He was raising money for an Aboriginal health programme. It made me feel that all my efforts were meaningless in comparison.

30 km from Coober Pedy the sun started setting. 5 km from the town it was almost dark. By the time I rolled into reception at the Opal Inn Motel and Caravan Park it was 7 p.m. and pitch black. But I'd made it, and had managed to avoid hitting any marsupials in the process. It had taken twelve and a half hours to do the 733 km and I was a wreck. In European terms, I had ridden the equivalent of London to Switzerland.

I'd picked a different caravan park this time, as I didn't want to have to pitch my tent on the exposed concrete wasteland of the other one again. It had been a fair bit cooler all day and as soon as the sun started to set the temperature had really dropped. I was freezing by the time I arrived in Coober Pedy and I really didn't want to be battered again by the cold winds of my previous visit. I also wanted to be closer to the centre of town so that I wouldn't have far to go to the shops to get some food.

The tent area was behind a high wall and was quite sheltered. It also had a nice soft grassy surface. This was definitely a better campground than the one I was in before. It was also quite a bit cheaper.

I put up my tent, blew up my airbed and transferred everything into the tent. Just as I was about to collapse from hunger and exhaustion, a couple at a picnic table nearby said, "We've made too much food – would you like to finish it for us?" I'd hardly had more than a twenty-minute stop all day, and nothing more substantial than a sandwich to eat. It was manna from heaven and I couldn't thank them enough.

And what was the reason for this insane dash to Coober Pedy, you may ask? Well, I had found a way to do the Oodnadatta Track that didn't involve taking Ruby along it – the Mail Bus Run. But it only ran twice a week and I'd got the last place on the bus the following morning.

THE MAIL BUS RUN

Every Monday and Thursday, Australia Post runs a Mail Bus service from Coober Pedy to Oodnadatta in the north, then William Creek in the south, dropping off mail and parcels to the various communities along its route.

We set off at 9 a.m. and took the Oodnadatta Road (not to be confused with the Oodnadatta Track) out of Coober Pedy and followed it north-east. I got to sit up front with the driver, Peter Rowe. He was a fascinating gentleman, who had come to the outback in 1966 on a three-week holiday, fallen in love with the place and stayed. As well as doing the mail run he had also been a potter and an opal miner, and he was an extremely good photographer. His knowledge of the history of the region was phenomenal and he regaled us with numerous stories of how people had overcome the adversities of the land to set up reliable homesteads there.

Our first stop was the Dog Fence. If I'd had any doubts about the need for the fence before, these were quickly dispelled by Peter. He explained that dingoes don't just kill for food, they kill for fun. As a result, they do about $40 million worth of damage to sheep stocks every year.

As we crossed the cattle grid and passed through the Dog Fence, we entered the Moon Plain, so named not because it has anything to do with the moon, but because it looks like the surface of it. It is a flat, empty, desert plain, littered with chunks of black gypsum and fossilised shells. It is scattered throughout with hundreds of pieces of petrified wood, where a vast forest once stood. It was part of the inland sea of Gondwana 120 million years ago. Its lunar features had made it the set for many movies, including *Mad Max – Beyond the Thunderdome*, *Priscilla, Queen of the Desert*, *Pitch Black* and *The Red Planet*, among others.

A few miles further on, we came to the water-pumping station that I'd seen from the Breakaways viewpoint during my tour of Coober Pedy. It was tiny, just a small white tin shed that looked no bigger than a double garage. It had a water tank outside, together with a gas cylinder. A ute was parked in the driveway. I couldn't believe it pumped sufficient water to support the town's population.

Peter explained that inside the shed, water from 60 metre deep artesian bores is pumped up to the surface into an underground pipeline that carries it 24 km to the desalination plant in Coober Pedy. Here it is treated by reverse osmosis and pumped through a reticulated water supply system to homes and businesses. The treatment process is expensive and as a result water costs $5 for 1,000 litres. Visitors can purchase 40 litres for 30 cents from a set of water dispensers, which look like petrol pumps, outside the tourist office.

Peter reassured me that the town wasn't about to run out of water anytime soon, as the bores tap into the Great Artesian Basin (GAB), the huge underground lake which covers over 1,700,000 sq km. The basin is estimated to contain 64,900 cubic kilometres of groundwater – that's 132 times the size of Sydney harbour. I still had my doubts, as I wasn't sure if the GAB was one huge pool or if it was made up from a series of small, interconnected chambers. But I had to assume that the engineers responsible for the pumps knew what they were doing, and took Peter's word that the water would keep flowing.

Our next stop was Mount Barry Station, a cattle ranch about 100 km along the Oodnadatta Road. As Peter unloaded a series of boxes of food into their refrigerator, I had a wander about the grounds.

The station was made up from a selection of buildings, including a house for the owners, cabins for the workers, barns, water tanks and various outbuildings and equipment. It was like a small village. The cattle have approximately 5,000 sq km of bush to roam and produce very lean beef, owing to the number of miles they have to cover to find sufficient sustenance.

About 100 km further north was the Pink Roadhouse at Oodnadatta. I'd been wanting to go there for years. It wasn't that different from most roadhouses – it had fuel, a restaurant, a post office and a reasonable sized store – it was just unmistakably pink. Everything, from the walls to the floors, was bright pink. This gave it a unique character and I liked that. The owners were responsible for setting up a series of road signs along the length of the Oodnadatta Track, giving travellers information including the number of kilometres to the next town or point of interest.

We had time for a quick look around the town before leaving, including the old railway station where the Old Ghan had been extended from Marree, the outdoor cinema (which consisted of four benches set around a small white screen in a clearing off the main road), the Transcontinental Hotel, and Australia's first outback hospital (established by John Flynn of RFDS fame). This had been relocated to a new building next door. The original hospital was still intact but no longer in use.

From there we joined the famous Oodnadatta Track south. The whole track from start to finish is 578 km but we were just doing the section from Oodnadatta to William Creek, a modest 199 km.

Peter told us a bit about how children on cattle stations were educated. Until the 1950s, children living in remote communities would either have to attend a boarding school or complete their lessons by mail. In 1954 the School of the Air opened and, for the first time, children were able to receive a formal education at home via the RFDS radio network.

By 1986 most outback properties had telephone lines, enabling assignments to be faxed instead of posted. By 2003, following a commitment by the Government to subsidise the provision of broadband to remote Australia, internet services became available. The last ever radio broadcast was transmitted over the airwaves in 2003.

The School of the Air deals mostly with primary school education, with students progressing to boarding schools for their secondary studies. Peter told us that 80% of students with a School of the Air education achieved better results than students receiving traditional methods of schooling.

As I'd ridden down the Stuart Highway I had noticed there were a lot of what appeared to be radio masts by the side of the road. Peter advised that these were booster stations for the new fibre optic cable that had been installed between Darwin and Adelaide. They are 300 m high and 70 km apart, and provide superfast broadband to rural central Australia.

Our first stop on the Oodnadatta Track was Allandale, a station that covered 5,000 sq km and was home to 3,500–4,000 head of cattle. This might sound like a huge amount of land but, Peter told us, the quality of the grazing is very poor, so a lot of extra land is needed to support the high numbers of stock.

The track runs parallel with the Old Ghan Railway line so there were some interesting sights to see, like the Algebuckina Bridge. This is a steel bridge made up of nineteen 30-metre spans and is the largest single bridge in South Australia. It was opened in January 1892 and crosses the Neales River. You can walk onto it along the old track, but after a few metres there is a gate which, I presumed, was supposed to stop people going any further. However it was open, so I stepped through and ventured a bit further out. The railway sleepers quickly became unevenly spaced and when I looked down to the riverbed below and had a sudden rush of vertigo, I realised why they didn't want people going any further. I backtracked quickly.

Back on the bus, we continued down the track. In the distance we could see ruins of the old station buildings at Peake Creek and Warrina sidings. When the Old Ghan was originally built, it followed John McDouall Stuart's route to Alice Springs because it was the only one that had sufficient water available to power the steam locomotives. We could see the remains of the water towers which had provided the large quantities of water needed. There were also some demineralisation towers. These had been built so that bore water could be used to supply the increased number of trains that ran during World War II.

When the Ghan was re-routed in 1980, diesel locomotives replaced the old steam ones, meaning far less water was needed. This allowed the line to take the much drier route to Alice Springs via Tarcoola.

The Oodnadatta Track itself was in a similar condition to the Birdsville Track, in that it was quite badly rutted in places. There were also some sections with long, hilly undulations and sweeping bends. I felt glad I hadn't attempted to do it on Ruby, as it would have been easy to have a spill. Given how far it was between homesteads, I could have been waiting a long time for help.

We passed Peake Station and continued on to Nilpinna Station, where we stopped for tea. Here some of our group disembarked to take a scenic flight over Lake Eyre, about 150 km to our east. Lake Eyre is the lowest natural point in Australia, at approximately 15 m below sea level. Most of the time it is a huge salt lake, but on the rare occasions that it fills, it is the largest lake in Australia. It was named after Edward John Eyre, an English explorer who was the first European to see it in 1840.

During the wet season, the rivers in south-west and central Queensland flow towards the lake through the Channel Country. The volume of water from the rains determines whether water will reach the lake and, if it does, how deep the lake will get.

We also stopped at Anna Creek Station, owned by the Kidman family (distantly related to the actress Nicole Kidman). Sir Sidney Kidman was another great conqueror of the outback. He was born in Adelaide in 1857 and left school aged thirteen with only five shillings and a one-eyed horse to his name. He joined a drover, who taught him the tricks of the trade.

Kidman worked as a roustabout and bullock-driver, and later as a stockman and livestock trader. He made money trading whatever was needed to the new mining towns springing up in outback New South Wales and South Australia. Eventually he and his brothers ended up working on the same station, and then bought their own.

Gradually Kidman extended his holdings, eventually owning an enormous area of land, variously stated to have covered from 220,000 to 280,000 sq km and including some sixty-eight separate stations stocked with about 176,000 head of cattle and 215,000 head of sheep. He'd become a millionaire by World War I and was knighted in 1921 for his support of the war effort. He also had interests in many other rural industries, such as transport. *S. Kidman and Co* is still the largest private landholder in Australia, although now on a much smaller scale.

Anna Creek (which included the Peake Station we'd passed earlier), is the largest cattle station in the world at 24,000 sq km – approximately the size of Belgium!

Our last stop was William Creek. As we approached the town we could see the small aeroplane our companions were flying in, coming in to land on the gravel airstrip. After parking the plane, the pilot transferred her passengers into a 4 x 4 and delivered them to the pub where the airline's offices were located. This really made me smile – where else but Australia would you find an airline based in a pub?

We had dinner at the William Creek café, then made our way back to Coober Pedy. By this time it was dark, so again we were breaking the outback law by driving at night. Unfortunately, this time we weren't so lucky and hit a kangaroo, which sadly didn't survive the impact.

We finally got back to town at 10 p.m. Peter dropped me, and a couple called Glenda and Merv, at the campsite. They were very friendly and, it turned out, were in a big campervan not far from my tent. In Australia, many people on reaching retirement get themselves a mobile home and go travelling around the country. Merv and Glenda had joined the ranks of these "grey nomads" and were now about to start making their way home to Perth. I had a quick peek inside their van, but we were all too tired to stay up chatting and soon I was safely snuggled up in my sleeping bag, dead to the world.

TENDER LOVING CARE

It was Friday 3 October 2014 and, after my two big days, it was time to have a rest day. Both Ruby and I were in need of some TLC. I hadn't done any maintenance on Ruby since I'd bought her in Adelaide – Dan would have had a fit – mainly because the one attempt I'd made to put her on the centre stand (with my sandals on) had, not surprisingly, failed. It was time to put things right.

With my riding boots on it was much easier to get her up onto her stand and I spent the next hour lubing her chain, checking her oil, pumping up her tyres and giving her a bit of a clean. I then went off to town to do some shopping.

First stop was the pharmacy to get some bandages. The idea was to wrap them around Ruby's handlebars to pad them out a bit so that my accelerator hand didn't cramp up so much.

During my previous trip to Australia I'd had a lot of problems with my hand cramping from having to hold the accelerator for such long distances. I had bought a device called a Cramp Buster, which solved the problem. You connected it to your right handlebar and it had a flap that stuck out which you could rest your hand on. I had brought this with me and tried attaching it to Ruby's handlebar, but because she was a much smaller bike in all dimensions than the Suzuki I'd had before, her handlebars were much slimmer and the Cramp Buster had given way as soon as I put any pressure on it. Therefore I needed another solution, and winding bandages around her grips was the best thing I could think of.

From there I went to the post office to send the postcards I'd bought at the Pink Roadhouse. As I wrote them, an English girl I'd seen in the market at Alice Springs came in. She introduced herself as Jan and said she was planning on taking her car down the Oodnadatta Track. I told her that the track was pretty rutted but if she was careful she should be okay.

She asked where I was off to and recommended I should go and see Karajini National Park in the north of Western Australia, if I got that far.

Next I went to the library to use their internet connection. As I was leaving, in walked Coen Tate, the guy I'd met walking down the Stuart Highway. Delighted to see him, I bounded over to see how he was doing. He'd arrived in Coober Pedy the previous evening and was now looking for some work so as to earn some cash before starting the next section of his walk.

"How far do you walk each day?" I asked.

"About 50 km," he replied.

"Blimey, that's a lot. Don't you get sore feet?"

"No, not now." He'd been wearing flip-flops when I'd met him on the road and was wearing them now, but I couldn't see any blisters or other damage.

"What do you do for food?" I continued.

"I've got some rice and I usually find some bush food to supplement it with."

He was very slim but didn't seem emaciated, so I guessed he must have been doing okay.

"And people stop and give me food, too, when they see me."

"And where do you sleep?"

"Just in the bush."

He was a gentle, unassuming guy and I was astonished at his resilience. I wanted to stay and ask him more questions, but he needed to get on with the task of finding a job.

I tore myself away and returned to the campsite to wrap my bandages around Ruby's handlebars. Glenda and Merv were at their camper and we chatted some more. They even invited me to come and stay with them in Perth if they were back before I got there, which would be in about a month's time. I was so grateful, but felt somehow undeserving of their kindness. The fear of running out of money was rising in me again and I wasn't sure I'd make it that far.

Nonetheless, it had been another great visit to Coober Pedy and it now ranked as one of my favourite places in the world.

AGAINST THE FLOW

While out and about in Coober Pedy doing my errands, I'd noticed that there seemed to be quite a lot of motorbikes cruising about the town. Many had a small flag attached to a rod on the back of them. I hadn't thought too much about it, but when I stopped at the petrol station to fill up before leaving Coober Pedy, it was crawling with bikers.

"What's going on?" I called out to one at a pump near mine.

"We're doing the Long Ride to Ayres Rock," he replied.

"The what?" I asked.

"We're raising awareness about prostate cancer. Bikers from all over Australia are making their way to the Rock, raising money as they go. There's a big rally there this weekend."

Typical! The one time I'd bumped into a huge pack of bikers, I was going in the opposite direction.

I was almost tempted to go all the way back to Uluru, just to be with them, but thought better of it and rejoined the Stuart Highway south.

I was on the road reasonably early and thanks to a good tailwind managed to get my speed up to about 90–100 km/h. I stopped at Glendambo for breakfast and to see if my neck sock, which I'd lost after stopping there on the way up, was there.

Alas, it was gone forever. Not that it really mattered because when I stepped back outside it was like a furnace.

When I got to Pimba the temperature was 36°C. I staggered into the loos and dowsed myself in water, then returned to the café and drained a litre of chilled water.

Here was the turnoff to Woomera. Glenda and Merv had been going there next and had told me a bit about it. The RAAF Woomera Test Range (WTR) is the largest land-based weapons test facility in the western world.

Following Germany's use of rockets in World War II, the British and Australian Governments joined forces to establish a rocket testing program. Australia provided a site with a long testing corridor containing minimal population, and Britain supplied most of the scientific equipment and personnel. At its peak, the range, known as the Woomera Prohibited Area, covered 270,000 square kilometres and included the infamous Maralinga Prohibited Area. Here, from 1953 to 1957, nine nuclear devices were detonated in the Great Victoria Desert – two at Emu and seven at Maralinga. All of them were atmospheric tests and deposited radiation across the continent. The effect these blasts had on the desert Aboriginals will never be known and I was horrified that so little thought seemed to have been given to their wellbeing before their lands were decimated.

If it had been cooler I would have made the 5 km detour to see the Test Range and learn exactly what had happened, but I still had a long way to go. I knew the heat would mean I'd have to stop more often, so I decided to give it a miss.

From Pimba to Port Augusta there was a marked increase in the number of road trains. I'd noticed this on the way north as well, and figured they must have been coming from either the WTR or the Olympic Dam Mine at Roxy Downs, further north along the Woomera road. The Stuart Highway was good here, however, with a tarmac shoulder, and anytime I saw one coming in my mirrors, I would ride on the shoulder to give them plenty of space to pass.

It was barren desert, with only a few salt lakes, emus and the odd eagle soaring overhead. I began to understand why, back in the 1950s, the Government had thought this land was so dispensable. Not that that made it right, but I could see that at first sight it would be easy to assume it was uninhabited.

By 3.45 p.m. I'd covered the 532 km and was back in Port Augusta. I went back to the same campsite as before.

There was a couple unloading a giant Triumph Tiger Evolution motorcycle from a trailer so I went over to say hello. Mark and Kim were a fun couple and I spent most of the rest of the day talking to them.

They lived in Perth and had just towed the bike across the Nullarbor so that they could ride it to Bathurst to watch the motor racing. They were then continuing on to Phillip Island to see the Moto GP races, before returning to Perth. Mark ran a dirt bike club and when I told him about my experience on the Birdsville Track and how Anthony had saved me, his response was, "That's brilliant. It costs nothing to stop and give someone a lesson. What a top bloke." I had to agree.

Before they left the following morning, Mark came over and gave me a box of eggs they no longer needed and some "hundred miles per hour tape" to stick over Ruby's paintwork to stop my panniers from rubbing it.

"It's called that because it will stay stuck up to 100 mph," he explained.

It was bright blue and didn't exactly match, but I was happy to have some way to protect Ruby.

He also gave me his contact details. "We should be back in Perth in about three weeks, so give us a call if you need somewhere to stay."

"Really? That would be wonderful," I replied happily. I'd met so many lovely people on this trip so far.

On the Sunday I headed over to the tourist office to get some information on riding across the Nullarbor. I'd forgotten there was a golf course, the Nullarbor Links, which runs the length of the Eyre Highway, with a hole or two at each roadhouse. I decided that this would perhaps be a good time to take up the sport and I should attempt to strike my way across the desert. But the universe had different plans for me.

Crossing the Nullarbor

SOBERING EVENTS

On Monday 6 October 2014 I left Port Augusta with the intention of starting my traverse across the Nullarbor Plain to Perth. It was 1,675 km from Port Augusta to Norseman (the official end of the Eyre Highway) and a further 704 km from Norseman to Perth, making the total crossing 2,379 km (roughly the same distance as London to Athens). I reckoned it would take me about a week to cover that ground at my sedate pace and that Ceduna, 467 km away, should be my first overnight stop.

The Eyre Highway leaves Port Augusta on a south-westerly heading. After 26 km the road splits – the Eyre Highway turning west and going across the Nullarbor and the Lincoln Highway going south down the Eyre Peninsula. It had been a dull, cool day with a nice strong tailwind when I left the campsite, but as soon as the Eyre Highway changed its heading, the wind became a raging crosswind.

Now crosswinds are all right if they're steady, as you can bank the bike over into them. But if they're gusting it becomes really dangerous, as you never know when the next gust will hit and how long it will last. If you're banked over when the wind stops blowing and don't bring the bike upright again quickly enough, you can end up ploughing into the tarmac.

If you've got enough weight or power, you stand a better chance of blasting through it, but even with my luggage,

Ruby was not a heavy bike and didn't have the engine capacity to bulldozer the gusts, so I was getting slammed across the carriageway. I couldn't hold her steady and the thought of having to do this all the way to Ceduna scared the hell out of me. After about a kilometre I realised I would probably die if I continued. I did a U-turn and went back to the junction with the Lincoln Highway, where I headed south, thus regaining the tailwind.

I decided to go as far as Whyalla (where I'd done a house-sit during my trip in 2010) and then take the road to Iron Knob, where I knew I could rejoin the Eyre Highway further along. It would be on a more southerly heading here and hopefully the wind wouldn't be so bad.

As I rode along I remembered that Walshy, one of the guys from the Postie Bike Challenge, lived further down the peninsula in Tumby Bay and had said if I got into trouble to give him a call. I texted him from Whyalla and he said he was currently in Cowell, a town about 100 km away, and that he'd meet me there.

Cowell wasn't a big place, having one main road where all the shops were located. I went into the bakery to have some breakfast and to text Walshy to let him know where I was. But before I'd even got my phone out of my pocket he'd spotted Ruby and come in to find me. It was great to see him again and I practically fell into his arms with relief. The wind had really rattled my cage.

He had some very upsetting news, though. Greg, the guy from the Postie Bike Challenge who'd got badly injured, had died. Dave in Alice Springs had been right all along.

It really shook me up. Greg had been such a big, strong man, I couldn't believe he hadn't survived. It really made me question what I was doing. *What if something like that happened to me? Was it really worth it?* It was only by the grace of God that I hadn't come to any harm that morning, and I might not be as lucky next time.

Walshy offered me a bed for the night, but as it was still another two hours' ride to Tumby Bay I agreed to meet him there as he had some things to do. I took a wander round the town and bumped into Glenda and Merv in the town hall. They'd decided not to bother visiting Woomera either, and to explore the Eyre Peninsula instead.

By the time I got back on the road it was noon. The wind had changed direction and was now blowing a gale across the Lincoln Highway. Ruby was being slammed across the road and it was scaring the pants off me. I got 20 km out of Cowell and had to give up. I pulled into a rest area and texted Walshy to let him know I probably wouldn't make it.

As I sat at the picnic table waiting for the wind to die down, the news of Greg's passing kept coming back to me. News like this makes you question the wisdom of what you're doing. Do you let the prospect of potential injury or death put you off what you came to do, or do you plough on regardless? Again, I was questioning my self-indulgence and whether it was right to pursue my idea of fun. What effect would it have on my family and friends if I ended up injured or dead?

I guess I had been questioning the trip right from the start. It seemed I was so dissatisfied with my life that the only way I could improve it was to undertake these extreme adventures and face the risks they posed.

But it had seemed I was "meant" to do this. I didn't know why – I'd just felt that once I dropped the veterinary nurse idea, everything had come together. And, up until now, I had been loving it. Look how many people I'd met and how my life was expanding as a result. I was experiencing more fun, love and laughter than I'd had in years, so surely that couldn't be a bad thing? It seemed that, for me, the appeal of adventure was how much it enriched and expanded my life. It was only through dealing with the risks, no matter how frightening, that true growth and change occurred. And that's why I did these things, because they gave me the chance to grow – something I hadn't been getting at home.

As time went on and the wind continued raging, I contemplated staying in the rest area overnight. I had two boiled eggs and a tin of stew, which would see me through to the morning. But the idea of trying to put my tent up on a hard, gravel surface with the wind doing its best to blow my flimsy home to oblivion wasn't a tempting prospect. I waited for four hours before the wind subsided enough to let me return to Cowell.

The day's events made me realise that crossing the Nullarbor was not a feat to be undertaken lightly. If I was to do it, I would have to be prepared to stop when the winds got up – I simply didn't have the power to combat them. And if I did have to stop, I'd better have plenty of food and water with me in case I had to wait out a storm overnight. I had the capacity to carry 3.5 litres of water, which was enough, but only a tiny amount of food. I needed to think how I could increase that.

Returning to Cowell, I couldn't face the thought of a night in the expensive, windy foreshore caravan park. There was a hotel nearby which was only a few bucks more. It was a no-brainer and I checked in. I'd continue down to see Walshy the next day and then, winds permitting, tackle the Eyre Highway again the day after that.

SOMETHING IN THE EYRE

My night in the Franklin Harbour Hotel in Cowell was a riotous affair – honestly, you'd think they'd never seen a woman before. There were about three groups of men scattered about the bar in various states of inebriation. No sooner had one lot come up and quizzed me about who I was, what I was doing there and where I was going, the next lot would do the same thing. After a couple of hours of this, I retired to my room for some peace and quiet.

Next morning I was on the road for 10 a.m. and in Tumby Bay by midday, the wind having finally blown itself out. Walshy came and met me at the jetty.

Every town I'd passed through seemed to have one of these. "How come there are so many jetties?" I asked.

"Well, back in the old days, before they built the roads, the sea was the only way to bring goods in and out. Every town needed to have a jetty or they'd be cut off."

He took me round to his place to dump my stuff. It was a big bungalow with four bedrooms, only one of which appeared to be occupied.

"Do you live alone?" I asked.

"Er, yes," he replied.

"I thought you were married?" I queried.

"I was. We broke up about eighteen months ago."

Really? This put a whole new slant on things. *Walshy was available!*

He showed me to my room and then took me for lunch at the Sea Breeze Hotel. I felt so relieved to see him. He was really easy to talk to and, after my battering the day before, it was nice to be with a familiar, friendly face again.

After lunch we went back to his place and he adjusted Ruby's chain for me – it was starting to look a bit loose. Now there's nothing like a man who knows what he's doing. Walshy had all the tools and knew exactly what to do with them. Apart from asking me to check the alignment every once in a while, he basically took control and had Ruby back in top shape in no time. *Ah, so nice to have someone help me.*

After a short nap he took me on a tour of the local area in his 4WD. My goodness, it was beautiful – white sandy beaches lapped by petrol blue seas on one side and huge swathes of wheat and barley fields on the other, merging into hillsides freckled with white sheep.

Up in the bush the sun was past its peak, casting that wonderful pristine light through the branches of every tree. Every leaf was clearly distinguishable and the colours were radiantly strong. It was one of the most beautiful places I'd ever been.

On the way back we stopped to see a couple of Walshy's friends. One of them had a huge Honda Goldwing, on to which he could attach a small caravan contained within a trailer, which could be towed along behind the bike. I marvelled at the scale and luxury of it all, while I don't think they could quite believe how I was travelling.

That evening Walshy cooked dinner for me.

"Would you like chips or mashed potatoes with your fish?" he asked.

"I don't mind – whatever's easiest," I said, not wanting to cause him any trouble.

"No, you decide."

"Really, I don't mind, I'll have whatever you're having," I replied, although I would have preferred mashed.

Walshy seemed to sense I wasn't being completely honest and pushed. "No. Chips or mash?"

"Okay, mashed," I decided. I liked the fact that what I wanted was important to him.

After dinner I showed him my Postie Bike Challenge photos. It was fun reliving the Challenge, and Walshy was really easy to be around.

When it came to bedtime, he suddenly sat bolt upright and turned to face me. My heart leaped and, for a moment, I thought he was going to lean over and kiss me. Instead, he said, "Right, that's it. I'm off to bed."

Bang! My heart crashed to the floor. I had hoped he might be interested in me, but if he was, he was far too much of a gentleman to make a move – and I had a rule about men having to make the first move.

I felt quite sad at having to retreat to my room alone. I hadn't set out to find romance on this trip, but Walshy was so warm, I couldn't help but think about it.

I lay in bed thinking. *Maybe I should rethink my rule. I mean, I'm pretty sure he likes me, but he's not going to want to make me feel uncomfortable by hitting on me, so of course he's not going to make a move. If a move is going to be made, then you're going to have to make it. Go on, go and see if he's interested.*

It took me three attempts to work up the courage to do it, but eventually I walked down the corridor to his room.

"Are you asleep?" I whispered.

"No."

"I can't sleep," I said, "Can I come in with you?"

And so ended my seven years of unintentional celibacy.

I hadn't realised until then that I'd been hiding myself from men for all that time. The last relationship I'd had was in 2007 and after my massage clinic closed in 2008 I'd put on a lot of weight. I loathed the way I looked. I had always been really skinny and now I had a stomach like a burst settee and bingo wings to match. I couldn't bear anyone seeing me like that.

But I didn't feel that way with Walshy. He wasn't your typically handsome man. He was six foot six and had an awkward gait due to knee problems, but he had kind, gentle eyes and that was very attractive to me. He seemed comfortable in his own skin and, being around him, I felt comfortable in mine too. For the first time in years, I didn't mind someone seeing me exposed.

We had a lovely night together and I was sad leaving the next day. It was so nice to connect with someone again, both physically and emotionally. Seven years had been a long time to go without being held.

Walshy escorted me into town to get some more bandages for Ruby's handlebars. The first set had kept coming undone. This time I managed to get some self-sticking crepe ones, which I wound round the existing ones to make nice thick pads for my hands to grip. Walshy then took me to the petrol station and bought me a tank of fuel before riding back to the main road with me on his Triumph America and waving me off.

I would have loved to have stayed for longer, but Walshy had just had a few days off and was due to go back to work in a town some distance away. It was a wrench to leave him, but such is the lot of the lonely traveller – ever moving onwards, never staying anywhere long enough to get too comfortable.

Having come this far, I decided I would go all the way to the bottom of the Eyre Peninsula and visit Port Lincoln before making my way back to the Eyre Highway. I was grinning like a Cheshire cat. Visiting Walshy had been an unexpected pleasure and I couldn't get him out of my head.

From Cowell onwards, I had been travelling through pastoral country interspersed with a few small coastal towns. Every town had a set of large concrete grain silos and Port Lincoln was no different. In fact, it had the largest set of silos I'd ever seen. There must have been about a hundred of them at the port. Port Lincoln has a natural deep-water harbour, therefore grain is brought in from miles around to be shipped out in large bulk grain carriers.

I took a ride around the town, down to the grain terminal, and discovered that the youth hostel was opposite. I considered checking in for the night but it was still early and as no one was around to take my booking I decided to carry on up the west coast of the peninsula.

It was a stunning ride. To my right were more fertile farmlands and to my left I caught glimpses of dusty sand dunes in the distance. Although the road ran parallel to the coast, it seldom actually overlooked it and more often than not I could only see the sea glimmering miles away. But the sun was out, enriching the landscape with strong, vibrant colours.

As I got further north, the farmlands petered out and were replaced with dry, grey salt lakes. It was more exposed on this coast, with the towns fewer and further between. I stopped at Elliston and Port Kenny and admired their long jetties and huge grain silos, but decided to keep going to Streaky Bay. Mark and Kim, the couple I'd met in Port Augusta, had told me there was a campsite there which was on the beach, and I liked the sound of that.

It was 5 o'clock by the time I got there. I stopped at the supermarket and stocked up with some things for dinner and for my onward journey across the Nullarbor. Then I made my way to the campsite. Mark and Kim were correct; it was right in the bay and I was able to find a spot on the edge of the beach. I pitched my tent and had a shower. Then I looked to the skies and waited.

When I was in Alice Springs, Dave had told me there would be a "red moon" on 8 October 2014 and if I was anywhere near the coast at that time I should get a really good view of it. I'd forgotten exactly when it was due to happen, but earlier in the day I'd stopped for petrol at a rather quirky general store that looked as though it would be more at home in the 1950s than the twenty-first century. It had a blackboard outside with a notice on it about the red moon.

A red moon occurs after a lunar eclipse has taken place. And a lunar eclipse occurs when a full moon passes directly behind the earth, into its shadow. This means the moon is no longer being illuminated by the sun, but some red light travels through the earth's atmosphere, reaches the moon and is reflected off it.

As the sky darkened and the moon started rising, I was suddenly aware of a large number of extremely long camera lenses appearing all around me. Everywhere I looked, people were looking skyward, waiting for the eclipse.

I'd never seen a lunar eclipse before, let alone a red moon, and didn't really know what to expect. But now I'd got the chance to experience it, I wasn't about to miss out. Gradually the moon started to reduce in size as the earth's shadow fell upon it, making it look as if someone was taking ever increasing bites out of it. But it was still iridescently white. Even when it disappeared altogether, there was no sign of anything red. *Perhaps I'd misunderstood.*

Then, as the moon moved out of the earth's shadow, it happened. The first sliver was orange. The more of the moon that reappeared, the redder it became, until finally the whole orb was blood red. It was miraculous. I'd been in exactly the right place at exactly the right time and had witnessed one of nature's rarest phenomena.

Although I'd originally cursed the winds for disrupting my journey, my detour down the Eyre Peninsula had turned out to be a wonderful diversion and I thanked my lucky stars for all the joy it had given me.

NULLARBOR NASTIES

I was on the road for 8.30 a.m. the next morning. I continued up the Eyre Peninsula on the Flinders Highway towards Ceduna. I hadn't gone far when a pilot vehicle with a sign on its roof saying "Oversize Load" came towards me and signalled for me to make way.

I pulled off the road and, sensing something enormous was about to appear, I started to fish about in my pocket for my camera. Suddenly two giant trucks materialised, each carrying an entire single-storey house. Immediately I could see that the loads exceeded the width of the road and if I didn't move further onto the verge I would be run down by them. They were going pretty fast and even if they'd wanted to, they wouldn't have been able to stop in time – with that load they had too much momentum.

I grabbed Ruby's handlebars, pushed with my feet and just managed to get her into the bushes as the juggernauts hurtled by. I'd had a narrow escape and made a mental note not to try and take photos of enormous loads as they headed toward me in future.

At Ceduna I rejoined the Eyre Highway. This, like Lake Eyre and the Eyre Peninsula, had been named after Edward John Eyre, the explorer. He was the first European to cross the Nullarbor, in 1840–1841.

One hundred years later, in 1941, construction began on the highway. Six months after that, a gravel track had been laid. During the mid-1960s, a programme to seal the highway began. The 462 km between Port Augusta and Ceduna was the first section to be completed, in December 1967. Then, in what seemed to be a somewhat random order, the section between Norseman and the South Australian border was upgraded in 1969. After that, they went back and started filling in the gaps, firstly Ceduna to Pedong in 1972, then Pedong to the South Australian border in 1976.

I stopped for petrol in Ceduna and parked up next to a couple of older gentlemen on enormous adventure touring bikes. They looked at Ruby.

"Is that a 125?" one of them asked.

"Yes."

"Which direction are you travelling?"

"West."

"You're crossing the Nullarbor on that!" he half-questioned, half-exclaimed. "Oh my God, you're brave."

"Well, so far it's been pretty good, apart from the wind."

"That wind the other day was hellish," he said, and I was glad I hadn't attempted to fight it. If these guys had struggled on big adventure touring bikes, then I'd never have made it.

We chatted some more. They were on their way to the Moto GP races at Phillip Island and had just come across from Perth.

As they were leaving, the one nearest me stuffed something in my pocket. It was a set of ear plugs.

"Oh, thanks, but I don't wear them," I said.

"The wind can get up to 100 decibels," he replied. "You'll need them to protect your hearing."

My hearing was already terrible so I didn't think they would make any difference. But it was a nice thought and, not wanting to seem ungrateful, I put them back in my pocket.

Back on the road, this time there was only a bit of a headwind and not the gale I'd encountered a few days earlier. A series of road trains kept me bobbing up and down over my tank to avoid the tail winds, but otherwise it was a good ride.

I was surprised to see that the farmlands of the Eyre Peninsula extended as far as Nundroo, a good 150 km into the desert. Thereafter, it went back to bush.

Just after the Nundroo Roadhouse – quite possibly the shabbiest roadhouse I'd ever seen – there was a set of three amber, diamond-shaped signposts, warning travellers to beware of camels, kangaroos and wombats on the road. I was at the end of civilisation again and not long afterwards I reached the sign for the start of the Nullarbor Plain – the vast, unpopulated desert that spans southern Australia. There are hardly any trees on the plain, hence the name Nullarbor, from the Latin for "no trees" (and not from an ancient Aboriginal tongue, as I had thought).

I had a stop at the Head of Bight, where there was a whale watching station. Before entering the station, I needed the loo – and if you're of a nervous disposition, you may want to skip the next bit! It was a composting toilet and as I sat down to do my business a moth flew out of the toilet roll holder, through my legs and off to some place I did not see. As I walked over to the visitor centre I felt a strange fluttering from my nether regions, but didn't think too much about it.

It was hot by now and I had an ice-cream to cool down. There was that flutter again. A lady started talking to me as I ate my ice-cream. Flutter, flutter. *What was that?*

I went back out to the bike and put my helmet on. Flutter. I adjusted my trousers and it stopped. *Must have been imagining things.* I swung my leg over Ruby's saddle and pulled off. There it was again – flutter. *What the hell was that?* I pulled over and wheaked down my riding trousers – nothing there. Flutter. *Could it be in my underwear?* I pulled them down too, shamelessly, in the middle of the road, not caring if anyone went past.

ARRGGHH – a moth flew out.

"Jesus", I screamed in horror, jumping about like a lunatic. I'd had a moth in my pants for about fifteen minutes!

"ARRGGHH! ARRGGHH! ARRGGHH!" I screamed. I thought I was going to be sick. I'd never been so disgusted in all my life.

Mind you, it was probably a lot worse for the moth.

It had been cold when I set off from Streaky Bay, but it had been heating up all day and by the time I got to the Nullarbor Roadhouse, where I planned on camping for the night, it was so hot I thought I would collapse. I could feel my heart racing as I attempted to whack my tent pegs in, and had to keep stopping to catch my breath, it was such an effort.

As soon as my tent was up, I threw myself into the shower in an attempt to cleanse myself of any traces of the moth. *YUCK, had that really happened?*

Apart from the Whale Watching Centre, the Nullarbor Roadhouse is the only populated structure for miles around. The people who work there live there as well. It offers a caravan park, motel rooms, backpackers' quarters, a café, a restaurant and a shop, as well as the petrol station and another hole of the Nullarbor Links golf course.

In the campsite there was no camp kitchen or any-where particularly sheltered to cook up a meal so I decided to keep my supply of food for an emergency and went to the roadhouse for a hamburger. I'd managed to squeeze a packet of couscous, some croissants and a couple of pots of yoghurt into my chill bag, as well as my can of stew, and hoped this would see me through, should I get marooned by a storm again.

Just as my meal was served an almighty dust storm blew up out of nowhere. The view from the window was completely obscured by a brown curtain of swirling dust outside. When I got back to the tent, I discovered I'd left one of the doors open and my tent was now completely full of the earthen powder. I'd had enough. I transferred to a "backpackers' room" (a room in a portacabin with two beds and nothing else), where I spent the next hour shaking dust out of all my gear. Sometime around 4 a.m. the winds finally died down. By morning you'd never have known there had been a storm at all, apart from a marked drop in the temperature.

RIDERS ON THE ROAD

I had a big day ahead of me. I wanted to get to Caiguna, 531 km away. But I had something I was particularly excited about seeing. I was going to pass by the end of the Dingo Fence. I'd bought a book about it called *The Dog Fence* by James Woodford. In it he mentioned that the fence crossed the Eyre Highway and that most people drove right past without noticing it or recognising its cultural significance. I was determined I was not going to be one of those people.

Up until now I hadn't met, or even seen, many other bikers, but today was to be different. First, a guy on a multi-coloured sports bike, who I'd noticed in Ceduna and also at the Nullarbor Roadhouse, kept catching up with me. He was with his family, who were towing a caravan and setting an even slower pace than mine – hence the reason I kept meeting him.

Loads of bikes seemed to be going in the opposite direction, too. I presumed they were going to the Moto GP races at Phillip Island, which Mark and Kim in Port Augusta had been heading for.

It was a beautiful ride, but after the storm at the Nullarbor Roadhouse it was freezing and I ended up wearing my liner and windproof jacket beneath my riding jacket all day. About 30 km from the roadhouse, the road comes within a few metres of the coast. I stopped in a parking area and walked down to the cliff's edge.

It was a magnificent sight. Sheer white rock faces plummeted into deep aquamarine waters, where white foaming waves crashed against them. Acres of stunted bush formed a coarse headdress for the cliffs. A signpost advised that the cliffs were limestone and because salt water dissolves limestone, out of sight, a labyrinth of caves and underground channels had formed.

The next 200 km had me on and off Ruby continuously, taking in the views. By lunchtime I had reached the West Australian border. To prevent the spread of disease, you are not allowed to transport fresh fruit or vegetables from one state to another.

"Anything to declare?" asked the customs officer as I rolled into the checkpoint.

I only had my can of stew and packet of couscous on board, as I'd eaten the croissant and yoghurt for breakfast, so I didn't have anything to worry about.

"No," I replied.

He stood for a moment, looking at Ruby. "Is that one of those postie bikes?" he asked.

"No, it's a 125, but I've just done the Postie Bike Challenge and I had one for that."

"I was reading somewhere that the postie bike has just been voted the best motorbike ever made."

"Really? Well I loved mine. It's amazing how hardy they are. We had them down dirt roads and everything." I was just about to launch into an account of my experience on the Birdsville Track when another traveller pulled in behind me and the customs guy moved me on.

I felt thwarted. I hadn't had many people to speak to, and now I'd finally met someone with a similar interest, I couldn't talk to him.

Crossing the border, I entered a new time zone and gained an hour and half. This was great as it gave me even more time to get to Caiguna.

The road started to rise and at Eucla it swept round a big bend onto a straight which followed the base of the Hampton Tablelands for miles. I was pretty sure I also passed the end of the Dingo Fence, which crossed the highway round about Eucla, though it wasn't signposted.

As soon as I crossed a cattle grid, I stopped to take a photo, thinking this was it. I later found out that the reason it hadn't been signposted was because it wasn't actually the end of the fence at all. I'd misread my map and it had actually finished back at the Head of Bight, where I'd been somewhat distracted by the moth that had stowed away in my underpants and had completely missed it. I'd seen the start and the middle but not the end as I'd hoped, and I hated loose ends.

At the Mundrabilla Roadhouse I stopped for brunch. A lady and her husband were already in the restaurant, she with a cup of tea and he with a golf club. After a few minutes the man got up and left, taking his golf club with him.

"Is he doing the Nullarbor Links?" I asked.

"Yes. It's been on his bucket list for years, but now he's doing it, he's actually finding most of the holes are pretty rubbish."

I laughed.

"Is that your motorbike outside?" she continued.

"Yes."

"My, that's brave. Are you travelling by yourself?"

"Yes. I've come from Brisbane and I'm going to Perth, then Darwin," I explained.

"Doesn't it worry you, being alone?"

"Sometimes, especially when it's windy. But when it's calm like today, it's just glorious."

We chatted some more, then her husband returned and they left. Shortly after, so did I.

After a while the road headed over the tablelands at the Madura Pass and led into a much more wooded area. At Cocklebiddy I was keen to get off the highway and go and have a look at the Eyre Bird Observatory and the Old Telegraph Station (this was not part of the O/T Line; it was a different telegraph line that ran from Port Augusta to Perth). But this involved a trip down a 5 km dirt track so I gave it a miss. I'd like to put this decision down to prudence, but if I'm completely honest, the dirt still scared me a bit. I may have attempted it on an empty bike, but I didn't want to do it on a fully laden one.

When I reached Caiguna I filled up Ruby's tank ready for an early departure the next morning. A guy on a Triumph Sprint pulled in behind me. We chatted for a bit, then another biker I'd noticed having a cup of tea came over, followed by two other guys towing bikes on a trailer. After that, the guy following the caravan turned up. For ten minutes or so it was like having a little bikers' party at the pumps.

After they'd all moved on, I was left with the guy who'd been drinking tea, Ed. He was trying to decide whether to continue east or stay in Caiguna for the night.

"I'm staying," I said.

"Well, in that case, I'll join you," he said. Then, realising his faux pas, he added, "Well, not in a biblical sense."

"Ha." I laughed.

He was travelling around Australia on a huge 1400 cc Suzuki and was wearing only shorts, a T-shirt, a thin Drizabone raincoat and a pair of workman's boots.

"Aren't you worried about coming off?" I questioned. "Your legs will be ripped to shreds."

"Naw, I've been going for two years now and I don't really think about it anymore."

As we pitched our tents, a guy called Doug on a 650 cc Honda turned up and rolled out a swag to sleep in. Usually these have a mattress and sleeping bag included, but he only had the mattress and no sleeping bag. It was already cold and I wondered how he'd manage through the night. I invited him to join us for dinner, which he accepted but then disappeared.

At dinner it turned out that Ed was very political and seemed to have a bit of a conspiracy theory going on about something that had happened in his home town. He also complained vehemently about the cost of everything. Australia was very expensive, but as there was nothing I could do about this, I'd just accepted it. However it seemed to be upsetting Ed greatly. He had the potential to be quite an interesting guy, but seemed to have difficulty focusing on what he was saying and kept losing his thread.

Back at camp, Doug had reappeared.

"What happened to you?" I asked.

"I'm a psychiatric nurse and I can tell when someone has mental health issues," he said, nodding his head in Ed's direction. "I thought I'd give it a miss."

I hadn't thought about it in those terms. Ed had just seemed a little eccentric to me.

That night the temperature dropped to almost zero and, for the first time, my two sleeping bags didn't keep me warm. When I got up the following morning, Doug had been up for hours, drinking coffee in the roadhouse to keep warm, having had a back seizure and almost frozen to death in his swag.

END OF THE ROAD

I started the day with the "Ninety Mile Straight", the longest piece of straight road in Australia, which starts/ends just outside the Caiguna Roadhouse. And boy, was it straight. It had two RFDS emergency runways on it, it was so straight.

When you do these huge distances you start to go into a kind of trance. It was only when I saw a bunch of people crowded around a signpost on the other side of the road, followed by a bend, that I realised I'd come to the end of the Straight.

A few km further on, I arrived at the Balladonia Road-house. I ordered some breakfast and as I waited at my table I noticed an elderly gentleman in a business shirt, smart trousers held in place with bicycle clips and a pair of shiny brogues covered in duct tape. In his hand was a cycle helmet. *Was this guy cycling across the Nullarbor?* A lady came in behind him and he latched onto her like a starving man.

Yes, he was cycling the Nullarbor and, judging by the desperation in his eyes, he'd been on his own too long. When the woman managed to break free, his eyes fixed on me. *Uh-oh, here he comes.*

It wasn't that I wasn't interested in his story – it was just the way he told it. For the next ten minutes he barely paused for breath. To summarise: he'd flown in from New Zealand to Perth and was cycling back to Sydney, from where he would fly home. He didn't so much talk *to* me as *at* me. I couldn't tell you most of what he said; he was babbling incessantly. By the time I'd finished my meal, I was exhausted.

I felt bad excusing myself but I had a fair bit of distance to cover and couldn't spend all day with him.

Back outside at Ruby, a man came up to me. "Were you at Streaky Bay?" he said.

"Yes, but it was a few nights ago."

"Yeah, we saw you there, at the campsite. Is that a 125?"

"Yes."

He and his wife were in a car, towing a caravan. "We're going about the same speed as you!"

I wasn't sure if he was trying to be funny or having a dig at me.

Another 200 km on, I came to the end of the Eyre Highway at Norseman. I stopped at the roadhouse for a break and to check something out. The previous year, my friend Isabel's son had worked there during a year's working holiday.

"Have you been working here long?" I asked the lady behind the counter.

"A few years," she said. "Why?"

"Do you remember a guy that worked here from Glasgow, called Ross?"

"Ross McKeown!" she exclaimed. "Oh yes, I remember him." She laughed. "He's the only person I know who could come to work with a stinking hangover, serve someone, throw up in a bin, then carry on working!"

I grinned.

"Yeah, he was a great guy," she added fondly. "Tell him Paula said hello if you see him."

It was a further 187 km to Kalgoorlie and I swithered about whether to continue. I'd already done 372 km, but the promise of a nice warm bed in the youth hostel for the night kept me going.

Taking the Coolgardie-Esperance Highway north, it was stunning riding. Tall groves of gum trees exuded gorgeous smells, and huge salt lakes flanked the road to my right. The Esperance Branch Railway followed the line of the road, occasionally crossing it when the terrain dictated. For the first time in ages, there seemed to be a lot of motorbikes passing me on the road south. I wonder where they're going? I thought wistfully.

Just north of the Widgiemooltha Roadhouse, I got to a junction for the Goldfields Highway. I could either go straight on to Coolgardie and then continue to Kalgoorlie, or I could take this road. The signpost indicated that this was the more direct route, and as it also meant I wouldn't retrace my footsteps through Coolgardie on the way over to Perth, I chose to take it. It was another pretty, tree-lined road, with barely a house in sight.

After about 20 km I came to the small village of Kambalda. Although Kambalda had started off as a gold mining town back in 1897, by 1908 the gold had dried up and it was all but deserted. However, in the mid-1960s one of the world's largest nickel sulphide deposits was discovered, resulting in the opening of Australia's first nickel mine, and the town was reborn.

I stopped for an ice-cream in the petrol station.

"It's two for the price of one," said the lady behind the counter.

"Oh, I only need one," I said.

"Are you on your own?"

"Yes."

"Well, in that case, you can have it for the cheaper price."

It was a kind gesture and, as I was really starting to tire by now, it almost brought tears to my eyes.

Even more motorbikes were here. I asked the lady what was going on and it appeared I'd just missed the annual *Nickletown Car, Ute and Bike Show* earlier that afternoon.

"I thought that was what you were here for," she said.

"No, I'm just passing through on my way to Kalgoorlie."

I followed the Goldfields Highway for the last 56 km to Kalgoorlie. The road rose up into hilly forests and I could see clues as to Kambalda's nickel mining industry. A sign pointed in the direction of the nickel mine and various barriers across dirt tracks warned passers-by not to enter.

At 5 p.m. I reached Kalgoorlie, utterly exhausted. But I'd done it – I'd made it across the Nullarbor safe and sound and I hadn't seen a single camel, kangaroo or wombat for its entire length... or much more than a two-trailer road train, for that matter.

Part of me felt slightly disappointed – cheated, even. It had been easier than I'd thought. It had taken four days of riding and 2,249 km. From Kalgoorlie it would take another day or so to Perth, and then I'd have made it across Australia.

The hardest part was now over, or so I thought. I should have known better.

Golddigging

COUNTING THE COSTS

Arriving in Kalgoorlie was like riding into a Wild West frontier town. The main street, Hannan Street (named after one of the first people to discover gold there), was full of old hotels and shopping arcades, built in the Federation style of architecture. This is characterised by long verandahs, slated or tin roofs and what I call Scooby-Doo haunted house towers.

The Exchange Hotel on the corner of Hannan and Maritana Streets was a fabulous example of this. Wrapping itself around the corner, a red tin-roofed portico spread out over the pavement. A second floor verandah sat atop the portico, with slatted cream balusters and dark green balustrades hiding a walkway on to which the rooms opened. Above was another red tin roof, with small peaks where vantage points had been built out for guests to admire the views from under the shade. A tall, Scooby-Doo-style tower sat over the corner, with further red roofs and chimney pots to complete its facade.

Within seconds of making my way down the main street, I knew I was going to like it here. This was a town that definitely had some stories to tell.

Kalgoorlie, or Kal as it's known by the locals, was founded in 1893 when three Irish gold prospectors, Patrick Hannan, Tom Flanagan and Daniel Shea, stumbled across 100 ounces of alluvial gold nuggets when their horse cast a shoe. Hannan rode through to Coolgardie and registered the claim, thus sparking a gold rush to the area.

Gold mines sprang up all over the place and by 1903 the population had swollen to 30,000. At this time, the neighbouring town of Boulder was founded. The mining area between the two towns became known as the Golden Mile and is still considered to be the richest square mile of earth on the planet. In 1989 the Golden Mile became the Kalgoorlie Consolidated Gold Mines (KCGM) Super Pit, the world's second-largest gold mine. That year also saw the amalgamation of Kalgoorlie and Boulder into one twin city called Kalgoorlie-Boulder.

I had arrived on a Saturday evening after everything had closed. As I was keen to see the Super Pit, the first thing I did on the Sunday morning was go to the Tourist Office to book a place on the tour. I had hoped to arrange this for the Monday, but was told that the first available tour wasn't until Wednesday and I'd have to book it directly with the tour operators when their offices re-opened on Monday morning. This left me three days to learn a bit more about the town.

The first thing I learnt was that Kalgoorlie has no Sunday trading and hence the supermarkets were shut. I'd eaten my tin of stew the night before and had absolutely nothing left to eat. There was a McDonalds just round the corner from the tourist office, which provided enough sustenance to see me through the morning but I still needed something decent for the next few days.

Back at the tourist office, they advised me there was a small supermarket on the edge of the city. It would be open but it would take about half an hour to walk there. I set off, equipped with a street map, and followed the line the lady had drawn on it to the supermarket. It took me past more beautiful old buildings, some fairly ugly modern ones, the pretty old train station, a cricket oval, a very dodgy looking pub and a residential area. It eventually brought me out at a store swarming with shoppers – obviously I hadn't been the only one caught out by the Sunday trading laws.

I'd been fantasising about fresh food for ages. Eating in roadhouses keeps you alive, but it's hardly the most nutritious form of sustenance and I hadn't eaten anything better than bacon and eggs and hamburgers for days. As I was on foot and it was a long way back to the hostel, I decided just to buy enough for one day and then do a proper shop from the supermarket nearer the hostel on Monday. I loaded up with salad and made my way back to town.

Walking back, I crossed the footbridge over the railway tracks again and decided to have a look at the train station while I was there. It was opened on 8 September 1896 and has the longest platform in Western Australia. Given that the town was only founded in 1893, this showed how quickly its population had grown. Originally it provided a connection to Perth as well as some smaller towns in the eastern goldfields, but nowadays services run west to Perth, east to Sydney via the Indian Pacific and south to Esperance on the southern coast of Western Australia.

Back at the hostel I devoured the salad I'd bought. Vacuuming down lettuce and tomatoes and cucumber and green beans and ham and feta cheese and olives, I felt as though my body was sucking the nutrients into every cell of my being. I'd never been so happy to eat salad in all my life.

As most of the town was closed, I decided to get on with some domestic chores. My bike gear was covered in dirt and stinking from days of alternately freezing and sweating my way across the Nullarbor. I did a couple of loads of washing and hung out my tent and sleeping bag to air. I took out my map and budget spreadsheet to see how my funds were holding up and whether they'd see me through the remaining journey to Perth and up the coast to Darwin.

Although I'd been looking at my map every few days and plotting my progress, it was only now that the whole map was spread out in front of me that the enormous distance between Perth and Darwin struck me. It was 5,000 km. I hadn't added up the mileage before. It was over twice the distance I'd just done crossing the Nullarbor and it was going to start getting a lot hotter. Oh my God, I'm never going to make it, I thought.

My hands had been giving me terrible trouble ever since I strained them on the Postie Bike Challenge. I hadn't had more than a couple of days off riding since leaving Adelaide and the pulled tendons in my fingers weren't getting the rest they needed to heal. Spending eight to ten hours a day in the saddle was putting awful pressure on them. I knew I was developing repetitive strain injuries and that, if I kept going, they might never recover.

Additionally, my funds were running low. I only had about $3,000 left. I had twice the distance of the Nullarbor to cover and seven weeks to go. I wasn't sure if I had the health or the funds to get much beyond Perth. But I couldn't give up halfway between Perth and Darwin. I'd never be able to sell Ruby in the middle of the outback and it would be very difficult to organise a flight out from some remote desert outpost. Either I went for broke and continued all the way to Darwin or I gave up at Perth. There could be no half-measures.

LUST AND GOLD DUST

On Monday morning I was waiting outside the Kalgoorlie Tours & Charters office at 8.30 a.m. They didn't open until 9 o'clock but I was determined to get on the Wednesday tour of the Super Pit and didn't want to run the risk of it selling out before I'd secured my place. I needn't have worried, though – all the people waiting were accommodated.

Next I went to the supermarket and bought enough fruit and veg to last me for my stay. With these two essentials dealt with, it was time to take a proper look at Kalgoorlie.

I wandered around the elegant shopping arcades on Hannan Street and then came across the Western Australia Museum. This gave an interesting history of gold mining: how the miners lived and how the town had developed. It also had a gold vault, in which nuggets of various sizes were displayed behind a security-protected plate glass screen.

Outside there was a large red "headframe". In the bigger mines these were used to power the elevators which lifted and lowered miners and machinery into the main shaft. In this one, a new elevator had been installed to take visitors up to a viewing platform which offered fantastic views over the town. Unfortunately I couldn't see the Super Pit from it.

While I was there, I overheard an English couple asking one of the assistants about the Brothel Tour. I had picked up a leaflet about this at the tourist office and noted that tours were held at 3 p.m. every day. What I hadn't realised, until I heard them talking, was that you needed to book a place on the tour. I headed back to the tourist office and did just that.

At 3 o'clock I was outside Questa Casa, one of two surviving brothels in the town (the other one, the Red House, was next door). Back in Kalgoorlie's heyday, there was an influx of single men seeking their fortunes in the gold mines. Goods and services were needed to support them and one of these services was provided by the local brothels. Questa Casa is the only one left from these times and is over 100 years old.

Initially brothels were located all over the town and there were also many independent prostitutes, who operated from local bars and hotels. But after the town decided it wanted to be seen as a "family town" the police regulated the industry. Prostitutes were no longer allowed to solicit business in bars and hotels, and had to be registered with a specific brothel. Each brothel had to be licensed by the police and all the brothels were moved into Hay Street so that they didn't sully other parts of the town.

To avoid prostitutes mingling with the regular townsfolk, they were not allowed to leave their brothel. The only way they could leave a brothel was to move out of town altogether or to get married, in which case they would be accepted as a regular citizen.

This seemed to me like a complete denial of their freedom but the Madame assured me the girls were happy to comply with this rule, as the best money was to be made in Kalgoorlie and a few years' working there could set them up for life. It was an arrangement that seemed to work well for everyone involved.

However, about twenty years ago, the industry was deregulated. An influx of Asian sex workers started operating from the bars and hotels and the market fell out of the brothel business. Hence the Hay Street brothels, which numbered eighteen at their peak, gradually reduced down to the two which remain today. There had been another one which survived until quite recently, Langtrees, but that had been converted into a motel two years previously (although it still sported a visual history of its notorious past on the walls).

The Madame of Questa Casa showed us the "starting stalls" in which the girls would sit with their doors open and wait for potential clients to come by. The clients could then discuss what they were looking for and whether the girl wished to provide it. Apparently the girls were not forced to do anything they did not want to do or with anyone they didn't like the look of. They could, to a degree, pick and choose their clients. Once the client's requirements had been established and a fee agreed (time was sold in fifteen-minute units), the client would pass through the starting stall into the main house and onward to the girl's room.

Madame showed us two rooms that were in use. One was the S&M room, the other just a regular bedroom. The S&M room was filled with various sex toys, apparatus and costumes, and the Madame informed us that most men needing such extreme forms of arousal were punishing themselves for something. It made me feel sad to hear that. The other room was used for more conventional forms of intercourse.

There were eleven starting stalls at Questa Casa, meaning that up to eleven girls could be on duty at any one time. However, the Madame told us there were currently only two girls working there. I couldn't help feeling that the Madame probably made more money from the tours than she did from sexual services these days. There were about thirty people on our tour, which at $30 each made $900. Multiply that by thirty days and you have $27,000 – not bad for a month's work.

The tour was quite interesting from a historical per-spective but it left me feeling somewhat unsettled.

GOLDFIELDS ENGINEERING

The next day I needed to take Ruby for a service. I'd been told when I bought her that she would need her first ser-vice at 1,000 km and should then be serviced at 4,000 km and at every 4,000 km thereafter. She was now up to 5,750 km.

I'd noticed a Honda dealer, Goldfields Bikeworks, on the main road into Kalgoorlie when I first arrived. I re-turned to see if I could book her in and they asked if I could bring her back at 2 p.m.

This gave me a free morning and, as I was already kit-ted up for riding, I decided to take a ride to some of the more distant attractions the town had to offer.

First stop was the Mount Charlotte Reservoir, a cov-ered reservoir on the outskirts of town. Its cover made it seem quite small and insignificant, but underneath lay one of Australia's three international historic civil engineering landmarks (the other two being the Snowy River Scheme and Sydney Harbour Bridge).

Kalgoorlie, like Coober Pedy, is located in the des-ert, which means it has a very limited water supply. In the 1890s after Hannan, Flanagan and Shea discovered gold and sparked the gold rush, men came to the area in their thousands. However, there was insufficient water to sup-port them all and many of the early gold seekers, driven more by greed than common sense, died of thirst. A solu-tion was needed.

Enter C. Y. O'Connor, Engineer-in-Chief of Western Australia. He designed and oversaw the construction of the Goldfields Water Supply Scheme (aka the Goldfields Pipeline), an ambitious scheme to provide the town with five million gallons of fresh water every day. It consisted of three main components – the Mundaring Dam and Reservoir, constructed in the hills above Perth, a steel pipeline which ran from the dam to Kalgoorlie (a distance of some 530 km), and a series of eight pumping stations and two small holding dams to control pressures and lift the water over steep ridges.

In 1896, construction began. Sadly, due to much unwarranted criticism by the press, O'Connor committed suicide in March 1902, less than twelve months before the pipeline was completed. The scheme was opened in 1903 and still provides the town's water supply today.

Originally the pipeline was laid in underground trenches, but because of a high number of leaks, in the 1930s it was re-laid above ground on concrete pillars to prevent corrosion. After World War II the Mundaring Dam was raised ten metres to increase its capacity, and the pipeline was extended to service farms and communities in the wheat belt east of Perth. Currently a network of 8,000 km of pipe extends north and south of the main west-east pipeline and only 30,000 of the 100,000 people served by the scheme actually live in Kalgoorlie itself. Water takes one to two weeks to reach the Mount Charlotte Reservoir.

Once again I was amazed at man's ability to overcome his environment. But this was nothing compared to Kalgoorlie's other great feat of engineering.

My next stop was the Super Pit Lookout and I got my first view into the mine. My goodness, it was colossal. A monstrous hole descended for hundreds of metres into the earth. I couldn't wait for the tour the next day, to see it all up close and learn how the gold was extracted.

From there I had a quick look around the neighbouring town of Boulder and the Loopline Railway Museum. This was located at the old Boulder Railway Station and told the story of the Loopline Railway.

During the early 1900s the Eastern Goldfields Railway ran from Perth to Kalgoorlie, but there was no public transport in Kalgoorlie or Boulder themselves or between the two towns. As the goldfields spread, there was an increasing need for a railway to transport goods and workers to the various mines.

Mine management on the Golden Mile wanted direct access to the Eastern Goldfields Railway, as did the merchants and townsfolk of Boulder. The Government arranged for an "ore tramway" to be built to the mines.

This was, in effect, a railway line, but was called a tramway until the appropriate legislation could be passed for its legal establishment as a railway line. The tramway opened on 8 November 1897 and immediately proved popular, with trains running regularly to Boulder and then looping on around the mines and back to Kalgoorlie. With the goldfields being so busy and more people arriving daily, this railway became their main means of transport to work.

However, with the introduction of trams to the city in 1903, the Loopline began to lose money and services were reduced.

By 1954, emphasis was shifting to road transport, which was considered to be more efficient than the railway, and in 1976 the Loopline ceased operation. In 1982 the Loopline Tourist Railway took over running what was left of the Loopline. However, in the late 1980s the Super Pit was developed, and since 1989 the mine's operations have spread to the extent that very little remains of the Loopline's extensive railway system. The Tourist Railway closed in January 2004, when it was necessary for KCGM to claim the track to expand the Super Pit operations further.

Apparently KCGM made a substantial donation to assist with the redevelopment of the track up to the Super Pit Lookout, but there didn't appear to be any building works to confirm this or timescales for its construction.

I dropped Ruby off at the garage at the appointed time and went to a nearby bakery for a cup of tea and a sandwich. There was a picnic table outside and I sat down to eat my lunch and read my book while I waited. But it was no use – my mind kept drifting.

I'd been feeling sad about Walshy, and men in general. All those lonely hours on the bike had given me too much time to think. I'd had such a great time on the Postie Bike Challenge and then it had been lovely re-connecting with Walshy. I knew there could never be any future for us, but I had really liked him and was nursing a hole that had been left behind. I so much wanted to have a relationship again.

A couple of hours later, I collected Ruby. They had done a fabulous job, right down to giving her a wash.

"I've done the service," said the guy behind the counter. "The chain was getting a bit loose so I've tightened it for you, but there's a stiff bit developing so you'll need to get it replaced soon. But it should see you through to Perth."

I paid my bill and headed back to the hostel.

That night my mood fell further. Walshy and I had talked about meeting up in Broome in November, when he was going to be there on holiday. However, after I left I realised the timescales weren't going to match with my schedule so I'd suggested meeting in Perth instead. I'd got a message back saying he couldn't do this and wishing me luck for the rest of my trip. It felt as if he was giving me the brush off, and left me feeling strangely rejected.

Thankfully I had the Super Pit tour to look forward to the next day.

THE SUPER PIT

Kalgoorlie's Super Pit has to be one of the modern wonders of the world. Of course, it is a huge scar on the face of the earth and uses a massive amount of energy to power the mining operations, but if you ignore that for a moment and just look at the engineering involved, it's quite staggering.

Back at the end of the nineteenth century when gold was first discovered in Kalgoorlie, men with pick axes and shovels would dig shafts by hand to extract the precious metal. By the 1980s, Kalgoorlie was riddled with thousands of shafts going from the surface to 1.5 km underground, and most of the easily accessible gold had been extracted.

At this time Alan Bond, a prominent Australian businessman, saw an opportunity to get at the less accessible ore between these shafts by creating one big pit from which ore could be extracted at far less cost. He started buying up all the individual land leases. Bond's company failed to complete the takeover, but in 1989 all the leases were combined and Kalgoorlie Consolidated Gold Mines (KCGM) was formed to operate a gigantic, ever-descending pit in which massive equipment could tear out the old underground workings and access the unmined gold in between.

The tour set off from town and took us first to the Mount Charlotte mine, a traditional hand-dug mine on the outskirts of town. This was part of KCGM's operations and was linked to the Super Pit via an underground tun-

nel. Beyond this was an area where extensive tree planting had been undertaken. Our guide explained that one of
the resources needed for operating the original mines was
timber. This was needed to generate electricity for lighting
and power, to power the steam-driven winders that hauled
ore to the surface, and to heat the furnaces in which the
gold ore was roasted. Structural timber was also required
for the shafts and passageways of the underground mines,
which amounted to 3,500 km (the distance from Kalgoorlie to Sydney). The demand for timber was so high it resulted in virtual deforestation of the area for miles around
Kalgoorlie-Boulder – hence KCGM had undertaken a large
replanting programme.

Heading into the Super Pit, one of our first stops was
the dumper truck service area. Forty of these massive $4.4
million Caterpillar 793C beasts transport rubble from the
pit to the processing areas twenty-four hours a day, seven
days a week, 365 days a year. About 200,000 tonnes of rock
is mined every day, and each truck can carry 240 tonnes.
That means over 800 dumper truck trips per day. It takes
three triple road trains worth of diesel every twenty-four
hours to keep the fleet going.

Inside the pit we stopped at a lookout and peered into
the vast chasm below. Currently the Super Pit is 4 km long,
2 km wide and 600 m deep. They are in the process of increasing the depth to 1.5 km, the level of the original hand-
dug mines, by expanding the width of the mine. They can't
just dig a hole this size with straight walls, as this would
collapse into itself, so they have to go down in steps. It has
taken three years to expand it to its current width and will
take another four years to take it down to the target depth of
1.5 km. They then have until 2021 to get as much gold out
as they can before the lease runs out.

As regards gold recovery, geologists determine where the gold is located and explosives are set to blow this out. Blasting occurs about three to four times a week and creates thousands of tonnes of rubble. Each blast is given twelve hours to settle, after which the geologists mark up the ore zones. Four gargantuan $18 million PC8000 face shovels then fill a continuous series of dumper trucks with the rubble. Each shovelful weighs 68.5 tonnes, so just three and a half of these fill a dumper's tray. The high-grade rubble goes to the ore crusher; the low-grade goes to the stick picking areas, where the old mine shaft workings are removed and recycled before being taken to the waste rock dump.

Only about one in seven truckloads actually carries ore, and even then it is only about the size of a golf ball of gold, at about 500 grams.

At the processing plant our guide showed us how the high-grade ore was deposited into one of two stock piles, where it was transferred into the ore crushers – huge steel barrels filled with steel balls that crush it into a powder. This is mixed with water to form slurry, which is pumped into flotation cells where air is added. The gold floats to the top, where it is removed to storage tanks and dried. When it is dry it is sent for roasting. This converts the concentrate into calcine, which is then leached and absorbed into carbon.

The gold is removed from the carbon by an elution process which leaves a concentrated solution of gold. Electrolysis is then used to plate the liquid gold onto steel cathodes. Once all the gold is plated, high pressure water jets are used to remove the gold. The gold is collected and dried in large ovens. The dried "cake" is then placed in crucibles and put in a furnace at over 1,000°C, to melt the gold before it is finally poured into gold bullion.

About four gold bars are produced each day, each fetching about $690,000, which is $2.5–$3 million a day. Considering how much rock has to be milled every day to produce this, and the vast amount of energy used, it didn't seem like a great return on investment to me, and I had to wonder if it was really worth it.

When Paddy and his friends first discovered gold in the area, I don't think they could ever have imagined how their small shafts would morph into such a vast pit, changing the landscape forever.

I'd enjoyed seeing the mine and learning how it all worked, but I was horrified at how wasteful it was. Even though the Super Pit seemed to be run as energy-efficiently as it could be, the whole concept of open-cast mining struck me as the most wasteful industry on the planet. How could we possibly justify boring colossal holes into the earth for the sake of a few grams of gold?

I am a conservationist at heart, though I find industrial processes fascinating and can't help being impressed by man's ingenuity. However the whole experience left me feeling very torn. Surely we should be putting our skills and imagination into preserving our beautiful planet, not destroying it?

When I got back to the hostel I got the surprise of my life. Four years ago, when I'd last been in Australia, I'd stayed in a youth hostel in the northern beaches area of Sydney. I met a lady in her sixties there. She was on a break from her boyfriend, who had some behavioural issues that she hoped the break would make him rethink. And now, here she was in the kitchen at the hostel in Kalgoorlie. I couldn't believe it.

I recognised her straight away and went up to introduce myself. I'm not sure she really remembered me, but she said she did. Apparently she was on a break from her boy-friend, who had some behavioural issues that she hoped the break would make him rethink!

BACK TO CIVILISATION

I did the 600-odd km to Perth in two hops, stopping overnight in Merredin. The ride along the Great Eastern Highway started well. It was perfect riding weather, not too hot or cold and with just a light breeze.

Not far along the highway I ran into a series of road works that spread over 20 or 30 km. At various points the road was diverted onto clay tracks, which had been damp-ened down by a water truck. It wasn't until I felt my feet be-coming wet that I realised mud was being sprayed all over me and Ruby. I hadn't even managed to last a day without Ruby or my nice clean riding kit getting mucked up again.

I passed through Coolgardie, which was surprisingly small. It too had been the site of gold finds in the late 1800s. Because it was established before Kalgoorlie, I'd imagined it would be a much bigger place. But it just had a wide open main street with a few hotels, shops and a roadhouse, and some side streets with houses on them. Otherwise there didn't seem to be much to it.

A series of wooden telegraph poles, and the Goldfields Pipeline, ran parallel for the entire length of the highway. At various places, signs pointed to the pumping stations used to drive the water east. Originally there were eight pumping stations but now there are twenty. Only a couple of the original ones are no longer in use. I thought about stopping off to have a look but it was too early in the morn-ing and the first ones weren't yet open.

I stopped at the roadhouse in Yellowdime for breakfast, where I got talking to a cyclist, Mario, who was on his way east. We swapped info about the road ahead and when I stepped back outside half an hour later, the temperature had sky-rocketed. Not only that, the wind had got up and I was now being pummelled across the road. I did think about calling it quits at Southern Cross, where a huge dust storm was underway, but as it was only 10.40 a.m. it seemed a bit early to be clocking off. I pushed on, though when I saw a sign saying it was still 108 km to Merredin I wondered if this had been such a good idea.

After Southern Cross, we were joined on the roadside by the Trans-Australian Railway line. Now I had three services running parallel to the road and somehow it comforted me. If I got blown off here, someone was bound to pass by soon and come to my aid.

A few miles further on, I came to a signpost for the No. 1 Rabbit-Proof Fence. This was another of Australia's long-distance pest control barriers. In 1859 rabbits were introduced to Australia, when Thomas Austin, a grazier in Victoria, imported twenty-four rabbits from England and released them on his property. The rabbits soon multiplied and spread throughout the eastern states. This had a severe impact on farming and by 1901 the situation was so serious that a Royal Commission was held to find a way to stop them spreading into Western Australia.

Explorer and surveyor Alfred Canning (who later established the Canning Stock Route) was hired to determine a north-south route for the barrier fence. According to the sign: "The longest fence in the world commenced here in 1901, length 1837 km (1139 miles), completed 1903 at Esperance on the south coast and 1907 at Port Hedland on the north coast".

This seemed odd to me. The Dog Fence had been 5,400 km, so surely that was longer? Even if you took into account the No. 2 Fence (which is smaller and further west) and the No. 3 Fence (which is smaller again and runs east-west), it still only came to a total of 3,256 km. Either someone couldn't count or someone was trying to lay claim to something that wasn't rightly theirs.

The need for the rabbit-proof fence diminished in the 1950s, following the introduction of myxomatosis to control rabbits. However, since then it has been renamed the State Barrier Fence and helps prevent migrating emus and dingoes from entering the state's agricultural farmlands.

Thankfully the winds subsided enough to keep me on the road and I got into Merredin at 12.30 p.m. I could have carried on to Perth, but the heat was too draining. By now it was 38°C and the prospect of putting my tent up and having to spend the afternoon with no means of cooling down was more than I could bear. The caravan park had a single ensuite cabin available for $70. It was a bit of an extravagance but it had air-conditioning and I couldn't resist.

The next morning it was freezing again and I needed to wrap up all the way into Perth. The area between Southern Cross and Northam is known as the Eastern Wheatbelt and the highway passed through acre upon acre of blond wheat fields. Beyond Northam, the road began to rise and made its way into the Perth Hills.

According to the *200 Top Rides* supplement which had come with my *Hema Motorcycle Atlas*: "It's hard to miss the Mundaring Weir Road, given the extensive signposting!" In actual fact, it's very easy to miss the Mundaring Weir Road sign because there are so many signs stuck on the post it's difficult to pick it out. Which is exactly what happened to me.

Ever since I'd learnt about the Goldfields Pipeline, I'd been looking forward to stopping off and seeing the weir on my way into Perth. But I ended up only seeing the sign when I was level with it, and as I was going too fast to make the turn and there was a road train behind me, I missed the turning and couldn't turn around and go back.

The approach to Perth was actually easier than I expected, being well signposted, and I managed to make it all the way to the hostel with only one stop to check the map. It was 11.30 a.m. and check-in wasn't until 1 p.m, so I decided to take Ruby for a wash. It took a few attempts to find the car wash the receptionist had told me about, but when I did, I was dismayed to find that wherever mud had stuck to the chrome, small spots of rust had appeared. I'd only left it a day, and already Ruby was corroding.

After checking into the hostel I went to explore the city. From a distance it looks very modern and clean, but from street level there is a lot of poverty visible in Perth. All the main shopping streets were filled with down-and-outs, and it made me feel uneasy.

THE WALL

It's hard when you're travelling not to form attachments to people, especially when you're spending long periods of time on your own. You long for the company of friends, and when you meet people you like it's hard to move on. I'd met so many wonderful people since arriving in Australia – the postie bikers, Pete & Suzie, Dave & Cec, Mark & Kim and Walshy – that by the time I arrived in Perth, I was a bit of an emotional, as well as a physical, wreck.

I didn't know what to do. I was at the start of the final section to Darwin. I had 5,000 km ahead of me and six weeks to do it in. I'd also be riding into the heat and humidity of the wet season and wouldn't see anyone I knew until Darwin, where Phil the postie biker lived and had invited me to stay.

My hands were completely shot, too. Every morning I would wake up and they'd be so stiff I could hardly straighten my fingers. Then, at the end of a day's riding, they would be so strained it was almost impossible for me to lift or grip anything. Financially, I was down to $2,500 and Ruby needed a new chain. I didn't know if I had the strength or the money to carry on.

It wasn't that I didn't want to do it. I was just feeling a bit daunted by it all and with so many miles of potential solitude ahead of me, I was experiencing a bit of a traveller's low. I'd hit the wall.

I had arrived in Perth on Friday 17 October 2014. The youth hostel was fairly central and in a nice building, but it was full of hell raisers, running around banging doors and screaming their lungs out at all hours of the night. None of the people who'd offered me a bed in Perth (Merv & Glenda and Mark & Kim) were back yet, and the thought of spending at least another couple of weeks in the hostel, if I decided to go home, was not in the least bit appealing.

Plus going home early would mean I'd need to sell Ruby and I didn't know anyone in Perth who could help with this. Martin Guppy in Adelaide had said to call him when I got to Darwin and he'd give me the name of the Honda Dealer there. He would also explain to him why the bike wasn't registered in my name, which would make things a lot easier. I didn't have that option here.

With the weekend ahead of me, I decided to spend my time exploring. I had been to Perth in 1989, but hardly remembered anything about it. In fact, there seemed to have been considerable development since then, which was probably what was blurring my memories.

A storm that had been threatening to break for days finally caught up with me, too. While I explored the city, thunder roared, lightning flashed and rain deluged the streets, externally representing the turmoil I was feeling inside. The dark skies added to the gloom of the place and by the Sunday night I'd abandoned all thoughts of selling Ruby and flying home early and decided to get out of Perth as soon as possible.

West Coast Wonders

COAST TO COAST

Looking at my map, there were three main options for going north. I could take the Great Northern Highway, which went inland through the interior of Western Australia, the Brand Highway, which after about 350 km would end up on the coast, or the Indian Ocean Drive, a new route which ran most of the way up the coast until it met the Brand Highway about 75 km south of Geraldton.

I'd seen enough of the interior for the time being and I had read something in my *200 Top Rides* book saying that the Indian Ocean Drive to Lancelin and beyond was gorgeous. The allure of sea views and sand dunes seduced me, and the coast road won my vote.

To get there, though, I first had to take the Mitchell Freeway out of Perth. Now the trouble with using maps instead of GPS to find my way on a motorbike is that I tend to forget everything beyond the actual landmark I'm aiming for. I had no way of mounting my map on Ruby's tank. If I wanted to check it, I had to stop and get it out of my backpack, which wasn't always possible if no lay-bys were available.

In this case, I'd seen the green line of the Mitchell Freeway leaving Perth northwards and another red line (indicating a highway) beyond it, but I hadn't noticed that the two lines didn't meet. When I got to the end of the Mitchell Freeway, it just petered out and led to an intersection in the middle of a housing estate.

Now who builds a freeway that ends up in the middle of a housing estate? I didn't know which way to go. I caught sight of a petrol station to my left and aimed for that. I pulled out my map, which indicated that the red line went through Wanneroo, slightly to the south-east. As this was roughly the direction I needed to go, I turned back onto the road I'd just left, but in the opposite direction, and followed it east. A few left turns later I got to a big intersection which offered access to the Great Northern and Brand highways straight ahead, or another minor road to my left.

I panicked. *Which way should I go?* Then, just as all the traffic started to move forward, I saw a mileage sign down the minor road with what looked like "Lancelin" listed in the destinations. In a split second I threw my weight to the left and Ruby veered onto the Indian Ocean Drive. We'd found it.

And what a fabulous discovery it was. The Indian Ocean Drive has to be the most exquisite road I've ever travelled in Australia. For the first few miles, the road rose up through tall gum forests and then, as I came round a bend, suddenly the sea was before me. It completely took my breath away. The dark skies of the last few days had passed and the sun was shining, with the ocean sparkling below. Stunning white sand dunes lay to my right and two emus were chasing each other over their glistening surfaces. For some inexplicable reason I kept singing *Moon River* in my head. I was so happy to be leaving the city behind.

There was another reason for my good mood that morning. I'd had another message from Walshy, which made me realise I'd misinterpreted his previous one and that our friendship was still intact. I hadn't been expecting undying love from him, but I had hoped for a degree of amity and this message re-established that.

It was a heavenly ride to my first port of call, Lancelin. During my first trip to Perth my friend Sue and I had taken a 4WD trip to Lancelin, the Pinnacles, Kalbarri National Park and Monkey Mia. At Lancelin our guide took us for a drive on the sand dunes. I was sitting in the front seat and at one point he turned to me and said, "I seem to have got a bit lost. You'd better put your seatbelt on, just in case."

Like the innocent abroad that I was, I did what he said, just before we careened over the top of a massive dune and dropped down the other side. He hadn't been lost at all – he'd wanted to make sure I didn't go flying through the windscreen as we plummeted over the edge. Of course, he knew exactly what he was doing and slammed on the brakes, leaving us halfway up the slope, dangling at a precarious angle, as he howled with laughter.

So I knew there were sand dunes at Lancelin. But I couldn't take Ruby on them – their sandy surface would provide absolutely no resistance and I would, no doubt, be catapulted out of Ruby's saddle within seconds. Instead I took a ride around the town.

It was a gorgeous place. Hidden behind the main road was a long white sandy beach with turquoise waters and a few men launching tin boats to go fishing in. The buildings were a bit run down, with weathered beach houses and tired old shops that had obviously been there for years and hadn't seen a paintbrush since the day were built, but I liked that. I liked slightly shabby towns. Somehow they appealed to my sense of freedom, something the more homogenous modern housing schemes seemed to lose. It would probably have been a perfect place for me to live.

In fact there was a youth hostel there and I was severely tempted to stay for the night, but it was only about 9 a.m. and seemed a bit early to be knocking off for the day.

I stopped at the roadhouse on my way back to the main road, filled up Ruby and had what was quite possibly the worst bacon and egg toasted sandwich of my life. I think it must have been deep fried in whale blubber, as it was dripping with fat. I could practically feel my arteries clogging up with every bite.

I rejoined the Indian Ocean Drive, which headed inland for a short time through the Nambung National Park. Glorious shrubs with flame-red flowers lined the roadside, and a lookout gave fantastic views over the plains ahead. A few miles further on, a signpost pointed towards the Pinnacles, a collection of rock pillars located in the desert. As I'd seen these before, I rode on by.

Back on the coast, I had a stop at Hangover Bay and walked down to the ocean's edge. I'd been to Cottesloe Beach in Perth, which was also on the Indian Ocean, the day before, but had had no sense of achievement there. Maybe it was because it was so isolated here, but this time, as I gazed out to sea, it suddenly struck me. I had ridden from one side of Australia to the other – from the Pacific Ocean in Brisbane to the Indian Ocean right here. I'd done approximately 10,000 km in seven weeks, on no more than 125 cc of power. I was overjoyed. Suddenly all my worries evaporated and I knew I'd made the right choice in carrying on.

The small seaside towns of Cervantes and Jurien Bay were next. They were a bit more touristy than Lancelin, with modern concrete beach houses gathered into well-kept estates and smart shops selling a variety of beachwear and water sports paraphernalia. But pretty as they were, they didn't have quite the same wild energy about them that Lancelin did.

I carried on up the coast, the road edging ever closer to the sea until it eventually met the Brand Highway a few kilometres south of Dongara. I was loving every inch of the ride and didn't want to miss a thing. I detoured off the highway through more white sand dunes towards Dongara. Coming round a bend I saw a tour bus I'd passed a few times that day, which was now pulled over at the side of the road. Its occupants were making their way up a tall dune, with surf boards under their arms. I stopped to watch as they surfed down the dune. It looked like fun.

Dongara was another seaside town, but much bigger than the ones I'd seen on the Indian Ocean Drive. It seemed to have a bit of a sewerage problem, as there was a rather unpleasant odour coming from the beach.

The final 65 km from Dongara to Geraldton was through rich farmlands. Like the towns in the Eyre Peninsula, Geraldton had a huge bank of grain silos at the port. It was the biggest town in the area and probably amounted to a city by Australian standards.

I arrived at 4.30 p.m. It had taken me nine and a half hours to do the 485 km ride but I didn't care – it had been a fantastic day. I couldn't believe I'd almost been going to quit in Perth and miss all this stuff.

I pulled in at the first campsite I came across, but at $40 a night it was over twice what I'd been paying up until now. The lady behind the counter was very helpful, though, and suggested another one near the port. It was cheaper but was still the most expensive one I'd stayed in yet – $30 for a tent for the night. It would have been cheaper in a youth hostel, if there had been one. It was a very nice campsite, I'll give you that, but the price seemed a bit steep. If I'd known what was coming I'd have thought it was a bargain.

FIFTY SHADES OF PINK

The next morning I was up with the larks, or seagulls in Geraldton's case, at 5.30 a.m. and on the road by 7. I followed the North West Coastal Highway through miles of luscious farmlands to Northampton, where I took a loop off the main road to Kalbarri National Park. The road wound gently through more farmlands until, after about an hour and half, it came to a junction where I could either go straight on to a place called Port Gregory or turn right towards the park.

There was a huge pink salt lake ahead, as pink as Lake Bumbunga in South Australia had been the first time I'd seen it. Who knows when you'll pass this way again, I thought to myself, and ploughed forward. The road ran alongside the edge of the lake, which became richer and pinker the further I went. I stopped to take some photos, but as with so many vast landscapes, putting a frame around it stunted the effect. However it was a wondrous sight and as the only person on the road I could dawdle along as slowly as I pleased, absorbing its lustrous colours and hues.

Port Gregory was just a small town, with a single shop, a caravan park and a few houses. I rode up to the car park and had a look at the view out to sea, then made my way back along the pink lake to the junction and continued round to Kalbarri.

As I got closer, signposts alerted me to various tourist spots I could turn off and visit. Kalbarri's most famous attraction is a rock formation called Nature's Window. A striated rock with a hole in the middle gives spectacular views across the parklands, but as I'd seen it before I wanted to use this visit to see new sights. I took one of the side roads down to Eagle Gorge, where a small sandy beach was flanked by huge auburn limestone cliffs with lines of striations forming steps up their sides.

I hadn't realised there was actually a town in the park, called, strangely enough, Kalbarri. It sat on a gorgeous sandy bay with cyan blue waters, protected by a high sandbank.

I pulled into the car park to have a look and use the Ladies. When I got back on Ruby she wouldn't start. *That's funny, she was all right a moment ago.* I tried again. Still nothing. I stood there, perplexed.

A couple of guys who had been loading a boat onto a trailer bounded over to lend their assistance but couldn't figure out what was wrong either. They looked at her engine, wiggled some wires and scratched their chins, but nothing seemed to work. After a while they wandered off, looking somewhat dejected. Just as they got back to their trailer I figured it out. The kill switch was on. This is a big red switch all motorcycles have, which can be used to quickly switch off the engine in an emergency. I must have knocked it when I dismounted. As soon as I flicked it back into its correct position, Ruby started straight away.

"It was the kill switch," I yelled happily at the two guys as I left.

By now it was mid-morning and, as it was a pleasant spot, I filled Ruby up and treated myself to eggs Benedict in a foreshore café. It was a lovely day and, again, I was tempted to stay, but if I stayed at every place I stopped I'd never make it to Darwin in time. Reluctantly I clambered back on Ruby and set off for the remainder of the loop back to the highway. It was only 70 km, but it seemed to take ages as I kept getting distracted.

The road passed through some exquisite bushland filled with thousands of shrubs with bright magenta-pink flowers. They were stunning, and even though the heat was rising rapidly I couldn't resist stopping over and over again to take pictures of them.

The loop added an additional 200-odd km to my route, meaning it was already noon by the time I rejoined the NW Coastal Highway. There was a huge 130 km section to the next roadhouse. As I rode along, without a single building in sight and the temperature soaring, I started to remember all the reasons I had been worried about doing the west coast – the heat, the wind, the humidity, the distances, the solitude, the expense, the flies and my own vulnerability in such extreme conditions. What would I do if I had a break-down or, worse still, an accident?

It took me until 2 p.m. to get to the Billabong Road-house. It was 38°C when I arrived and my face was scarlet as I went inside to pay for Ruby's fuel.

"Are you all right?" asked the guy behind the counter. He was a tall man who appeared to be of Maori descent, probably in his forties, with a big friendly smile.

I lurched for the fridge and pulled out a chilled bottle of water. Unscrewing the cap, I raised the bottle to him as if toasting his health, then poured it down my throat.

"Just a bit overheated," I finally spluttered.

"Well, have a seat and take your time. You know, it will only get hotter, the further north you go?"

"I know!" I cried. I sat down, gasping for breath.

"All the road crews are off the road now," he told me.

"Really?" I questioned, not really understanding the significance of his statement.

"Yeah, once the sun reaches its peak you've not only got its heat, but the heat is reflected off the road surface, too. Even though it's only 38 on the thermometer, with the reflection it's nearer 60 degrees on the road."

"Oh, that explains why it's so freaking intense."

"Where are you going?" he asked.

"Monkey Mia."

I almost decided not to continue, but if I wanted to see the dolphins in the morning I'd need to get there tonight.

"Well, it should get cooler as you get closer to the coast," he advised.

It was enough to give me the push I needed. I stayed a bit longer, then climbed back on Ruby.

It took me another forty-five minutes to do the 48 km to the Overlander Roadhouse and the turn off for Shark Bay. I gulped down some more water, then took the turn. I still had 150 km to go.

I split the journey into three sections of 50 km each. The first was reasonably easy, and fortunately the second took me to Shell Beach, which was made from millions of tiny white shells. From a distance it looks like white sand; it's not until you get up close that you can see its real formation. I stopped to have a look, and a few minutes later the tour bus I'd seen at Dongara pulled in behind me.

"I've seen you before, haven't I?" said the driver. "Back at the sand dune in Dongara?"

"Yes," I said.

"Is that a 125 you're on?"

We had the usual conversation and he wished me luck with the rest of my journey. "We'll probably see you at Monkey Mia," he called as I waved him goodbye.

The exchange had lifted my spirits and the last section to Monkey Mia wasn't too bad either, getting me in for 6 p.m. I just had time to put my tent up before sunset. Myriad shades of pink painted the sky, as the sun set on another beautiful day.

ANIMAL MAGIC

Monkey Mia is located in Shark Bay, a World Heritage Area. Its combination of natural beauty, ecology, history and biological diversity meant it met the criteria required by the United Nations Educational, Scientific and Cultural Organisation (UNESCO) to qualify for World Heritage status, and it was inscribed on the list in 1991.

One of Monkey Mia's main attractions is its "Dolphin Experience". Every morning, wild bottlenose dolphins swim into the beach at Monkey Mia to visit and interact with humans.

In the 1960s, fishermen at Monkey Mia began sharing their catch with local dolphins. Over the years, the dolphins grew to trust them and were fed at the jetty and later the beach. News of the phenomenon spread and increasing numbers of visitors came to see the dolphins.

The Parks and Wildlife Department now run the show and every morning the dolphins are offered small amounts of fish to encourage them to swim in to the shore. To ensure that the dolphins continue to behave and hunt naturally and teach their young to hunt, the feeding is strictly monitored by Department staff.

The first feed is at 7.45 a.m. I was there at 7 a.m. to have a look around and see what had changed since my previous visit in 1989. I was glad to see there had only been a few, minor changes, but when I went to pay my National Park entrance fee one of the Rangers told me about some less obvious changes that had taken place.

"I was here twenty-five years ago, you know," I said.

"So you know what happened to the dolphins then?"

"No," I replied, "what happened?"

"It's really sad. Between 1987 and 1994, eleven of the twelve calves born to handfed females died. We didn't realise it at the time, but dolphins that get dependent on hand-outs lose their wild instincts, such as their ability to hunt and their interest in teaching their calves natural behaviours so they know how to survive in the wild. We were feeding them too much and too often, and visitors were feeding them all sorts of rubbish, like hamburgers."

"Hamburgers? You've got to be joking. People are idiots – what on earth made them think that would be good for a dolphin?" I said in disgust.

"You'd be surprised. The mothers became overfed and their calves starved to death because of neglect by their mothers. This wiped out a whole generation of dolphin calves. It's only now that their numbers are returning."

"That's awful," I cried.

"But there's been a lot of research done since then and we now understand the consequences of overfeeding. Since the feeding programme was changed in 1995, only three of the thirteen calves born to handfed mothers have died, and one of them was killed by a shark. Visitors are no longer allowed to feed them, except when supervised by the Rangers."

"Can we still touch them?" I asked. "I remember we could do this when I was here before."

"No, we found this was starting to stress them. The dolphins were starting to nip people. In fact, there was one incident when a dolphin grabbed a man's arm between its jaws. It didn't bite him as such, it was just a warning, but we had to take that on board. I mean, how would you like it if people kept coming up and touching you for no apparent reason?"

"Fair point," I agreed.

I was distressed to hear what had happened to the dolphins, but glad the Parks and Wildlife Department now had a better understanding of how to treat them. With this knowledge in mind, I made my way down to the beach to join the thirty-odd other visitors who had come to see them being fed.

As we waited, the Ranger told us what would happen. Only adult females with good survival skills would be fed. Males (including male calves) would not be fed, because they tended to be more aggressive towards other dolphins and humans. The dolphins were never fed more than a third of their daily food requirements, so that they still had to hunt for most of their food. Although they were fed three times each morning, there were no set feeding times, to prevent the dolphins from becoming conditioned, which would affect their natural wild behaviour.

As he talked, I looked out to sea. Suddenly, by the jetty, I saw a fin. It was a dolphin. Almost immediately, it ducked back under the surface. It was a few minutes before another one appeared. Gradually, in ones and twos, more dolphins swam into shore. Cautiously, they'd get closer. Some were braver than others. Some were more playful, bumping the Ranger's legs. Some had babies with them. It was delightful to watch and I remembered why I had enjoyed being here so much before.

After a while, three volunteers with buckets of fish chose onlookers to come into the shallows and feed the dolphins. I hung back. After my chat with the Ranger, I didn't want to do anything that could disturb them. But it was fun to see that the dolphins seemed to enjoy interacting with us just as much as we did with them.

Once the fish had been eaten, the dolphins swam off again. It had been a magical experience and I returned to my tent full of wonder at the natural world.

Back at camp, a daddy emu and its chick were making the rounds (apparently male emus do the child-raising in emu families). When I checked in I'd been handed a leaflet about how emus can come and scavenge when conditions in the bush are harsh, warning that food should be kept out of their sight and reach. A large tent nearby had left its door open and the emus were having a look inside. They were really comical and when a man appeared and shooed them away I couldn't help laughing out loud.

I decided to spend the day at Monkey Mia. I had a look around the visitors' centre, took a stroll along the beach and, when the temperature got too hot, plunged into the swimming pool. It was nice to relax after two big days on the road.

Later that afternoon, the man whose tent had been raided by the emus returned from taking his red setter dog for a walk. It was a beautiful youngster, just five months old. It bounded over to say hello and I patted and rubbed it happily.

"What's his name?" I asked.

"Big Vicious Dog," said the owner.

"That's a strange name. Wouldn't something like Charlie be better?"

He didn't answer.

"Is that you on the bike?" said the man.

"Yes." I knew what was coming.

But it didn't. Instead, he spent the next thirty minutes telling me how this was his second red setter and how the first one had become an internet sensation when he'd started dressing it in a tutu and posting photos of it online.

"A tutu?" I said in disbelief. "Why would you put it in a tutu?"

"People love it."

He went off to retrieve a yellow tutu from his tent and proceeded to put it on this dog. The dog clearly didn't like it and immediately tried to pull it off with his teeth.

"I don't think he likes it," I said, appalled.

"Aw, he'll get used to it. I'm going to set up a website for him, too."

I was incensed. Any form of animal cruelty, no matter how mild, really upsets me, and because this was purely for the owner's benefit and not the dog's, it drove me nuts. I wanted to rip the stupid skirt off the poor animal and slap the guy around the face with it. I had to walk away.

He clearly didn't pick up on my anger, as he kept coming over to chat for the rest of the day. No amount of uninterest seemed to deter him, and no arguments from me about the wrongs of dressing dogs in tutus seemed to put him off the idea. I was not impressed.

That evening two Irish women arrived and attempted to put their tent up. Clearly they'd never done this before and were having a hilarious time trying to figure it out. When they attempted to whack in the poles (not the pegs) with a hammer, I felt I had to intervene.

"See this pin?" I said, picking up a metal pin attached to the corner of the tent. "You slot that into the bottom of the pole." I demonstrated. "Do that with each corner."

They did, and up it popped like an igloo.

"Oh, so that's what they're for. I thought they were for putting the pegs through."

It turned out they had been living in Australia since they were teenagers (one was now retired, the other nearing retirement), but they hadn't lost their Irish accents at all. I could have sworn they'd just arrived.

The next morning I wanted an early start and had my tent down by sunrise. As I was packing up, one of the Irish ladies came over to say goodbye. Then, just as I got on Ruby, the man with the dog came over.

"Are you leaving?"

"Yes."

"That's a shame. I really enjoyed talking to you."

Talking at *me, don't you mean?* I was still too mad to return the compliment. I just nodded my head, kicked Ruby into gear and rode off.

FEELING THE STRAIN

I was grumpy and Ruby needed petrol, so we stopped at Denham, 30 km away, to refuel. It was 6.45 a.m. and the petrol station didn't open till 7. The wait did nothing to improve my mood, even though the view out to sea was gorgeous. The surface was flat calm with a clear blue sky above.

There is only one road in and out of Monkey Mia, which meant I had to retrace my steps down the peninsula for 150 km before getting back to the NW Coastal Highway. From there I was aiming for Carnarvon, a further 219 km away.

The strain was really starting to show. My right hand was seizing into a claw and, as predicted by everyone I'd spoken to, it was getting hotter and hotter. I was having to ignore the "don't ride at dawn" rule more and more often and get up at 5 a.m. to try and do as many miles as I could before 10 o'clock, when the heat soared.

Ruby was feeling the strain, too. Her chain was now like a piece of wet spaghetti and her rear wheel was almost completely bald. I needed to get her to a big town where I could find her the attention she needed.

Rejoining the highway, I filled up at the Overlander Roadhouse and started the long haul to Carnarvon. The road was a few miles from the coast and was the most like a sandy desert that I'd yet seen. Tufts of spinifex and stunted bushes scattered the ground and for the first time I was seeing long stretches of sand. About 50 km north, a flat-topped mesa rose out of the plain. A signpost indicated a lookout at the top and I turned off the road and up the track towards it.

It was magnificent and instantly my bad mood evaporated. Huge, dry salt lakes spread out to the horizon, with the faint dark hue of the sea in the distance. Other sandy outcrops poked up above the desert floor and I could see the road snaking its way through them for miles ahead. Down at ground level again, herds of wild goats kept running out in front of me. I stopped to watch them as they skipped and jumped through the thicket. It was delightful.

Further on, I stopped in a parking place for a drink. I could see two huge road trains coming towards me. I ran over to the middle of the parking bay and snapped a picture of the first one, then up to the edge of the road to get a close-up of the second. Admittedly, I was pretty close to the edge, and the second one honked its horn loudly as it hurtled past. I wasn't sure if it was a greeting or a rebuke.

I made it to Carnarvon by 12.30 p.m. – not bad for a 369 km journey. I found a campsite, pitched my tent and went to the tourist office to see if there was a Honda dealer in town who'd be able to nurse Ruby back to health. I was given directions to Sandy McGinn's Motorcycles, a few miles out of the town centre.

Unfortunately, they couldn't fit us in at such short notice, but Mrs McGinn told me there was another Honda dealer in Karratha, a couple of days' ride north. She gave me the number to call them, to make sure they could take me.

It was Thursday 23 October 2014 and I reckoned that if I booked Ruby in for Monday 27 October, it would give me plenty of time to get there. Fortunately, they had sufficient space to take her and I made the booking.

With Ruby's needs in hand, I left her at the campsite and went off to have a look around the town on foot. Although Carnarvon is on the coast, the town is actually set back from it, on a sea inlet. Back in the olden days, to get goods in and out, they needed a way to get them to the actual sea. Hence a tramway was built across the inlet to a jetty on the coast. Even at the coast, shallow waters prevailed and a one-mile-long jetty was built to get goods to ships moored at greater depths.

I started to walk along the tramway, but it seemed it might also be in the region of a mile long and I quickly abandoned that idea, deciding to come back on Ruby the next morning.

The campsite was very nice, with a swanky stainless steel kitchen and a swimming pool, but there were no picnic tables and I needed something to sit on when I was at my tent. I found a sports shop on the high street which had a small, lightweight, collapsible stool for just $15. I bought it and headed back to camp. The campsite wasn't very busy and there was no one to talk to; everyone was on their way south to avoid the heat and rains of the imminent wet season. I knew I was in for a long, lonely ride to Darwin.

Before leaving town the following morning I took Ruby for a ride to the One Mile Jetty. It was so long I couldn't even see the end of it. It had a set of railway tracks along it, which enabled a small train to transport goods and passengers from one end to the other. It was built in 1897 to accommodate ships that bought supplies and passengers from Perth, and allowed the export of livestock and wool from the region. Its merchant days were over now, but the train still ran as a tourist attraction – although not at 6.30 in the morning.

Leaving town I passed rows and rows of banana plantations. This, it would seem, was one of Carnarvon's main industries, tourism being another. I crossed the Gascoyne River, which flowed through the town and whose mouth opened into the sea inlet. The riverbed was currently dry but an indicator on its bank showed the levels of various floods, the highest being in 1960 when the waters exceeded 7 metres.

Coral Bay was my next destination. It was only 252 km and I was there by 11 a.m. It had been a bit of a boring ride. Apart from crossing the Tropic of Capricorn and thus officially entering the Tropics, and seeing some unusual termite mounds, there hadn't been much to entertain me. It was hot and sticky and I was in a stinking mood when I arrived. I hadn't spoken to anyone interesting in days and was in dire need of a good conversation.

I found the campsite and paid the $32 for my pitch. *Thirty-two dollars! Bloody rip-off.* I sulked.

At my pitch I couldn't decide what to do. *Put my tent up or go for a walk? Tent or walk? Tent or walk?* Just when I was about to go mad with my own indecision, a guy on a monster Triumph Tiger Evolution (just like the one Mark had had in Port Augusta) came riding in, and like a bee to honey I buzzed around him, desperate for company.

Phil was an ex-pat from the UK, who'd moved out to WA with his family twelve years before, but you wouldn't have known it. As soon as he took his helmet off, he donned an Akubra. With his stubbly beard, dark-tanned skin and jeans he looked every bit your typical outback Aussie. Even his accent was decidedly Australian. But there were still strains of UK English in it, and as time went by this seemed to become stronger and the Aussie less obvious, but that was probably due to my influence.

He was a great guy and spent the whole day with me, showing me around (he'd been there before) and letting me drivel on endlessly about life on the road. It was good to have someone who understood the ins and outs of motorcycle riding in Australia and who was happy to explain some of the mysteries I'd encountered, such as the hundreds of diagonal trenches that ran off the side of every highway (they're used to drain water off the road surface when it floods).

He also understood the fixation I'd developed with numbers. When there isn't much else to think about, reading road signs becomes an obsession. At major junctions there is usually a sign that tells you how far it is to the next outcrop of humanity. Then the way-markers count down the kilometres to the largest town. In the outback they are usually every 10 km, nearer the cities, every 5 km. But you start longing for these, mentally subtracting them from the total distance to see how far you've got to go. I'm not sure if this was keeping me sane or driving me insane, through all the vast spaces I was covering.

As I babbled on, I felt I was turning into the cyclist I'd met on the Nullarbor who had been on his own for too long. But Phil didn't seem to mind.

Coral Bay sits on the Ningaloo Reef and is incredibly beautiful. A flat white sandy beach extends into shallow turquoise waters that glitter in the sun. It's just a small resort, but it seems to absorb its many visitors without too much evidence of them being there, and it didn't feel busy at all.

We wandered about its perfect beaches and walked up to its petite harbour, then looped round the back of the campsites to a café on the foreshore to have some ice-cream.

Phil had been up in the Pilbara, a big mining region further north, to visit his son, who was working in one of the mines. Phil's wife had been worried that the son would blow all his earnings on wine, women and song, but Phil was proud to report he'd actually been very sensible and invested it in real estate, which for a twenty-year-old was quite impressive. Phil was now heading home to Bunbury, south of Perth, and I made him promise he'd tell the guy at the Billabong Roadhouse that not only had I made it to Monkey Mia but I was still alive and kicking here at Coral Bay.

Back at the campsite, we split up for a while to have showers and dinner, then met again for a drink. Phil collected me from my tent and had a closer look at Ruby.

"So you've really been riding a 125 all round Australia?"

"Yep."

"That's pretty impressive. Can I take a photo of you? I want to send it to my mate. He couldn't believe it when I phoned and told him what you were doing."

I let him take a photo and posed as best as I could. I am not the slightest bit photogenic but he'd been so nice – how could I refuse?

We went across to the bar and had a drink. We'd been talking pretty much constantly since 11.30 a.m., with only a couple of hours off. It was great to meet someone I had so much in common with, and had he not been happily married I think I could have spent the rest of my life with him. But before I did anything under the influence of alcohol that I'd live to regret, I took myself off to bed.

I was up at 5 a.m. again the next morning and, not surprisingly, Phil was nowhere to be seen. I thought about leaving my business card on his bike so we could stay in touch, but something held me back and I rode off without being able to tell him how much I'd appreciated his company.

I had a big day ahead of me. I was going to try to do the 525 km to Karratha in one go, but I almost didn't even make it back to the NW Coastal Highway. At the last fuel stop the previous day I hadn't filled my tank right up to the top so I had a few litres less than usual. Then I'd used 91 km worth of fuel getting to Coral Bay. This meant I had approximately 140 km worth of fuel left in my tank, with another 100 km worth in my jerry, giving me enough for 240 km.

There had been an unmanned 24-hour petrol station at Coral Bay but it only sold Premium Unleaded or diesel. The guys at Moto Adelaide had given me strict instructions only to use Regular Unleaded. I had added up the mileage on my map and worked out that it would be 143 km back to the highway, then a further 105 km to the Nanutarra Roadhouse (I was going a different way back), which meant I should have just enough to cover the 248 km ride.

As I rode along I could see the fuel gauge dropping rapidly. At the 140 km mark there was still no sign of the NW Coastal Highway and I was almost on empty. I started panicking. "Never ride past fuel," I kept saying to myself. *Surely it couldn't be far now?* Another 2 km on, I finally rejoined the highway and emptied my 5 litres of spare petrol from my jerry into the tank. According to the signpost, it was only 101 km to the next roadhouse. *I should make that, shouldn't I?*

As it turned out, I was able to do a bit more than 100 km on 5 litres of petrol and sailed into the Nanutarra Roadhouse with fuel to spare. But it had been a bit of a close call and I swore never to ride past fuel again, no matter what grade it was.

Just beyond the roadhouse was the turning to the mining town of Tom Price and Karijini National Park. Karijini was the place Jan in Coober Pedy had told me about. I'd since seen brochures about it, and it looked very appealing, with waterfalls plunging into cool rock pools. But I couldn't do everything. Ruby needed to be at the garage in Karratha for 8.30 on Monday morning and I had to put her needs first. Plus it would have been over 300 km each way, which would have added an extra two days' travelling time to my journey, not to mention the time I'd need in the park to look around. Even if I had been willing to do the extra distance I probably wouldn't have been able to see that much, as most of the waterfalls were down dirt tracks. I'd then need to take the same road out to get back to Karratha, by which time Ruby would have missed her appointment. It was an easy decision to make really, and I rode on by, adding it to my list of things to see if I ever came back to the Pilbara.

Somewhere during the remaining 283 km to Karratha, I hit the humidity I'd been dreading ever since leaving Perth. While with dry heat your sweat evaporates as soon as it reaches your skin's surface, with humidity it clings to you, soaking your clothes but providing none of the cooling properties of cold water. I was riding in a blistering inferno of heat, through parched desert plains. It was beautiful country and I loved the wide open spaces, but the heat was bleeding me dry.

I stopped to look at a mine by the side of the road and my camera, which had been giving me problems ever since I arrived in Oz, gave up the ghost. 30 km from the Fortescue Roadhouse, Ruby almost gave up, too when she suddenly coughed sharply, twice in a row. I thought she was going to cut out but she recovered and kept going.

Another kilometre on, she did it again. I immediately pulled over, switched off and took a look to see what was happening. It seemed to me as though there had been a blockage in her fuel line but I had no idea how to check this. I opened her tank to check I wasn't running out of fuel, but there was still plenty. I wiggled her wires and these all seemed to be securely attached. Her chain didn't look any worse than when I'd left Coral Bay. I didn't know what else to try. I started her up again and continued to the roadhouse with no further incidents.

This time, it was my turn to collapse. It was 38°C and I was so overheated I practically staggered into the café. I gulped back a litre of chilled water, sat down for half an hour in the air-conditioned room and tried to stop shaking. I was on the verge of heatstroke – I knew the symptoms from my previous trip. Even in my delicate state, I found it interesting to note that water was actually more expensive than petrol here. It cost $1.66 for a litre of unleaded, compared to $5 for 1.5 litres of water (that's $3.33 per litre) – exactly twice as much.

When I got back outside, the heat hit me again and I knew I'd never make it if I didn't take some additional precautions. I went to the Ladies and soaked my T-shirt, face and hair under the tap. At that moment my phone bleeped. It was Walshy, replying to a message I'd sent him earlier. It said, "Ruby and you are winners, you will both get there in one piece…"

His timing couldn't have been better and it gave me just the boost I needed to keep going. By the time I got back to Ruby I had almost dried out again, but I felt better for having heard from my friend, and managed to push through to the outskirts of Karratha.

As I approached another petrol station, Ruby coughed again, just as before, twice in a row. I stopped, had a rest, then restarted her and rode into town. Riding into Karratha, I saw hundreds of pre-fabricated houses flanking the road. These were villages that had been built to house workmen deployed in the mines nearby.

It was 3 p.m. when I arrived and I desperately needed to cool down. I found the campsite and almost fainted at the $42.00 a night fee. Seeing my reaction, the lady reduced it to $37.80. I put up my tent and threw myself into the pool.

Within minutes of getting out I was sweating again. *Was it ever going to cool down?* I was tired and very irritable.

Later, spotting Ruby, a guy came over and said, "I've got one of them at home."

I told him about her coughing fits and he said it was probably the fuel overheating in her tank.

"Bloody hell!" I exclaimed. "If that's the case, I'm going to have a hell of a ride to Darwin!"

244

THE PILBARA WANDERER

I only had one full day scheduled in Karratha and I wanted to make the most of it. Apart from locating the Honda garage and buying a new camera, the thing I wanted to do more than anything else was find the statue of Red Dog in Dampier.

Dampier was a town located 21 km west of Karratha. Its port was developed in 1963 when Hamersley Iron (now Rio Tinto) established an iron ore mine at Tom Price and needed a port on the coast to export its ore from. A private railway line was also built, to link the mine with the port.

During the 1970s a Red Cloud Kelpie known variously as Bluey, Tally Ho and, most famously, Red Dog, roamed the outback and found his way into the hearts of everyone he met. After the death of his owner, who lived in Dampier and worked at the port, Red Dog was taken in by the local community and became known as the Pilbara Wanderer, owing to his travels through Western Australia's Pilbara region.

He had such an impact on the people of the town that after he died (of what was suspected to be deliberate strychnine poising in 1979) the townspeople erected a statue in his memory.

Several books have been written about him, including Louis de Bernières' *Red Dog* in 2001. In 2011 a film based on this book and also called *Red Dog* was made on location at Dampier. I had read the book and seen the film and loved both of them, so I couldn't come this far and not see the place where it all happened.

The statue was located in a parking bay just after the railway passes under the road on the approach to the town.

It was a beautiful sculpture, with Red Dog atop a stone plinth in mid-stride, looking purposeful and friendly. It was so realistic I found myself patting his face and it brought tears to my eyes as I remembered all the touching stories of how he'd brought people together.

While I was there, I took a look around the town. There wasn't much to it; it was mostly houses and there didn't appear to be any obvious town centre or shopping area. An esplanade followed the line of the beach. It led to the port and its loading facility at Parker Point at its western end, and back up through the housing area at the other. Several clubs had sports fields or club houses on the Esplanade, and a caravan park was also located there, together with several banks of workers' apartments. Following the road up through the town, more apartment blocks looked out over the bay. These looked like 1960s/70s architecture and I couldn't make out if they were still in use or not. Some had cars outside, while others seemed to be completely deserted.

I went back along the Esplanade towards the port, but access wasn't allowed to the general public and I had to content myself with taking pictures of the massive ships moored at its extensive jetty.

As I was leaving the town, a mile-long train passed under the bridge, hauling its load of iron ore in numerous open wagons to the port. Further on, to my left, going north, I saw a sign for the Burrup Peninsula. This contains the North West Shelf Project, Australia's largest oil and gas development. The Project comprises three main components: (1) three offshore extraction facilities, (2) two sub-sea pipelines and (3) an enormous onshore processing plant.

The offshore facilities lie about 135 km north-west of the peninsula in the Carnarvon Basin oil and gas fields. The processing plant is on the peninsula. It is one of the world's largest liquefied natural gas (LNG) producers, supplying oil and gas to Australian and international markets. Two additional pipelines supply natural gas to customers in southern Western Australia, via the 1530 km Dampier to Bunbury Natural Gas Pipeline, and to customers in Port Hedland via the Pilbara Pipeline. A fleet of nine specially designed ships transport LNG to international customers.

Between Dampier and Karratha, on the water's edge, lay Dampier Salt. Originally established by Hamersley Iron, it is now run by Rio Tinto and comprises several long salt flats where salt is extracted from seawater by evaporation. The resultant product is also exported from Dampier, but from a point east of the Esplanade called East Intercourse Island.

Karratha was a much more modern town than Dampier, with a large shopping centre, some modern high-rise apartments and numerous new housing schemes. It was established in 1968 in response to the development of Dampier Salt and the continued expansion of Hamersley Iron's operations, and now acts mostly as a service centre for the area.

Given that the Pilbara had seemed so barren on my approach, it was astonishing to see how many resources were being extracted from it.

That evening I opened up my budget spreadsheet to see how my funds were lasting. I had $1,300 left. That would only last me about two weeks, three at the most. I began to realise that I might not be able to spend as much time sightseeing as I'd hoped, and that I'd have to get to Darwin as quickly as possible if I wasn't going to run out of money altogether. If necessary, I could then bring forward my flight home.

But first I needed to leave Karratha. Even this wasn't going to be quite as straightforward as I'd hoped.

A CATALOGUE OF ERRORS

I had arranged to drop Ruby off at Northwest Honda at 8.30 a.m. When I arrived, a lady came running out looking very apologetic and explained that the mechanic had phoned in sick and they wouldn't be able to work on Ruby after all, and could I bring her back tomorrow?

I didn't really have any choice. It was 600 km to the next large town, Broome, and I felt I'd already pushed my luck enough with Ruby's chain. The mechanic in Kalgoorlie had recommended I only go as far as Perth with it, and I had done another 2,850 km since then.

I agreed to return the following morning. I had checked out of the campsite and couldn't stand the thought of going back there and having to camp again in the tortuous heat. Fortunately, I passed the tourist office on the way back into town and there was an advert there for a backpackers' hostel.

Immediately I made my way there and checked in. *If only I'd known about this place before.*

"Where are you from?" asked the manager.

"Scotland," I replied.

"Oh that's good. There's another Scottish girl in the room you'll be in."

He showed me to the room and introduced me to Suzie, a twenty-eight-year-old from my home town of Glasgow. We immediately hit it off and as soon as I'd moved all my stuff in, had a shower and got changed, she offered me a lift to the shopping centre so I could get some food.

Suzie and her boyfriend were on the second year of a working holiday. The boyfriend was working for a company based in Karratha that, as part of his package, provided accommodation for him. Unfortunately this did not extend to Suzie and she was having to stay at the hostel. She was looking for work in the town too, but had been finding it difficult to get anything.

However, later that day she got a call from an agency, saying they had some short-term cleaning work available, starting the next day. But she would have to provide her own protective clothing, so she went over to her boyfriend's to borrow some.

When she got back, I was in a bit of a state.

"How was your evening?" she asked as she came in.

"Not good. I've made rather a mess of something."

She raised an eyebrow, questioningly.

I decided to confide in her. Earlier in my trip, one of the places I'd been staying had been largely filled with men who were working in the town. They were a fun crowd and I soon found myself settling in comfortably with them. The night before I was due to leave, I was talking to one of them I'd become quite friendly with, Bruce. When I told him I was leaving the next day he said he'd get up and see me off.

I'd already packed up Ruby and was just getting ready to leave when he came out and kissed me goodbye – on the lips. It was the type of kiss I could have stayed in for hours – soft and gentle and heartfelt. It really took me by surprise and left me swooning all day.

He asked where I was heading. When I told him, he joked (or at least I thought it was a joke) that he might wave at me if he passed by.

Later that afternoon I got a call from the receptionist at the place I'd checked into, saying Bruce had phoned to see if I was there. She'd taken his number, if I wanted to ring him. Alarm bells went off in every fibre of my being. Given how much I'd enjoyed the kiss he'd given me earlier, you'd think this would have been welcome news, but it kind of freaked me out. *Was he here? I mean you don't just happen to "pass by" towns in outback Australia. Surely he hadn't followed me?*

I should have listened to my gut reaction – fear doesn't arise for no reason. But we'd got along well and curiosity got the better of me, so I texted him to see what he wanted. That was my first mistake – now he had my number. It turned out he was there with his work, which allayed my concerns a bit, and I agreed to meet up with him. That was my second mistake.

We met for dinner, where it became clear he was interested in a lot more than what was on the menu. He was nice enough, but I soon realised we didn't have much in common and that any romantic feelings I'd been feeling towards him had dissipated the moment I'd received the news of his unexpected arrival.

Nonetheless, given that I hadn't had much interest from men in recent years, I was flattered by his attention and ended up going back to his room with him. This was my biggest mistake yet. Now I was giving him a message I was interested, whereas I just didn't know how to get out of it without hurting his feelings. He was keen to take things further and, thinking I'd never see him again, I went along with it.

As far as I was concerned it was just a one-off, but unfortunately he seemed to rather fall for me. Despite numerous arguments on my part that I was only in Australia on holiday and there would be no future in getting together, he seemed convinced otherwise. To try and get my point across, I left shortly after.

Bruce had been phoning and texting me ever since. At first I was flattered, but it was becoming a bit over the top. Every message was full of sloppy sentiments and when I phoned to warn him about getting too attached, it seemed to make him think I was even more wonderful, and he told me he loved me.

As we'd only spent a few hours together, this seemed ludicrous to me and I knew I had to put a stop to it. I called him again and reiterated that there was no future for us. He seemed to accept this, and when he asked if it would be all right if he texted me occasionally, just to see how I was getting on, I made my final mistake. It had seemed like an innocent enough request and, not wanting to appear rude, I'd agreed. It was the worst thing I could have done.

Instead of an "occasional" message, he had been bombarding me with a barrage of texts. None of them enquired how I was getting on; he just mused on about how he felt about me. I'd stopped answering them weeks before, but he'd kept on sending them. Now they were really starting to wear me down. That evening he'd sent more texts and I'd finally cracked and sent him a message back, asking him to stop.

He immediately phoned me to find out why. I refused to answer his calls and ended up having to turn my phone off.

When Suzie got back, I was a nervous wreck. "What do you think I should do?" I asked, after explaining it all to her.

"I think you're going to have to speak to him. He's obviously not going to stop calling until you do."

So I called him back and explained I didn't feel the same way about him. After a long discussion he eventually seemed to accept this. But the whole episode really scared me.

The next morning Suzie was out early and we only managed a groggy farewell. I felt sad about this, as she'd been really fun and supportive and it would have been nice to keep in touch.

I packed up Ruby for the second time and was back at Northwest Honda for 8.30 a.m. This time the mechanic was there. Ruby was wearing out, too. As well as needing her 8,000 km service, a new chain and a new rear wheel, she'd been having these mysterious coughing fits. I told the mechanic about them and said that the guy at the campsite had thought it was due to the fuel overheating.

"Oh, I doubt that," the mechanic responded. "It's more likely to be something in the fuel lines. I'll flush the carbs out just to make sure."

Three hours and $704 later (thank God for credit cards), we were ready to go – carbs duly flushed. Apparently there had been a bit of grit in the carbs, which could have caused the coughing. Apart from this, the mechanic hadn't been able to identify anything seriously wrong with her.

SPONTANEOUS COMBUSTION

As I was late getting on the road, I decided only to go as far as Port Hedland, 235 km away.

Not long after leaving Karratha I could see huge plumes of smoke on the horizon. Believing that the next town, Roebourne, was another industrial centre, I thought it might be pollution from one of the processing plants there. But as I got nearer, I could see it was actually a huge bush fire. A base of flames enveloped the land and tall clouds of black smoke rose into the air. Even though it was some distance away, I could smell it from the road.

Bush fires are very common in Australia. Often they are started by lightning strikes, sometimes by arsonists and occasionally by spontaneous combustion. There hadn't been any storms for the last few days, but as it was still blisteringly hot it seemed the heat was the most likely cause of this one. It looked as if it had been raging for days. There was a whole section of burnt scrub and scorched tarmac a few kilometres further on.

I stopped in Roebourne for something to eat and was surprised to discover it wasn't an industrial town at all. It had originally been founded as an administrative and service centre for the pastoral industry, but now it seemed to be mostly residential, with a few hotels and shops lining the road.

A signpost pointed to Wickham, Point Samson and Cossack. Wickham was originally a private town, built by Rio Tinto to accommodate workers at the nearby Cape Lambert iron ore ship loading facility (which has one of the longest and tallest jetties in Australia). Point Samson was a deep-water port and Cossack was a port originally built to ship cattle but was now mostly a ghost town. They were all places I wanted to see, but it was already past noon and the heat was becoming insufferable. I knew I'd end up spending too much time there and possibly wouldn't make Port Hedland if I didn't keep going. My rapidly dwindling funds also meant I was having to make some tough decisions, and this was one set of attractions I couldn't afford the time or the money to see.

The next place I passed was Whims Creek, but instead of the highway going through the middle of the township, there was a turnoff for it. Unfortunately it wasn't signposted and I only caught a glimpse of a banner saying "Whim's Creek Pub – A Must See" out of the corner of my eye. This was the only indication that there was anything there at all, and I was past it before I could stop. I could have turned around and gone back but I decided it was one "must see" I could miss.

Charred remnants of the bush fires continued along the roadside for miles to the north, leaving just blackened stumps where some of the larger shrubs had managed to resist complete destruction. Smoke was still rising from their remains, filling the air with the smell of burning and raising the temperature further.

About 40 km from Port Hedland I entered quadruple road train country. Port Hedland is the highest tonnage port in Australia and serves the mining and resource industries. These massive trucks, together with mile-long freight trains, transport ore to the port. At one point one came up behind me and couldn't get past for the traffic in the other direction. I tell you, there is nothing scarier than several hundred tonnes of iron ore in a steel truck bearing down on you.

Port Hedland is a massive industrial town surrounded by iron mines, salt farms and God knows what else. As soon as I rode in, I knew I couldn't just spend the night and ride back out again. This was a place that needed exploring. *To hell with my budget.*

HEDLAND HIGHLIGHTS

The first thing you see as you come into Port Hedland is a long railway line to the left and a huge white mountain of salt, set amongst shining wet salt beds, to the right. Ahead of this are the monstrous drilling machines of the iron mines. A new road, resembling a freeway but not so wide, flies over the railway line, offering staggering views of the industrial landscape all around. In the distance I could see the coast and the sea beyond.

As I got closer to the town I saw a sign for the caravan park and followed it. It led me to Cooke Point, overlooking the sea. Great, should be nice and breezy here, I thought to myself, but I was wrong. It was just as hot as everywhere else.

I left Ruby outside as I went into the office to check in. A couple of guys in work gear came in after me. They looked at my helmet, put two and two together and exclaimed, "Is that you on the 125?"

I nodded.

"Bloody hell! Where have you come from?"

I told them my story.

"Wow, you're game. Must be pretty scary riding that thing when a road train passes?"

"Yes, but it's worse when a caravan tries to overtake you. Often they don't pull away after passing you and you get caught in their tailwind. They don't seem to notice and you get dragged all over the road. I feel like shouting 'pull away, pull away', but they'd never hear me."

A lady who had just arrived in a caravan and had been listening in said, "I didn't realise that. I'll need to tell my husband."

I went back out to Ruby and found my site. It was gravel and I practically needed a jack hammer to drive my pegs into the ground. Just as I finished putting all my stuff into the tent, my phone rang. It was Mark, the guy I'd met in Port Augusta, ringing to see where I was.

It was great to speak to him; he was such a friendly person and was so genuinely interested in what I was doing. He and Kim were now back at home in Perth, having had an excellent trip to the motor racing at Bathurst and the Moto GP at Philip Island. I reported that I was now in Port

Hedland and wouldn't, therefore, be needing a bed at their place after all.

Afterwards I thought I'd better tell Glenda & Merv I wouldn't be seeing them in Perth either, so I sent them a text message.

It was nice to hear from Mark, but it left me feeling a bit lonely. However, this wasn't to last for long. When I returned from the shower a bit later on, two fellow campers had arrived. It was the Irish ladies I'd met in Monkey Mia – Ethel and Kathleen. For such a big country, it's surprising how easy it is to bump into people you've met before.

They were having dinner in the camp kitchen and invited me to join them, giving me a can of soup/stew which they didn't want. I fired up my camping stove to heat it, but it ran out of gas a minute later. I transferred to the barbeque plate, which also ran out of gas. *Strange that two appliances should run out of gas at the same time. Was the universe trying to tell me something?*

When Ethel had first moved out to Australia by herself at the age of seventeen, she'd met and married Kathleen's brother, Paddy. He had found work in the Pilbara and they had spent several years living at the caravan park where we were now staying. Kathleen had arrived in Australia a few years later and she and Ethel, as well as being related, had become good friends.

Ethel was hilarious and was full of stories about her early adventures. When her husband had first moved to the Pilbara, she'd been left in Perth. Missing him, she packed up her old Holden station wagon with her young children and some supplies and drove up to see him. This was back in the 1960s, when most of the roads were still unsealed and cars didn't have four-wheel-drive. Miraculously, she'd made it and had ended up staying for the duration of Paddy's time there.

"Weren't you worried about breaking down?" I asked.

"Back in those days, if you had a puncture you'd wave the next motorist down and give them the wheel, and they'd take it to the next town to get it fixed. The garage would then give it to the next person going in your direction, to bring it back to you. When you got to the town, you'd go to the garage and pay for the repairs."

She and Kathleen were now on a Pilbara Revisited tour, returning to all the places Ethel had lived. Given how resourceful she'd been as a girl, I was surprised she'd never put a tent up before, but was glad to see they'd now mastered the technique.

They'd been over to Karijini National Park and informed me that it had been closed due to the bush fires. I was glad I hadn't attempted to go there.

We whiled away the evening, exchanging tales of our adventures, and I felt warmed by their company.

When I'd checked into the caravan park I'd noticed a small flyer entitled "Daytime Harbour Tours". I'd been spending a lot of time on land and the thought of a boat trip sounded divine, so I phoned up and booked a place. The tour wasn't till the following afternoon, giving me most of the day to explore the town.

I took a ride around Port Hedland and its sister town, South Hedland. Port Hedland is surrounded by iron mines and the town itself is largely residential, with a town centre bordering the harbour. The sprawling Esplanade Hotel takes up a full block and various other shops and offices occupy the remaining streets of the centre. South Hedland, by contrast, had lots of shopping malls but much less in the way of heavy industry.

It wasn't until I took the harbour tour that I fully understood the enormity of the harbour area. On the map you can see that the harbour lies between two promontories. The westerly one is called Finucane Island (although it's not strictly an island) and contains a number of iron ore mines. The easterly promontory, Nelson Point, contains the town of Port Hedland itself. To the south is Anderson Point, which joins the two promontories and contains more iron mines. The channel between the three areas looks like an upside-down Y and is called Stingray Creek. Each area contains berths for ships transporting a variety of cargos, including iron ore, copper, fuel, general goods, salt, manganese and chromite.

Given that the port started out as a jetty to serve the cattle industry in 1896, it was now a gargantuan complex. There were sixteen operational berths. The Port Hedland Port Authority (PHPA) had four, which were used by the smaller mining companies. BHP Billiton had eight and Fortescue Metals Group (FMG) had four. As if this wasn't enough, another berth had recently been completed to serve the new Roy Hill iron mine and railway project, and was due to open in September 2015. Additionally, FMG and BHP Billiton both had further berths planned.

I was interested to learn that the two bigger companies, BHP Billiton and FMG, transported ore to the port via their own private railways. The smaller mining companies trucked it in via road trains, which explained why I'd seen so many road trains full of ore on the way in. I also learnt that Rio Tinto had exclusive use of the ports at Dampier and Cape Lambert, which clarified why they did not have a presence at Port Hedland. Apparently Rio Tinto operates the largest privately owned heavy freight rail network in Australia.

The Harbour Tour was run by the Seafarers' Mission, a Christian charity set up to support overseas mariners. The

Mission provides a centre for the crews of the bulk carriers that come in to take the iron ore to China and other destinations. Often the crews of these vessels are at sea for months at a time and have little or no contact with their families. The Seafarers' Mission provides a ferry service that goes around all the ships, picking up sailors from their vessels and taking them to the Centre. From there, they can exchange money, go into town to buy provisions and use the internet services in the Centre to contact their loved ones. The Centre also provides a bus service to get them to the shopping mall and back. As a way to fund these services, the Mission offers tours on the ferry to visitors.

I was the only paying client on the tour. There must have been about forty mariners, jumping on and off ships. There were two other passengers, who both had some connection with the Mission, and our guide, but otherwise I pretty much had the tour to myself. It was fabulous being out on the open water, seeing these huge vessels up close and where a light sea breeze made the temperature much more pleasant.

The tour lasted about an hour and half and took us from one ship to another, collecting and dropping off sailors as we went. The ships were colossal and several berths were capable of accommodating Panamax-sized vessels – that is, the maximum size able to pass through the Panama Canal. Steep gangways were lowered from their decks to our tiny ferry, and the sailors had to hop over the harbour waters below onto the gangways to make their way up or down. It was a calm day, but I thought it would be quite scary if it was at all choppy.

I really enjoyed the tour and once again I was staggered by the engineering involved in extracting resources from the earth and distributing them around the globe. With the production of iron ore, salt, oil and gas, the Pilbara produces over a third of Australia's export income.

But I couldn't help being disturbed by the impact it was having on the environment. It seemed that care had been taken to ensure that the industries were as efficient as possible, and they had been secreted from sight as best they could be, but this didn't change the fact that vast quantities of natural resources were being shipped to foreign lands, to be turned into electricity or raw materials to feed mankind's addiction to consumer products.

It made me wonder if we'd ever be able to reverse the effects of global warning, if we continued to buy so many frivolous, pointless items. I'm not denying that many great advances have been made, which have improved man's health and welfare significantly. But there is also a lot of utter crap produced, like cushions and ornaments, that really isn't needed. It's this stuff that perhaps we should be cutting back on, so that the earth's precious resources can be reserved for more worthy purposes.

MAD DOGS AND ENGLISHMEN...

I'd been dreading the ride from Port Hedland to Broome ever since I left Perth... 606 km (only marginally less than the distance from Glasgow to London) in blazing sun and sweltering humidity.

Now 606 km was by no means the greatest distance I'd covered in a day. But, according to my map, after the Sandfire Roadhouse there would be no further service stations for 366 km. As Ruby's tank only held about 230 km worth of fuel and my jerry another 100 km worth (totalling 330 km), that meant I would almost certainly run out of petrol.

Knowing this, I'd bought a couple of stainless steel drinks canisters and filled them with an additional 1.5 litres of fuel.

I set off at 6 a.m. and got to the Pardoo Roadhouse by 8 a.m. Those first two hours were quite pleasant – with a relatively cool breeze and lots of cattle and road trains on the road to keep me on my toes. I even started taking some photos of a road train coming up behind me while I was riding along – something I would never have dared to do before this trip.

A serving of bacon and eggs for breakfast and I was back on the road for 8.45 a.m. Immediately, the temperature was up. By the time I got to the Sandfire Roadhouse at 10.30 a.m. it was 40°C and I was seriously starting to wonder about the sanity of continuing.

A man came up to ask me about Ruby, but I could hardly speak and had to wave him away as I stumbled into the shop to pay for my fuel.

I'd been so worried about running out of fuel, I didn't even think about topping up my water bladder and left with it half full. That meant I only had a litre of water on my back, 750 ml of Hydralyte in one of my drink bottles and 750 ml of water in the other. I still had 366 km to Broome, and at 80 km/h this could take another five hours. With nowhere to shelter from the scorching sun, I was really going to be in trouble if I ran out of water.

As I continued north I seriously considered turning back and leaving the remaining distance to Broome until the next morning, when it would be cooler. But it was only 11 a.m. and I was determined to get there in one journey.

An hour later I stopped in a lay-by for a break. Half an hour after that I came across a proper rest area, so I stopped again. As I headed over to the toilets I saw a dingo making for my abandoned kit. Oh no you don't, I thought, and raced back to my picnic table. The dog didn't run off, so I grabbed my camera and took a few shots.

He was quite cute, with a healthy light brown coat, and looked as though he might have been fairly young.

"Hmm, just mad dogs and Englishmen go out in the midday sun, eh?" I said out loud to my four-legged friend.

He looked at me and nodded.

Leaving the rest area, for the first time that day I suddenly had the sense that I was going to make it. I rationed my water and took a break every 50 km. It was barren country again, with little to keep my mind entertained. Then, about 50 km from Roebuck, the scrub ended abruptly and huge wide plains began, filled with cattle. This was the Anna Plains cattle station and it appeared to be very well stocked.

By 3.30 p.m. I'd made it to the junction with the Great Northern Highway at Roebuck. Turning left towards Broome, there was a roadhouse on the right. *That wasn't on my map.* But it was – I'd just thought it was on a different road. All that worry about running out of fuel was for nothing.

But now I was more worried about my own need for fluids. I bought a 1.5 litre bottle of water, drank half of it in one gulp and poured the rest into my water bladder before knocking off the last 33 km to Broome, where I checked into the youth hostel and collapsed in a cool, air-conditioned room.

I'd done it. I'd made it up the west coast of Australia – woohoo! Now all I had to do was get to Darwin.

Top End Meltdown

PEARL OF THE WEST

Broome found its fame as a pearling town during the 1850s, when European sheep farmers who had settled in the area discovered beds of giant silver-lip pearl oysters, the largest pearl shells in the world. By the late 1800s, Broome had developed into a major pearling centre. At this time, the town's 400 pearl boats (known as luggers), worked by 3,000 men, supplied 80 per cent of the world's mother of pearl. This was used mainly for buttons.

During the early 1900s, Japanese divers were brought in to dive for pearl shells. Ships' crews were recruited from Malaysia, the Philippines and Indonesia, thus establishing Broome as a multicultural town. The town centre is known as Chinatown, reflecting its Asian history.

The introduction of plastic buttons in the 1950s saw a decline in the pearling industry and by the 1970s Broome was struggling for survival. Enter one Lord McAlpine, who poured money into the place and restored many of the old buildings. More notably, he saw its potential as a tourist destination and set up a number of luxury resorts at Cable Beach.

Broome struck me as a somewhat disjointed town. It lies on a peninsula. To the east, on the shores of Roebuck Bay, is Chinatown with its restored buildings. About 5 km to the west, you've got the expensive resorts bordering Cable Beach. Various housing estates lie between, but it's way too far to walk from Chinatown to the beach, so most people shuttle between the two on scooters or 4WDs.

I'd arrived in Broome on Thursday 30 October 2014 and my plan was to stay for a couple of days and leave on the Saturday. But it occurred to me that I'd be travelling through the remote Kimberley area at a weekend and, after my experience in Kalgoorlie, I didn't want to be caught out by any Sunday trading restrictions. Therefore, I decided to stay for the weekend and leave on the Monday instead. This would give me a few days to see why Broome was considered one of Australia's top tourist destinations.

It was so hot and humid during the day, it was all I could do to drag myself from the hostel to the air-conditioned shopping mall and back. After about 4 p.m. it became a bit easier to move, but even then the air was so heavy it was like walking through wet cement.

The hostel was about a twenty-minute walk from Chinatown. On the Friday afternoon I summoned up enough energy to haul myself over there. As it was called Chinatown, I expected it would be filled with red and gold pagodas and Chinese-looking houses and shops. Maybe it was, at one time, but nowadays there was really only one block, Johnny Chi Lane, that looked even remotely oriental. Mainly there were plain wooden and corrugated iron buildings. Some of these still housed Chinese merchants but most were now restaurants, shops and pearl galleries.

The one thing that Chinatown did have to offer, I discovered, was the Sun Picture Theatre, the "Oldest Operating Picture Gardens in the World". It looked like just the type of shabby old building I'd love, and in an attempt to avoid the Halloween Party at the hostel that night, which the Scottish guy behind reception kept trying to persuade me to join, I decided to go and see a film.

I'd never been to a picture gardens before and it was everything I'd hoped for. Outside there was a double-fronted tin structure with a slanted portico, providing shade for waiting customers. Inside it had been beautifully preserved, with the entrance hall full of old projectors, posters of famous film stars and photographs of the Picture Gardens since it opened for business in 1916. Under the tin roof was a wooden floor with rows of wooden deckchairs.

There was no back wall; instead, the hall opened onto a grass lawn on which more deck chairs were placed. Ahead was the screen and above, a starlit sky provided a crystalline ceiling. I gasped with delight. It was beautiful and it exuded olde worlde charm.

I found a seat under the stars and sighed with joy. This was exactly the type of place that appealed to my sense of nostalgia. After a while, we could hear some adverts playing, but there were no pictures. Someone shouted, "Take the lens cap off!" and the pictures appeared.

Gone Girl was the film that was playing – a slightly disturbing movie about a wife who fakes her death and tries to frame her husband for her murder. As the film got underway, I realised that the Sun Picture Gardens had one other unique feature. It lay right under the flight path for Broome airport and every twenty minutes or so, a plane would roar overhead as it came in to land. This just made me love it even more.

Walking home, however, I felt uneasy. I was alone and the film had been a bit scary, making me jumpy. A group of Aboriginals were gathered on the town oval, either drinking cans of beer or passed out on the grass. And when I got back to the hostel, a few people were slumped over tables, dressed as vampires or ghosts or in some other form of fancy dress. It was definitely the witching hour.

At four in the morning I had another text message from Bruce. It was harmless enough, but left me feeling a bit shaky. *Would he ever give up?*

On Saturday I spent the morning doing laundry, then used every ounce of energy I had left to walk down to a camping shop to buy a new gas cylinder for my camping stove. It only took about an hour and half there and back, but the humidity left me utterly drained, and even the prospect of another outing to the cinema wasn't enough to make me leave my room again.

I'd been feeling a bit low since I arrived. The girl in my room wasn't very friendly and didn't want to talk. Neither, it seemed, did anyone else. I was down to my last $1,000 and I still had 2,000 km to go. *How was I ever going to make it, with so little money and in such unrelenting heat?* Between the unsettling film, the late-night messages and my ever-decreasing pool of money, I was starting to feel quite vulnerable and thinking that maybe I wanted to go home.

On Sunday, after another message from Bruce, I knew I needed to do something about it. I decided to visit the Blue Buddha Temple to try and clear my karma about the whole affair. I took Ruby and rode in normal trousers and a T-shirt. Much to my disappointment, it wasn't much cooler in these than in my full riding gear, but in some ways that was good to know, as I could stop fantasising about how much cooler I'd be if I was in jeans.

The temple was near Cable Beach and provided a lovely, tranquil setting for me to meditate. Instead of endearing him to me, the messages of love and affection that Bruce had been sending had been scaring the crap out of me. I tried to focus on the good intent behind them – he wasn't trying to scare me, he was trying to attract me. But I wasn't interested in him and I had to honour that as well. It took a while to reconcile the two opposing sets of feelings, but eventually I imagined the universe enveloping each of us in the type of love we needed and my heart began to feel at peace.

As it was close by, I went from the temple to Cable Beach. It was named after the third sub-sea cable from Java was landed there in 1889. Due to volcanic activity in the Timor Sea, frequent breaks had occurred in the original Java to Darwin cable laid for the Overland Telegraph Line. A second sub-sea cable was laid on the same route, but suffered the same fate. Therefore an urgent need arose to lay a third cable from Java to Australia, away from the seismic zone. Broome was chosen as the site for this, as there was direct telegraphic communication with Perth and thence with the rest of the country, via the telegraph line across the Nullarbor to Port Augusta.

Cable Beach was heralded as one of the best beaches in Australia, but I wasn't overly impressed. I think it was because it was bordered by car parks and a landscaped boardwalk full of cafés and tourist amenities.

Further on was the port, with a long T-shaped wooden jetty stretching out into shimmering, celestine-coloured waters. I liked this much better, as it had more of a wild, untamed naturalness about it.

I took a zigzagging route back to the town centre, through the luxury resorts and housing estates. I discovered another small beach at Roebuck Bay, called Town Beach, which I much preferred to Cable Beach because, like the port, it was more rugged and undeveloped. I rode past museums and hotels, the police station, courthouse and jail, cricket ovals and schools, and back up to Chinatown for a final circuit before returning to the hostel to collapse in my temperature-controlled haven once again.

Broome had been an interesting place, but apart from the Picture Gardens it didn't quite live up to its billing, I felt. Perhaps if it hadn't been so intolerably hot it would have been more enjoyable.

That evening I called my friend Rod, who lived in Bateman's Bay on the east coast. I'd been meaning to phone him since my arrival in Australia but things kept getting in the way. He seemed really happy to hear from me and it lifted my spirits. *Maybe the last section to Darwin wasn't going to be so bad after all?*

IF YOU CAN'T STAND THE HEAT

Have I mentioned how hot it was? I was up at 4.30 a.m. on Monday 3 November 2014 and on the road by 5.30 to do the 402 km to Fitzroy Crossing. It was like an oven by 8 a.m. and there was absolutely nothing I could do about it. I tried riding without any tights under my riding trousers but, as I'd suspected, this only resulted in my much thicker and stiffer riding trousers sticking to my legs and making it very difficult to move. I'd need to keep wearing my tights for the rest of the trip.

I was going east now, which meant I was riding into the sun. Up to this point I had mostly been riding away from it and had managed to survive without a pair of sunglasses. Now that I'd be going east I'd bought a pair of cheap sunglasses in Karratha to stop my eyes from being burnt out. I'd tried them on with my helmet in the shop and although it was a tight fit, I'd reckoned they should work okay.

Unfortunately, when I wore them on the bike for the first time, the legs started pressing into my skull. After a few minutes it was too sore to continue so I had to stop using them. However, when I was in South Hedland, I'd passed an optician and asked if they could remove the legs.

The lady asked why, and I explained that they were pressing into my head when I had my helmet on.

"How are you going to stop them from falling off your face, without the legs?" she asked.

"Er, I was just kind of hoping they'd sit on my nose like a pince-nez."

She took the legs off and we tried it. As soon as I moved my head even the smallest amount they fell forwards. It was obvious that this wasn't going to work.

"Why don't you get some elastic thread? We can feed it through the holes where the screws were and then you can loop it over your head. The thread should be thin enough not to press into your skull."

"Where can I get some?" I asked.

"Try K-Mart."

A few minutes later I was back at the optician's with the elastic. The lady fed it through the holes and adjusted it to fit my head.

I tried them on. "This is great," I said. "These should work perfectly."

I hadn't used them since, but with the sun in my eyes I pulled over and put them on.

As I pulled away, visor open, they seemed to be working fine. But as soon as I flipped my visor down, I couldn't see properly. The sunglasses had Polaroid lenses which, when used with the visor, seemed to create a spectrum of colour on the visor, making it difficult to see. Ethel, in Port Hedland, had warned me this might happen. As it was dawn and kangaroo breakfast time, I had to pull over again and remove them. *Damn!* I thought I'd been so clever.

Once I got past the Roebuck Plains Roadhouse, I left the last vestiges of humanity behind and hit the open bush again. It's amazing how different the bush can be from one place to another. The two things that seem to differentiate one type of bush from another are height and density. If the bush is small, stubby and thin on the ground, it tends to look more desert-like. The taller the trees get and the more densely set they become, the more forest-like it appears. Initially, on leaving Broome, it was very dense and, with a few palm trees thrown into the mix, it almost looked like jungle. But beyond Roebuck it became sparser, until I suddenly came upon a huge plain of termite mounds. There were hundreds of them, all different shapes and sizes.

Termites look like ants but aren't, and they work together to survive. They divide labour among castes, produce overlapping generations and take care of their young collectively. To do this they build subterranean nests. In order to keep the nests cool and well ventilated, they build mounds on the surface which incorporate an extensive system of tunnels and shafts leading down to the nest below. I'd read that the mounds occur mostly in well drained areas, but as virtually all of outback Australia seemed to fall into this category, I wasn't sure why they appeared in some places but not in others that, to me, looked exactly the same.

Just beyond the Willare Bridge Roadhouse the road forked, one branch following the Great Northern Highway east, the other going north to Derby, where the Gibb River Road begins. The Gibb River Road is another famous outback track and comes out just before Kununurra.

I'd done part of it during a 4WD adventure tour Sue and I did in 1989, and there had been lots of gorgeous gorges to go and cool down in, as well as rivers to cross and steep hills to negotiate. When I'd planned this trip I'd intended on doing the whole thing, but at the Broome Visitors' Centre there had been a notice warning travellers that the last two cattle stations offering fuel on the road were closed. There was only one roadhouse for the 667 km length of the track, meaning that food would not be plentiful either and I'd need to find a way to carry my own.

Together with the inherent danger involved in riding dirt roads alone in remote areas at a time of year when few other people would be doing the same thing, this led me to conclude that it wouldn't be a good idea. That left the Great Northern Highway as my only option.

After another hour or so, I pulled into a rest area for a break. There was a huge Boab tree there. Boabs are remarkable for their extremely wide trunks. In fact, there is one in Derby that I'd seen on my 1989 trip, called the Prison Boab Tree, whose trunk is so wide it is thought to have been used to lock up Aboriginal prisoners on their way to Derby for sentencing during the 1890s.

Coming into Fitzroy Crossing, I could see the town across a low, flat plain. From a distance, it was like an oasis in the desert, though up close it was a bit run down. But it didn't matter; I was so glad to have finished my ride for the day. It was only 11.30 a.m., but the sooner I got off the road and cooled down, the better.

I pulled into the roadhouse to fill up Ruby's tank and noticed that her odometer had now reached 10,059 km. This meant I'd done about 13,500 km including the Postie Bike Challenge. That is a *very* long way... about the same distance, in fact, as from London to Darwin!

It was a moment for celebration, but as there was no one to celebrate with, I just patted Ruby's tank and thanked her for all she had done for me. She had been the best bike I could have hoped for.

Fitzroy Crossing had three caravan parks to choose from. The first looked pretty rough, the second, I was advised by the tourist info guy, was equally bad, so I went for the third, the Fitzroy Crossing Lodge. It was full of little wallabies bouncing about, so I pitched my tent and retreated to the camp kitchen to try and cool down. It was no use though – the temperature just got hotter and hotter.

After a while a small campervan drove in and its owners set up camp near my tent. The couple, Iain and Anne, came over to the kitchen and joined me. They were retired and had spent a few months touring Western Australia; now they were on their way back home to Darwin.

We chatted for a while, but when I started shaking I knew I was in a bad way and might collapse if I didn't cool down. I left them, walked the half km back to the Lodge and spent the rest of the afternoon in the air-conditioned bar.

When I got back to the tent at dusk, everything I owned, including Ruby, had been infested by ants and the campground itself had been invaded by a herd of cattle. It was too much – I was outta there. I moved all my stuff onto a picnic table under a gazebo at the edge of the campsite, took my ant-infested tent down and made a bed for myself on top of the picnic table.

After dinner, it was still sweltering. I climbed into my sleeping bag atop the picnic table but couldn't sleep. The table was only a couple of inches wider than my air mattress and every time I turned over I kept worrying I would plummet off the table onto the concrete plinth below. After sweating profusely for an hour, I moved the whole assembly onto the concrete floor and eventually got to sleep.

But I was up at 4.15 again and on the road for 5.15. I was aiming for Halls Creek, only a short hop of 291 km away, but my God, it took *five hours* to get there. The first 100 km I did in one go, but after that it all went pear-shaped and I had to keep stopping every half hour or so. And why was that? Oh yes, because of the bloody heat!

At one point I could feel myself starting to fall asleep. I pulled into a lay-by and lay down on the ground beside Ruby. Within seconds I was unconscious. I think I could have died in that moment. I don't know how long I'd been like that – it could have been seconds, it could have been minutes – but I was startled awake by the vibration of my phone going off in my breast pocket.

It was 007 Michael, replying to a message I'd sent him a few days before. It probably saved my life. I'm not sure I'd have come round again if it hadn't been for that message. I later found out that Michael had actually sent the message two days before, but it had only reached me as I lay there, dead to the world. It was as if the universe was shaking me awake and telling me to keep going.

I staggered to my feet, drank half my bottle of Hydralyte and got back on the road.

There were a lot of cattle about, which was good as it kept me alert. And masses more termite mounds, many of which had been dressed in T-shirts and hats, making me laugh. There were also some nice viewpoints overlooking rocky escarpments. One rest area took me off the road and over a small creek. A sign by its side said: "Crocodiles inhabit this area. Attacks cause injury or death". Thankfully the creek was dry and there was no sign of any man-eaters, so I rode over the concrete causeway and parked under a tree for another rest.

I arrived in Halls Creek at 10.15 a.m. There was no way I was going to camp. My tent was still full of ants. I had the whole day ahead of me and, after my scare in the lay-by, I knew I needed to cool down properly. (I think the combination of not being able to cool down the day before and the terrible night's sleep had left me weakened, and that was why I'd passed out in the lay-by.)

The tourist office advised that there were two hotels in town; one was fully booked and the other was $150 per night. *Damn, I was going to have to camp after all.* I checked into the local caravan park, took one look at the pitiful, unshaded camping area, and checked straight out again. Back at the tourist office I dusted off my credit card and said, "Give me the room at the motel."

Shortly afterwards I was safely ensconced in my "budget" room with the air-conditioning on full blast. For half an hour I just lay on the bed, wasted. Eventually I managed to drag myself into the shower, and its cool waters started to revive me. For such a short distance, it had been one of the hardest rides I'd ever done.

I had known this section to Darwin was going to be tough, but this was ridiculous. At least there would be a youth hostel in Kunanurra the next night. Then hopefully I'd have just one last night's camping in Katherine before hitting Darwin, where I'd be able to stay with Phil and his wife.

I went and got some lunch, then returned to my room to tackle the ant problem. Ants were everywhere – in my panniers, in my sleeping bag, in my clothes. One had even got in my bra, as I had two bites on my boob where it had clearly got trapped between the underwire and my skin, and, my God, are ant bites itchy. The only place they hadn't penetrated was my top box.

There was a notice in my room about Singapore ants being a problem in the motel. It said to get some spray from reception if any were encountered. I borrowed their bottle of ant killer and sprayed all my possessions with it.

Halls Creek was quite a nice little town, which had a busy high street with lots of shops and a few eateries on it. The hotel wasn't very full, with only a handful of cars parked outside rooms, but no one was around to talk to. Presumably they were all flaked out on their beds, soaking up the air-con like me. There hadn't been many other travellers on the road and those that there were seemed to be heading south, away from the heat. I was definitely going the wrong way.

I was travelling through an area called The Kimberley, which is claimed to be "one of the world's last great wilderness regions". I remembered that the section along the Gibb River Road had, indeed, been delightful, but so far the country along the Great Northern Highway was pretty dull. I was fed up and lonely, and hoped things would pick up in Kununurra.

KIMBERLEYS, CATTLE AND KUNUNURRA

Okay, I take it back. The Kimberley is not all dull. The road from Halls Creek to Kununurra was a much better ride than the preceding two days' had been. Almost immediately, the road started bending and twisting through rocky mounds and outcrops. Since it was dawn, the wildlife was out in force. Cattle were everywhere, strolling across the road without a care in the world.

Two cattle stations bordered the highway: on the left was Alice Downs and on the right, Springvale. Springvale had a large set of holding pens by the roadside, full of cattle, which I presumed were waiting to be transported to market. A kangaroo bounced out in front of me and herds of wild horses (known as Brumbies) frolicked in what was now becoming lush green scrub.

The Brumbies were beautiful. Most were dark brown, with long, slender legs and glossy coats. Apparently they are the descendants of escaped or lost horses which the early European settlers bought with them. Some have been rounded up and domesticated, but large "mobs" of them still roam freely in the Northern Territory and Queensland.

It was cooler, too. The previous evening, as I'd eaten my hamburger outside my room, I'd noticed huge hammerhead clouds building in the near distance, with flashes of lightning illuminating the sky. In the morning I'd noticed that Ruby was covered in splashes of dirt, so I guessed it must have rained during the night.

The first three hours to the roadhouse at Warmun/Turkey Creek were very pleasant riding. Warmun was a closed Aboriginal community, but the highway passed through it and as I looked down a side street I saw a mob of Brumbies charging down the road, clouds of dust behind them. I couldn't tell if they were being driven by human handlers or if they had somehow got lost, found themselves in the town and were panicking to get out. It was a captivating sight.

I'd arrived at 7.45 a.m. and the roadhouse in neighbouring Turkey Creek didn't open till 8. In just fifteen minutes the temperature went from reasonably pleasant to sauna-like. After that, despite the beautiful scenery, it got harder to ride. The road rose up through hilly ranges on either side and, after a diamond mine, widened and looked as if it had been resurfaced recently. No doubt the mine had contributed to the road's upgrade.

I stopped at the Doon Doon Roadhouse for breakfast.

"Is that a 125 you're on?" said a man sitting at the table next to mine.

"Yep," I replied and told him my story.

He was a road train driver on his way to Broome. I was tempted to ask him to show me his rig but he left shortly after and, as I was still in the middle of my bacon and eggs, he was gone before I had the chance.

I made it to the junction with the Victoria Highway by 11 a.m. As I pulled into a parking area for a rest, I hit some soft sand, went into a wild wobble and almost went over. Some workmen were gathered there for a break, and scattered as I lurched from side to side. I'd become so confident about riding into dirt parking areas, I hardly even looked at the surface anymore. Fortunately, Ruby proved to be as stable as my postie bike had been and we both stayed upright, but it gave me quite a fright and I was shaking for some time afterwards.

Coming into Kununurra, there was a change of scenery. A large dam spanned the road and green fields of crops lay on either side. A large lake flanked the edge of the town.

I made my way to the youth hostel, only to find it wasn't really open. It was owned by a private business who also owned a motel in the town. Because it was the low season, they were in the process of moving all the backpackers from the hostel into the motel so that the hostel could be closed for the season. The guy behind the desk told me I'd need to go to the motel instead.

I found my way to the Kimberley Croc Lodge and, as they didn't have any beds available in a female dormitory I was given a whole motel room to myself for the same price as a dormitory, $32, on condition that I didn't mind sharing it should another female traveller come along.

It was bliss. I threw off my riding gear and immersed myself in the shower, then went off to explore.

Kununurra was a pretty town. With the lake nearby, everything was very green and lush and tall palm trees lined the main road. There was a selection of shops and supermarkets and the usual roadhouses and caravan parks. There was another Picture Gardens and, as I made my way there, I passed the Kununurra Historical Society Museum. I went in to have a look.

Two men there told me all about Kununurra's history. Back in the 1940s the town didn't really exist, save for a handful of cattle stations nearby. By the end of the dry season, the farmers were finding their cattle were losing form due to a lack of foodstuffs, so they lobbied the government to help. In the 1960s the Diversion Dam (the one I'd seen on the way into town) was built to block the River Ord and provide the necessary irrigation to grow crops to feed the cattle. However, for some reason this never really took off and since then various crops have been tried in Kununurra, of which sandalwood seems to have been the most successful.

One of the men told me that the Chinese were currently proposing planting sugar cane there instead. Despite all this uncertainty, the town was now well established, with all the amenities you would expect. Both men were very well informed and suddenly I'd been there an hour and it was closing time. I thanked them for sharing their knowledge and one of them picked a flower off a tree and gave it to me. He'd obviously enjoyed telling me about Kununurra's history as much as I'd enjoyed listening.

Across the road was the Picture Gardens, but sadly it was closed for the wet season.

Back at Kimberley Croc, no one else had turned up to share my room and I got ready for another big ride to Katherine (503 km) the next day. It was listed as Ride Number 196 in my *200 Top Rides* book, so it looked as if it would be another good day.

THE ABORIGINALS AND THE ONION

Well, the *200 Top Rides* book was wrong. Kununurra to Katherine was not, in my view, anywhere close to one of the best motorcycle rides in Australia. It had its moments, but I'd say Halls Creek to Kununurra was far better.

One of the highlights, though, was Lake Argyll, the largest man-made lake in Australia. It meant a 70 km round trip off the main road to see it, but as it was unlikely that I'd pass that way again, I did the detour. And it was completely worth it. Following a beautiful ride up through more mountains, the road came out above the lake, giving panoramic views of the scene below. It was breathtaking. The water was petrol blue, with little sailing boats moored near the shore and small verdigris-tinted islands littered upon its surface. And, at 6 a.m., there was no one else to spoil the view.

I made my way back to the Victoria Highway and shortly afterwards crossed the border from Western Australia into the Northern Territory. A rather battered sign marked the spot. Although it was nowhere near as impressive as the monument at the South Australian border, I parked Ruby in front of the sign and took a photo. We were back in the NT and had gained an hour and a half in the process.

Unfortunately the rest of the journey wasn't quite so interesting. There were more flat bushlands for miles and only a brief bit of excitement passing through the Gregory National Park, when the Victoria River came into view.

I stopped at the Timber Creek Roadhouse for breakfast and to buy some more water. My water bladder had sprung a leak shortly after leaving Broome and it was getting worse. I could now only half-fill it, or I'd lose the rest before I had a chance to drink it.

An hour after that, I got to the Victoria River Roadhouse and had another break. There was an English guy serving behind the counter. I'd hardly spoken to anyone all day and found myself quizzing him for his life story, I was so starved of company.

A bit later on, one strange incident did brighten things up a bit. I'd stopped for a break at the junction with the Buntine Highway, where there was a memorial. As I stood there, a ute full of Aboriginals drew up. Four adults, a toddler and a baby piled out. One of the women took out an already-peeled onion and sliced the end off it with a knife. They then all piled back in again and one of them shouted over to me to see if I had some sort of paper.

"What, newspaper?" I queried.

"Naw," she replied.

"Toilet paper?" I continued.

"Naw, for cigarettes," she said.

"Oh, you mean rolling paper?" I replied. "Sorry, no, I don't smoke."

With that they shot off into the yonder.

About 50 km out of Katherine I stopped to use the toilet in a rest area. No sooner had I got off the bike and taken my helmet off, than a small campervan pulled in. It was Iain and Anne from the Fitzroy Crossing campsite. I was so happy to see them.

"We saw your bike at Halls Creek, outside the motel," they said. "So we knew you were all right."

I found it comforting to know that someone had been keeping an eye out for me. They gave me a glass of cold water and I recounted the strange event with the Aboriginals and the onion.

"Oh," said Anne, "they were probably using the onion skin as cigarette paper."

Mystery solved.

"Where are you staying tonight?" they asked.

"Katherine," I replied. "It's my last night on the road, so I'm going to treat myself to a hotel. I don't suppose you know any cheap ones, do you?"

Iain gave me directions to a hotel he knew and we got back on our way.

I got to Katherine at 5 p.m. (it would have been 3.30 p.m. if it hadn't been for the change in time zone). I found the hotel Iain had recommended but it looked a bit too expensive for me and was some distance from the centre of town. I did a couple of loops of the town and settled on the Katherine Motel, which was right in the heart of the shopping area. I pulled out my credit card for the last time and paid the $120 charge.

It was worth every penny. It was just a plain room, but it was cool and quiet and gave me a chance to reflect. Suddenly it struck me – tomorrow I would be in Darwin. I was almost at the end of my trip.

THE LAST LEG

The time difference between Western Australia and the Northern Territory totally threw me the next morning. Like every day for weeks before, I'd set my alarm for 4.30

a.m., which was when it was usually starting to get light. In Katherine, however, it was still pitch black at this time.

I had a cup of tea and a croissant to kill time and left at 6 a.m. to do the last 327 km to Darwin. I was a bit disappointed to be shooting through Katherine and heading directly for Darwin, as there seemed to be lots of interesting places to visit from there, but I'd been travelling for so long and in such heat, I just wanted to get to the end now.

It was a nice ride. For once, there was a slight chill in the air, at least for a while. I was back on the Stuart Highway – the one that runs up the middle of Australia and that I'd taken to Alice Springs.

I stopped at Pine Creek, where gold had been discovered in 1871, and peered into the remains of the Enterprise Pit, which had been active from 1906 until as recently as 1995. Now the pit was filled with water and I was astonished to learn that the base of the pit was actually 135 metres below the water level. That was deep. No wonder it had managed to produce $393 million worth of gold between 1985 and 1995 alone.

I also stopped at Adelaide River, where the old station building from the former North Australia Railway still stood, preserved as a museum (known as the Adelaide River Railway Heritage Precinct).

In 1883, construction began on the North Australian Railway from Darwin to Birdum in the Northern Territory. This was another narrow-gauge line and was completed by 1929, the same time as the Old Ghan. But as it did not reach Alice Springs, the two lines were not connected.

The township of Adelaide River became an important military base during World War II. However, after the war, and with the introduction of diesel locomotives, trains stopped for less time at Adelaide River and passenger numbers declined.

By 1958, only a single train stopped once a week at the station. Following damage caused by Cyclone Tracy in 1974, the decision was made to close the line in 1976, and the last passenger service stopped at the station on 29 June that year.

There had long been a promise by the Government to connect the Ghan and the North Australian Railway, providing one single track all the way to Darwin. However, this did not occur until 2001, when construction on a new standard-gauge line began between Alice Springs and Darwin (the new Ghan already providing the link from Adelaide to Alice). The new line runs near the route of the North Australia Railway in places, but uses very little of the old infrastructure. It was completed in 2003 at a cost of $1.2 billion, with the first passenger train reaching Darwin on 4 February 2004. There are now only fourteen stops between Adelaide and Darwin, as opposed to the seventy-nine stops there had been between Port Augusta and Alice Springs on the Old Ghan.

As I got closer to Darwin I suddenly started seeing motorbikes again – all going in the opposite direction to me, of course... apart from one, which had pulled into a rest area I'd stopped at and was on his way back to the city after a wee ride out for the morning. In this rest area was a sign giving some interesting information about the construction of the new Alice Springs to Darwin Railway.

The total length of track laid was 1,420 km. 146,000 tonnes of rail were transported in 27.5 m lengths from One Steel in Whyalla. 2 million sleepers and 2,835 million tonnes of ballast were used. There is a total of ninety bridges and the railway crossed the Stuart Highway four times and the Victoria Highway once.

Leaving the rest area, the road gained height and did a bit of weaving and twisting as it went. To allow traffic to pass, several overtaking lanes had been built. I was about halfway along one of them when I noticed two triple road trains coming up behind me. I slowed down to let them pass.

The first one went by very quickly, but the second one seemed to take a long time to catch me up. We were almost at the end of the lane when he pulled out to pass. The lane was going to run out. I slammed on my brakes to avoid crashing onto the gravel shoulder and the driver honked his horn at me as he hurtled past. *Bloody cheek!* He was the one who should have pulled up, if he could see he wasn't going to get past in time. But then I remembered – *road trains stop for no one.*

As the road got closer to Darwin, lots of old World War II runways bordered the highway. After a while I noticed the two road trains that had passed me parked on one of them. The drivers were out having a chat. I threw them a dirty look as I chugged past at 80 km/h. Typical! I'd made it all the way round Australia unscathed and on my last day I'd nearly been run off the road by one of these huge bruisers.

About 40 km from Darwin the road opened into a two-, then three-lane highway. Unfortunately, I missed the turn to Phil's apartment and had to do a series of U-turns to get back on track. I finally got there at 11.15 a.m. Phil came home from work to let me in. He showed me my room, gave me a set of keys and left me to it.

I'd done 11,656 km on Ruby and another 3,540 on Rosie, my postie bike, giving a total of 15,196 km for the whole trip. Strangely enough, this was only about 500 km less than the distance from Glasgow to Brisbane, my starting point.

I turned on the air-conditioning, put on a load of washing, lay down on the bed and fell asleep. I'd done it. I'd made it around Australia and I still had $350 to spare.

Decompressing in Darwin

HOT IN THE CITY

I was awoken by the sound of the washing machine banging from side to side. I sprang to my feet and ran over to the cupboard in which it was located. A lady was leaning over it, rebalancing the load.

"You must be Jenny?" I said.

"Yes. And you must be Jill," she replied with a big smile. I liked her immediately.

Phil's wife was tall and slim, with long blond hair tied up in a bun. "Would you like a cup of tea?" she offered.

"Oh, I'd love one."

We sat down to have tea. Phil and Jenny were originally from Queensland but had lived in Darwin for thirty-odd years. Four years ago they moved from their family house into this apartment. It was a gorgeous modern flat, with a balcony overlooking the city centre a couple of miles away.

"So how long are you staying?" asked Jenny.

"Well my flight isn't until 27 November." It was now 7 November 2014. "But don't worry, I won't impose myself on you for that long. I'm hoping to change it and get home next week, if that's okay with you?"

"Yes, that's fine. You can stay as long as you like."

We chatted for a while and then she took me on a tour of the city. We went to the school where she worked as a sports co-ordinator, then past a swimming complex and a big shopping centre at a place called Casuarina. From there we went past a beach that had an old gaol nearby, followed by a casino and an upmarket area "where all the millionaires lived" called Cullen Bay. After that we saw Fisherman's Wharf at Frances Bay, where all the commercial fishing boats were moored, then finally we went back to their apartment.

When we got home, I was completely disorientated. The intention of the tour was to give me an understanding of where everything was in relation to the apartment, but as I didn't know where the apartment was to begin with, I ended up totally confused.

Phil arrived home about 5 o'clock with some good news. He was a surveyor and had just been informed that the trip he was supposed to be going on the next week had been cancelled. This was due to the support vehicle with all his equipment not being loaded onto the ferry which was supposed to take it to the place where he'd be working. As he was due to retire the following year and there had been a lot of job losses in his department, he had been under a lot of pressure. This meant he could now get on top of some office work.

We reminisced about the Postie Bike Challenge. After pouring me a huge glass of wine, Phil said, "So, tell us about your trip."

I told them where I'd been and shared some of the highlights.

"And what are you going to do with Ruby, now it's over?"

"Well, the dealer in Adelaide said he'd give me the number of the Honda dealer here. I need to phone him on Monday. Because I couldn't register her in my name, he said he'd explain this to the dealer here and see if he could get him to buy her off me."

"How much do you want for her?" Phil asked.

"If I got $1,000 I'd be happy," I replied. Then, sensing there was something more behind this question than polite curiosity, I added, "Why? Are you interested?"

"Yes, I am."

"Really?"

"Yes. After the Postie Bike Challenge I'd been thinking I would like another bike, but I hadn't got round to doing anything about it. Ruby would be just the thing."

"Oh my God, that would be great." I couldn't believe my luck.

This was going to make life a lot easier and came as a huge relief, as I didn't want her going to someone who wouldn't honour her travelling pedigree, as I knew Phil would. I mean, in the first two months of her life she'd been all round Australia. Becoming a commuter bike for a sixteen-year-old learner rider would have been a bit of a comedown.

I told Phil I'd need to get Pete in Adelaide to sign the registration document so he could get it swapped over to Phil's name, and he was fine with that.

It was Friday night and Phil and Jenny had a tradition of cooking pizza every Friday and eating it down by the beach. They baked an enormous pizza, piled high with every topping you can imagine, then put it on a tray, covered it with a plastic lid and a blanket and loaded it, plus some other picnic items, into the car and drove down to the beach. Even now, I'm not entirely sure where that beach was, but it was a lovely evening, with the sunset over the bay creating glorious colours.

The next morning I took my panniers and my backpack down to the parking area and flushed them out with a water hose to try and finish off the last of the ants before I flew home – I didn't want to be bringing any nasty beasties back with me.

When I got back into the apartment Phil came through and gave me $1,000 in cash for Ruby. I hadn't expected such prompt payment. I immediately phoned Pete to ask if he could sign the registration document if I sent it to him, and return it to me as quickly as possible, so Phil could sign his section and I could post it off to the Northern Territory registration authority before I left.

Pete agreed to do this and I jumped on Ruby for what would be my last ride on her, up to Casuarina shopping centre to find the only post office that was open on a Saturday, before it shut at noon. Even though I hadn't quite worked out my orientation yet, it was an easy ride up a straight road and I made it with half an hour to spare. I posted the documents to Pete, then took a slow ride back, trying to figure out where on earth Casuarina was in relation to the rest of Darwin. It was no use, though – without knowing where the apartment was in relation to the city centre I had no chance of figuring it out.

When I got back, I had a good look at a map.

Darwin lies on a peninsula shaped like a shepherd's crook, so that the Stuart Highway comes in from the south, then veers west along the edge of the airport before turning south into the northern end of the city centre. The city centre then extends southwards into a promontory. In the north it merges into some suburbs, before the airport separates these from another set of suburbs (including Casuarina) on the northern side of the airfield.

Add to that the fact that there are beaches on three of the four sides of the peninsula, and you have a very confusing town layout. I had thought the highway arrived in the south of the city and that everything was north of it. Phil and Jenny's apartment was in the westerly section, meaning that the city centre was actually to the south of it, not the north as my inner compass was telling me.

Phil and Jenny had plans for the afternoon so I decided to spruce Ruby up before handing her over to Phil. I took off the bandages from her grips, peeled off the hundred miles per hour tape from her sides, removed all the sticky gunk that was left behind and washed her from top to toe. It was the least I could do – after all, she had been my best friend and trusted companion for the last two months. She may not have been very fast but she had been one hundred percent reliable and a diligent workhorse. She had been the perfect bike for me.

As I hosed her down for the final time another guy came round to the cleaning area with his giant 1,300 cc black sports bike. He was quite attractive and, as always with fellow bikers, we got talking. He was from the UK and had moved out to Darwin a year before. He was a child psychiatrist.

"So what's a child psychiatrist's view on guys who buy big powerful toys like that?" I said, pointing at his bike and raising my eyebrows.

He just laughed.

That evening Phil and Jenny took me on another tour, this time of the city centre. We walked along Bicentennial Park, which lay between the Esplanade and Lameroo Beach. I found a plaque which had been laid in 1972 to commemorate the centenary of the laying of the undersea cable from Java in 1872. I'd been following the Overland Telegraph's story all around Australia and now here I was at the point where it had come ashore. I felt a sense of completion.

On Sunday, I took the bus into town – I didn't want to end up walking around in my bike gear all day. The humidity was worse than ever here.

I'd phoned my travel agents the night before to see if I could change my flights home and they had advised that I needed to contact the airline directly. I went to the tourist information office to find out if Malaysia Airlines had an office in Darwin.

"No, they don't have one anywhere anymore. You have to phone their call centre instead." The woman behind the desk gave me the number.

I was on my own now, and decided to have a closer look at the town to see if it brought back any memories. I had been here during my 1989 trip to Australia but had only had one night in the city. Consequently I never really got to see the place and had only very patchy memories of it. Now I was back, I hardly recognised a thing.

Behind the visitor centre was Parliament House, a large building known locally as "The Wedding Cake", on account of the fact that "it's white and filled with fruit, nuts and alcohol". It was relatively new, having been built in 1994. Across from this was Government House, a whitewashed, wooden, colonial-style house in which the Administrator of the Northern Territory resided.

There was also the old Court House & Police Station and Survivors Lookout. From there I got a clear view over the waterfront area. This had been developed significantly and now included a host of new apartments, a beach including a man-made wave lagoon, the Fort Hill Wharf Cruise Ship Terminal and Stokes Hill Wharf. This was the wharf used in the film *Australia*, where all the cattle were driven down to the ship – although apparently a "wharf double" in Bowen on the Queensland coast had been used for the actual filming.

There was a huge cruise ship at the Cruise Ship Terminal and I took a wander over to have a look. Passengers were disembarking and spilling into the shops and cafés at the neighbouring waterfront complex. I followed the path round and had a look at the shops and cafés too.

From there I found the World War II Oil Tunnels, a unique part of Darwin's history. During World War II, Darwin had nine oil tanks located on a hill between Frances Bay and Stokes Hill Wharf. They were an easy target for Japanese air raids, so a plan was hatched to build nine steel-lined underground oil tunnels to store the oil instead. Construction began in 1943 but only five tunnels had been completed by the end of the war, so they were never really used. The original oil tanks still exist today, but now hold diesel instead of oil.

By mid-afternoon I was sapped of all energy and returned home to cool off in the block's swimming pool before tucking into a delicious roast dinner Jenny had cooked for us.

On Monday, I was a mess. I'd been on the go pretty much since I'd arrived in Darwin and I needed to slow down and take stock. Phil and Jenny were both at work and I didn't leave the apartment all day. My hands were wrecked. They were so sore I could hardly hold a pen to write. My ankles were stiff from having been locked into the same position for days on end and emotionally I was all over the place. On the one hand I wanted to get home; on the other, I was sad my adventure was almost over.

I'd missed a call from Walshy, too, and was dying to speak to him. I knew I'd probably never see him again, but I missed his kindness and had really liked the way he'd checked in with me every week or so to make sure I was still okay. He was always interested in what I was doing and how I was getting on and was happy to share what was going on in his life, too, when we spoke. Walshy was a man who hadn't asked too much of me, yet was grateful to receive what I had to give. I felt I could be myself with him and I would have liked to have spent more time in his company. But it wasn't to be and I was sad about that.

That night, after finding out that Malaysia Airlines couldn't access the conditions of my ticket, I phoned my travel agents back to tell them what the airline had said and to ask them to change the ticket instead. When I originally called I'd spoken to someone who seemed a little inexperienced, and I'd wondered if she'd given me the right information. This time I got someone who was much more on the ball and immediately knew what to do. I told her the dates I wanted to travel and she made the changes then and there.

I would now be flying home the following Monday, the 17th November. It was a relief to get that sorted and know I wouldn't overstay my welcome with my lovely hosts.

COOLING DOWN

Having spent the previous couple of days recovering from my intense ride from Broome to Darwin, by Wednesday I finally felt up to seeing something a bit further afield than the city centre and took a tour to Litchfield National Park, about 110 km south of Darwin.

The bus collected me from the Transit Centre at 7.15 a.m. As I climbed aboard and saw there was only one other person anywhere near my age, a German lady called Tina, I began to wonder if the 'AAT' in AAT Kings stood for 'Ancient and Aged Tours'. They were all very nice people, but since one of the main features of the tour was being able to swim in all the waterfalls and rock pools of the park, and none of them were fit enough to do this, it seemed that either Tina and I or the oldies had booked the wrong tour.

Not to be put off, our driver Gordon set out with a running commentary of the landscape through which we were travelling. We were on the Stuart Highway going south and a long steel pipeline, which I'd noticed on the way up, was running parallel to the road. This was the water pipeline that had provided Darwin's first water supply from the nearby Manton Dam. Prior to World War II, Darwin was largely dependent on bores for its water. With the advent of war and an influx of troops to be supported, a more reliable source was needed and in 1939 construction began on the Manton Dam. By the 1970s, an increase in population made it necessary to develop a new water supply for Darwin, and in 1972 the Darwin River Dam was officially opened. The Manton Dam is still operational and means that Darwin is in the enviable position of being the only city in Australia that has a backup water supply.

After a stop for a cup of tea at a caravan park near Batchelor, and another to look at Cathedral and Magnetic Termite Mounds, we continued to the first waterfall of the day, Florence Falls. Tina and I headed down the track and were soon immersed in the gorgeous cooling waters at the bottom of the falls. As we dried off afterwards, a water monitor lizard appeared at the edge of the swimming hole. At first I thought it was a snake, as it had a long, dark, narrow body, but when it moved I could see it had legs and feet. For once I managed to grab my camera and take a few pictures before it slithered into the pool and went for a swim itself.

After a stop for lunch, we continued to the next waterfall, Wangi Falls. This was considerably bigger than the first one and had several bus-loads of tourists all bathing in its waters. There was a sign warning visitors that: "Wangi plunge pool is home to smaller fish-eating freshwater crocodiles. However, during the wet season, larger saltwater crocodiles often move in". Given how many people were already swimming, it seemed unlikely that any salties had moved in yet, and Tina and I waded in. But, as we swam out to the bigger of the two cascades, I found myself jumping every time something brushed against my legs.

Our final stop was the Buley Rock Holes, a series of descending pools formed at the upper reaches of Florence Falls. A load of young Aboriginal boys were bombing into the largest of the pools, so my new best friend and I had to content ourselves with squirming around some of the higher, shallower pools.

There was one other fall we were supposed to see, Tolmer Falls, but alas this was closed due to maintenance work to the viewing platform.

On the way back, a huge thunder and lightning storm developed and by the time we got back to Darwin the city streets were awash with water and, for once, the air was cooler. It was a great way to end a great day.

THE DEVASTATION OF DARWIN

My last few days in Darwin were spent exploring. Although Jenny had given me a guided tour of the city, it took several days for me to relocate the places she had shown me and figure out where everything was in relation to everything else. To aid this process, I took the Hop-On Hop-Off bus tour, and after two circuits of the city felt I was finally sussing out the lie of the land. Having done this, I turned my attention to the history of the place.

Darwin was originally called Palmerston after the ruling British Prime Minister of the day, but was changed to Darwin when Charles Darwin's ship, the Beagle, moored at its harbour. Although Darwin himself wasn't on board, the town was renamed in his honour.

Two major events had shaped Darwin's history – the bombing of the city in 1942 during World War II and Cyclone Tracy in 1974.

On 19 February 1942 the same Japanese air squadron that had bombed Pearl Harbour attacked Darwin. They bombarded the city and 243 people were left dead. Over the next eighteen months a further sixty-four air raids were made.

Cyclone Tracy was the second major disaster to befall the city. On Christmas Eve 1974, a cyclone warning was issued to the townsfolk. This was the second one in a few days and as the previous one hadn't really amounted to anything, most people ignored it. That night the cyclone hit and for three hours 250 mph winds battered the town. Seventy-one people were killed and over 70% of the buildings were destroyed.

Both events devastated the town and called for virtual rebuilds. Most of the traditional architecture was lost, with only four of the famous Burnett-style houses surviving, along with some of the government buildings in the downtown area.

Architect Beni Carr Glynn Burnett had been responsible for designing many of the pre-war homes for the public servants of the Territory. He was charged with designing homes which would be "appropriate for Australia's tropical north". What he came up with was a range of distinctive two-storey houses with the sleeping area upstairs and the living and dining areas at ground level, opening onto shaded verandahs. They were timber-framed, with fibro sheeting cladding and glass louvre windows.

After the war, between 1950 and 1974, an extensive public housing program used the same materials in their construction. However, when Cyclone Tracy struck, these materials proved hazardous, shattering and causing great injury. Many residents had to shelter under the floor of their elevated houses because the upper storey had been blown away. Thereafter, strict building regulations (known as the Cyclone Code) were introduced, requiring homes to be built from reinforced concrete with their own individual cyclone shelters (usually a reinforced bathroom or central area). Gradually these regulations have been relaxed, with several public cyclone shelters being built around the city, but the new concrete architecture didn't appeal to me as much as the Burnett style, which was beautifully breezy and reminded me of the traditional wooden homes built on stilts in Queensland, known as Queenslanders.

Not to be discouraged by all this destruction, Darwin fought back and now has four main industries – tourism (especially cruise ships – the one I'd seen had had 2,700 passengers on board), defence (10% of the population work in this), oil and gas, and construction, to ensure there is enough housing for the oil and gas workers.

The Northern Territory occupies 1.3 million sq km and hosts a population of 250,000 people. Of these, 125,000 live in the Darwin area. The city has been experiencing something of a housing crisis and to combat this a new city called Palmerston (just to confuse everyone) has been built to the south of Darwin to accommodate the expanding population.

Phil took me over to the East Arm Wharf, located on another promontory south of the city near Berrimah, where a huge gas plant is located. A 502 km pipeline carries natural gas from the Bayu-Undan offshore gas and condensate field in the Joint Petroleum Development Area of the Timor Sea to the ConocoPhillips-operated liquid natural gas (LNG) plant at East Arm. Here it is converted to LNG and shipped to market in special purpose-built ships (like the ones I'd seen in the Pilbara).

From Phil's apartment there was a clear view of a large circular tower at the plant known as the Esky (after a brand of containers designed to cool beer). This was a huge compressor that turned natural gas into liquid form. Now I could see that there was a lot more to it than just the Esky, with lots of smaller towers scattered about the site.

Also at East Arm was Darwin's railway station. At about 20 km out of town, it didn't strike me as particularly handy for those people wishing to catch a train. However, it was a large industrial area and as most of its traffic appeared to be freight, I could understand why it was located there. It was the terminus for the Ghan and once again I had that sense of completion, having tracked its history all the way from Port Augusta.

With the city being such a target for military action, Darwin has a strong military presence, with army and navy bases in several locations. Additionally, Darwin Airport, which is actually a military airport but sublet to the civil sector, was originally sited much closer to the town centre. The old runway now forms a very long, straight road called Ross Smith Avenue. For some reason, the Qantas Hanger was not torn down and built on like the rest of the airport and now houses a vintage vehicle museum.

Numerous relics from World War II are scattered around the city, including a set of munitions bunkers in

Charles Darwin National Park and the new *Defence of Darwin* Military Museum at East Point Reserve. This is a former military base, where an anti-submarine boom net was stretched across the harbour to West Point on the Mandorah peninsula, to protect it from Japanese invasion during World War II. It was six kilometres long and was the longest floating net in the world.

Not far from East Point is Fannie Bay, where there is an old gaol which dates back to 1882 and is a thoroughly depressing testament to man's inhumanity to man.

Two blocks with sixteen stone cells, a washhouse and a kitchen formed the original goal. During the late 1920s a cell for women prisoners was added, followed soon after by another area for keeping Aboriginal detainees. In the 1950s a remand section for juveniles, a watch tower and maximum security wings were erected.

However, the thing Fannie Bay Gaol is most famous for is its execution chamber. Originally this was built in 1887 as an infirmary, but in 1952, instead of keeping people alive, it was dedicated to executing them. Following the construction of a new penal institution at Berrimah in 1979, the gaol discontinued operation and is now a museum.

Another thing I had to do while in Darwin was visit Fisherman's Wharf (or the Duck Pond, as it's also known) at Frances Bay. This is where my friend Lisa and I had managed to get jobs working on a prawn trawler when we first visited Darwin in 1989. Or at least, I thought it was. I couldn't be sure now. It wasn't really how I remembered it and I wondered if it hadn't in fact been Stokes Wharf we'd sailed from. But Jenny assured me that the Duck Pond was where the prawn trawlers had always been based.

FRIENDS, FILMS AND FAREWELLS

On one of my sorties around the city I had discovered the Deckchair Cinema, an open-air cinema bordering Lameroo Beach, which reminded me of the Sun Picture Gardens in Broome, although this one was completely uncovered. I had noticed that a film called *On Tour and Looking for a Feed* was going to be shown on Friday night and mentioned this to Phil and Jenny.

We all decided to go. What I hadn't realised was that it was one of about twenty films being shown that night as part of the *Fist Full of Films Festival*. It turned out to be a fantastic night, with loads of local film-makers showing their shorts. The *On Tour* film was about two Aussie blokes who pick up a pretty but spoilt French hitchhiker and do a road trip of outback Australia. It was hilarious, and the stars were even there at the end to meet and greet us.

On Saturday the registration documents arrived from Pete and I handed over Ruby's keys to Phil. I ran through all her foibles – like how the petrol tank could look as if it was full but if you waited for a moment the fuel would sink and you could then add another litre or so. I told him how she'd had a new back tyre and chain but that she'd probably need a new front tyre and would be due her 12,000 km service soon.

We took some photos to commemorate the moment and I bit back the tears. I'd always found it hard to let go of my motorcycles. Because you're so physically attached to them, it's as though they become part of you, and when you've shared such a big adventure together, it almost feels like a betrayal to sell them on. But I knew Phil would be a good owner and I was glad she was going to him, even if it was breaking my heart to leave her behind.

I'd had a great time in Darwin (humidity aside). It was a big enough place to have all the services you might require, but not so big that it was difficult to get around. And Phil and Jenny had been a wonderful couple, who had welcomed me into their home and provided me with everything I could possibly need. I cooked a couple of meals for them, got a photo of Phil riding his postie bike framed, bought Jenny some flowers and treated them to the Deckchair Cinema, but still it didn't seem like enough to express my gratitude for all their generosity and hospitality.

I'd probably stayed longer than they'd really wanted, but the extra few days had allowed me to recover from the tortuous ride through the Kimberley and to reconnect with all the fun I'd had on the rest of the trip.

At 1.30 in the morning on Monday 17 November 2014, Walshy rang to say goodbye. We'd been missing each other's calls for days and I was so glad to be able to speak to him before I left. I had really liked him and I wanted to thank him for all his support. He said my visit had done him the power of good and had come at a time in his life when he really needed it. I could have said exactly the same thing. He had reminded me how good it is to be held, and to be able to share even a small part of your life with someone.

Two hours later, Phil dropped me off at the airport and another two hours after that I was in the air, leaving Darwin and Australia behind.

Nirvana

Flying out of Darwin, I could see the coast of Australia below. Would this be the last time I would see this land I loved so much?

This had been my fifth visit and, like the others before it, it had touched my soul.

Australia is a very spiritual place for me. Maybe it's because there is so much space and so little interference between you and the sky, but it always feels as if God is a lot closer to me there.

Somehow my money goes further, help always turns up when I need it and my deepest needs seem to be met. Before my previous trip I had been badly wounded by the collapse of my massage clinic and needed healing – and that's just what I got. The kindness of everyone I met and my ability to overcome my fears on the huge Suzuki SV650 motorcycle I'd been riding had restored my faith in myself and helped me to like the person I was again.

On this trip I had been in a much happier place but had needed a new direction for my life. Thinking back on all the places I'd been and all the people I'd met, my conversation with Dave in Alice Springs drifted into my thoughts.

I'd all but forgotten about the idea I'd had about doing industrial heritage tours in Glasgow but now, I suddenly realised, I'd been given a new direction, too.

I'd also had some romance thrown in for good measure – and boy, had I needed that.

Oh yes, it had been tough at times. Slow riding had its downsides: taking twice as long to get anywhere, prolonged exposure to extreme heat and the dehydration and exhaustion that goes with it, and a tendency to fall asleep in the saddle. But these were far outweighed by its advantages.

Riding so slowly had given me time to take in a lot more detail and to think about life – about how I'd got to this point and where I wanted to be. Riding alone had meant I could visit the places I wanted to see and not have to compromise. And what a luxury that had been.

Rosie and Ruby weren't big or powerful machines, but they were stable and oh, so much fun. And there's something about feeling secure that gives you confidence, which meant this trip hadn't been overshadowed by the same fear as the previous one.

I had felt a lot more in control on this trip. To some degree I'd known what to expect – the heat, the distances, the discomfort. What I hadn't expected was how much more enjoyable it was when I was going more slowly and didn't have to worry about the weight of the bike toppling over all the time. It freed my mind to take in other things I hadn't really had time to notice before, like Australia's history and engineering. This added confidence had filtered into the relationships I'd made as well.

I hadn't realised it before, but Australia was where I went for inspiration and healing. Perhaps the same could be said for anywhere that's not home, anywhere that's away from all the usual distractions of daily life, where one can get the peace just to be. But for me, out in the open spaces of the outback there was nothing blocking my prayers getting to heaven. Back in Glasgow, I was going to have to shout them a lot louder, if I wanted not only the universe but other people to hear them.

Australia was my Nirvana.

EPILOGUE

Hopes and Dreams

LEAP OF FAITH

Arriving at London Heathrow, I was looking forward to getting home and getting on with my life. I felt sure everything was going to fall into place and that I'd soon be living happily ever after.

It didn't quite work out that way.

The day after I got back, I switched on my laptop to check my email and there was a message from Dan, the organiser of the Postie Bike Challenge. Andy, the mechanic who had helped me so much, had been killed on Saturday 15 November 2014 in a single vehicle accident during a group motorcycle ride.

My heart ached. Andy had been so kind and caring. I couldn't believe he was gone. The only consolation was that he had died doing something he loved.

On getting home, I had my new business idea in my head, but I'd need some money to make that happen and the only way I could make some money was to go back to work. So I went back to the Health Service.

It seemed like nothing had changed. I was temping again, I had a shed load of debt and a low income, and I still had no boyfriend. Additionally, my hands were wrecked. But one thing had changed – me.

In January 2015 I was due to start an eight-week contract based in one of the city's most deprived neighbourhoods. I took a drive out, the weekend before I was due to start, to see where it was.

It was horrible. I couldn't bring myself to work there.

Over the past few years I'd started to lose faith in my ability to get an interesting job, earn a good salary and find love. I was just grateful for whatever came along. But something had snapped inside me. I could no longer tolerate settling for second best. I needed something better.

I called the Health Service and not only withdrew from the contract but resigned completely. I didn't have anything else lined up – it was a complete leap of faith. If my life was going to change, I had to stop doing the things I'd been doing before. If Greg's and Andy's sudden deaths had taught me anything, it was the importance of making the most of the time we have on earth.

I started writing. I started meditating. I gave my hands the rest they so desperately needed. I started forgiving everybody and everything that had ever done me wrong and I joined an internet dating site. If I was ever going to get a boyfriend again, I would to have to reprioritise my life and stop putting work first.

It was a scary time. I had no money coming in and was living on my credit card. But riding a postie bike down the Birdsville Track had given me nerves of steel and, despite the mounting pile of debt I was accumulating, I hung in there.

If I'd been travelling slowly in Australia, it felt as if my life was now about to grind to a complete halt. Oh yes, I was enjoying indulging my interests, but I was no closer to manifesting my new idea.

But my trip had shown me how much I liked meeting new people, how much I enjoyed learning about the places I was visiting and how much I loved being in the great outdoors. I really needed to find a way that I could make my idea happen.

After two months, I realised I was going to go bankrupt if I didn't do something about my financial situation. I was determined not to go back to temping but I didn't know what to do instead. Then, my friend Carol suggested I claim unemployment benefit from the Government. It wouldn't amount to much, but it would be a lot better than the nothing I was currently receiving. Walking into the Job Centre felt like the lowest ebb of my life, or so I thought. But, miraculously, it actually became the turning point.

EVEN SLOWER RIDER

I still had the seed of my business idea in my mind and asked my advisor if there was any way I could explore this instead of looking for a job. She told me about the New Enterprise Allowance Scheme, which would let me investigate whether it would be a viable business or not. For eight weeks I was allocated a business mentor and was allowed to develop a business plan whilst claiming unemployment benefit.

The first version didn't work. It was going to cost a fortune to get a minibus and all the licences and insurances that would be associated with it.

Then I had a brainwave – I could do bicycle tours instead. This would be a much cheaper and more environmentally friendly option. I did the numbers, and although it meant I'd have to do a lot of tours to get the income I needed, it wasn't beyond the realms of possibility.

It seemed I had found the answer to my dream. But the disaster I'd experienced with my massage clinic still haunted me. Riding around Australia so slowly had shown me how much more enjoyable life is when you feel safe. If

I was going to start another business, I had to feel secure. I had to feel I was not going to risk everything and potentially end up in a worse position than where I'd started.

I looked at my business plan again. Diving into it as a full-time venture would be too scary. But if I got a job, I could build it up over time.

And that's just what I did. I got a job to cover my bills and started running bicycle tours around Glasgow at the weekends. It struck me as ironic that, after three months of riding two of the slowest types of motorcycle available, I was now opting for a career that would force me to become an even slower rider.

But that's the thing about slowing down – it's just a gentler, less stressful way of life and I liked that. Oh yeah, it takes longer to get where you want to go, as this way forward was going to do for me, but it would be a much safer, more interesting ride. It was exactly what I'd been looking for.

Further Information

To read the original blog of this trip, view the photo gallery or find out more about my past, current and future adventures, please visit my website at:

www.jillmaden.com

Acknowledgements

My thanks go out to my mum, Gina Gillard, and brother, Chris Maden, for helping me raise the funds needed to do this trip and for the encouragement and support of all my family and friends. To Carol Mayberry for looking after Cozy and making it possible for me to go away. To Dan, Andy, Scott, Mick, Richard and all the participants on the Postie Bike Challenge for providing me with one of the best experiences of my life. To my dear friend Lisa in Melbourne who checked in with me every week to make sure I was still alive, thank you, you'll never know how much that meant to me. To Pete & Suzie, Dave & Cec, Walshy and Phil & Jenny for putting me up and for helping with Ruby, I shall forever be grateful to you. To Lesley Currie-Sherwood for her invaluable feedback on the first draft of this book and to Sheila Glasbey for her impeccable copy editing, my thanks are given. To the staff at CreateSpace for their fabulous cover design. And to everyone I met along the way who made this the best fun adventure I've ever had.

Cover Photographs

Front cover: Rosie on the Birdsville Development Road
Copyright © Jill Maden

Back cover: Author riding Ruby in Adelaide Hills
Copyright © Peter Knights

Rosie on the road to Mitchell
Copyright © Jill Maden

Author and Ruby arriving in Darwin
Copyright © Jill Maden

Author on the road to Broome
Copyright © Jill Maden

Lightning Source UK Ltd.
Milton Keynes UK
UKOW06f1825161115

262866UK00007B/100/P